The Curious Death of the Novel

The Curious Death of the Novel

Essays in American Literature

LOUIS D. RUBIN, JR.

LOUISIANA STATE UNIVERSITY PRESS / BATON ROUGE

For
Donald R. Ellegood

Library of Congress Catalog Card Number: 67-26970
Manufactured in the United States of America by
The Seeman Printery, Durham, North Carolina
Designed by Jules B. McKee

Preface

These are general essays on aspects of American and Southern literature, but I hope they possess at least some unity of approach and theme. At one point I had thought to entitle this collection "The Experience of Difference," because if there is a recurring, central concern in my various commentaries on the national letters, it is probably that. The experience of difference of a Jew in a Christian society, a Roman Catholic in the Protestant, rural South, a Southerner in an industrial society, even the experience of an Edgar Poe in an optimistic, progress-worshipping civilization—the awareness of difference, the consciousness that one is not fully a member in good standing, gives form to a writer's insights into his experience.

Few of the pieces that follow are written specifically about that theme. Indeed, I cannot claim to have fully recognized the extent to which I had been exploring the matter, going at it from various vantage points, until it was pointed out to me. When a man is invited to collect some of his miscellaneous critical writings in a book, he faces some hard decisions. At a certain point in the process, I found myself at something of a loss as to just what should go in and what should not. So I sent the whole potential manuscript to a friend of mine, whose opinions about my work I have long since learned to trust more firmly than my own, and I asked him to see whether he could suggest a rationale for selection. It was, therefore, Robert D. Jacobs who indicated to me the extent to which so many of the essays and essay-reviews that I had published over the past decade or so were focused on the business of the writer's relationship with and alienation from his society. At his suggestion, I used the theme as the chief, though not the only, principle of inclusion for the book. It seems to me that the theme is clearly there; I am grateful to Mr. Jacobs for pointing it out, and at the same time I emphasize that he should in no way be blamed for the inadequacies of my handling of it.

For the most part the pieces I have included are not importantly changed from the way in which they originally appeared in periodicals and other books. Throughout the book I have sought to eliminate out-of-date references and to effect some judicious cutting here and there. In two instances, the essays included were originally prepared for oral delivery—"Edgar Allan Poe" and "The Difficulties of Being a Southern Writer Today"; while I have tried to remove the more obvious marks of oral presentation, the oratorical origins of each will doubtless be apparent to the reader.

I should like to express my gratitude to the following parties for permission to reprint material appearing in this book:

The Southern Review, for "The Experience of Difference: Southerners and Jews," originally entitled "Southerners and Jews."

The Kenyon Review, for "The Curious Death of The Novel."

The Hollins Critic, for "The Search for Lost Innocence: Karl Shapiro's *The Bourgeois Poet*."

The Fordham University Press and Messrs. Lewis Lawson and Melvin Friedman, for "Flannery O'Connor and the Bible Belt," originally published in Lawson and Friedman (eds.), *The Added Dimension: The Art and Mind of Flannery O'Connor* (New York, 1966).

Rice University, and Mr. Frank Vandiver, for "Notes on a Rear Guard Action," originally published in Vandiver (ed.), *The Idea of the South* (Chicago, 1964).

The Sewanee Review, for "H. L. Mencken and the National Letters" and "Edmund Wilson and the Despot's Heel."

Modern Fiction Studies, for "One More Turn of the Screw."

The Georgia Review, for "All The King's Meanings."

Doubleday and Co., Inc., for "Two in Richmond," originally published in Louis D. Rubin, Jr., and Robert D. Jacobs (eds.), *South: Modern Southern Literature in Its Cultural Setting* (New York, 1961).

The University Press of Virginia, for "The Image of an Army," which in its present form appeared first in R. L. Simonini (ed.), *Southern Writers: Appraisals In Our Time* (Charlottesville, Va., 1964).

American Quarterly, for "*Tom Sawyer* and the Use of Novels" and "The Southern Muse: Two Poetry Societies."

The Journal of Southern History, for "The Difficulties of Being a Southern Writer Today."

Because this time he is not associated with the publication of one of my books, and cannot therefore deny me the right to dedicate the book to him, it is my privilege to offer this book to the person so designated, in small recognition of his friendship and encouragement over the course of some fifteen years.

L.D.R.

Chapel Hill, North Carolina
July 15, 1967

Contents

PART I

The Curious Death
of the Novel:
Or,
What to do About
Tired Literary Critics

FABLE

Once upon a time there was a group of very talented writers known as Modern Novelists, who wrote books known as Modern Novels. The writers known as Modern Novelists were named Joyce and Proust and Dreiser and Mann and Faulkner and Fitzgerald and Hemingway and Wolfe, and while no one of these writers wrote books like those of any of the others, they were all considered very good Modern Novelists.

At the same time there was another group of people, some of them very talented and some of them not so very talented, who were known as Literary Critics. They read the books of the Modern Novelists, and they thereupon said to each other, "Aha! Now we know what a Modern Novel is." This was a very astute observation and they were most satisfied with it.

Time Passed, and after a long while every one of the group of people known as Modern Novelists was dead. There were now some new people around who also wrote books, and who kept insisting that the books were Novels and that therefore they too were Modern Novelists. "Heavens, no!" replied the people known as Literary Critics. "How can you be Modern Novelists? Modern Novelists are writers who write Modern Novels, and we all know what a Modern Novel is; it is a book written by Joyce or Proust or Dreiser or Mann or Faulkner or Fitzgerald or Wolfe."

"But we are not *those* Modern Novelists," said the new people; "we are Bellow and Malamud and Styron and Barth and Salinger and So Forth and So On."

"Don't be silly," the people known as Literary Critics declared. "Unless you write the same kind of books as those written by Modern Novelists, they can't be Modern Novels and you can't be Modern Novelists."

"But those people are all dead," the new people objected.

"True," admitted the people known as Literary Critics, "and so is the Novel."

"Then what do you call the books that *we* have written?" the new people asked.

"I couldn't say," the people known as Literary Critics told them, "because now that the Novel is dead, I don't keep up with current fiction any more."

Moral: Nothing is quite so dead as a dead definition, unless it is a dead critic.

EXPLICATION

One hears it all the time, and one gets tired of listening to it. The Novel is Dead. It has passed on into history with the Epic Poem and the Volstead Amendment. The Great Age of Prose Fiction which began with Fielding and Richardson and reached its flowering in the first several decades of the twentieth century is drawing to a tawdry close. Novels continue to be written, but they have nothing new to communicate, because the possibilities of the literary form have been exhausted, and without discovery there can be no survival.

Sometimes I wonder who it was who first discovered that the novel was dead. I suspect that it was some English literary critic who, having read *Pamela* and *Tom Jones*, happened upon *Tristram Shandy* and immediately afterward announced that the form had now been fully explored and that therefore no more works in that genre could be written. And when someone offered to lend him the new work by Jane Austen entitled *Sense and Sensibility*, he refused to look at it, declaring instead that the genius of his age lay in works of nonfiction such as Charles Lamb's *Recollections of Christ's Hospital*, or perhaps in the throbbing vitality of magazine journalism as exemplified in *Blackwood's* and the *Edinburgh Review*. But on second thought it was probably not an Englishman who discovered that the novel was dead; doubtless it was a Frenchman, for that is the sort of thing that the French are constantly discovering. No doubt it was some Parisian seer of the early nineteenth century who deduced that no one would ever want to write a novel any more, because no one would ever be able once again to bring himself to say, "The little town of Verrières may be regarded as one of the most attractive in the Franche-Comté."

So the novel is dead. Who killed the novel? There has been no lack of answers. We are told that the Age of Prose Fiction is over, that the Novel was a nineteenth-century phenomenon which depended for its life on the breakdown of the traditional class structure, and now that the class structure is permanently fluid (try that one at the Country Club), there is no place for the novel. The bewildering cacophony of modern times, with its continual crises, its everyday reality more weird than anything formerly portrayed in the most visionary works of fiction, has left no room for the mere loveliness of the belles-lettres. Actual events boggle the imagination; this is the age of nonfiction, of the quest for meaning involved in interpretive reportage. Furthermore, television and journalism have provided our culture with art forms that mirror contemporary reality far more accurately and faithfully than the leisurely prose of the novel could ever do. And besides, the discoveries of modern physics and of behavioral psychology have all but destroyed the old certainty of the human ordering of experience, so that there can be no solid basis, whether in finite matter or human reason, upon which the novelist can erect his commentary. The vast terror of the atomic bomb has rendered individual tragedy inconclusive and unimportant. And of course the helplessness of the modern human being, caught in the play of mass forces and the gigantic wheelings and evolutions of whole societies and cultures, is such that the distraught single citizen cannot of himself achieve the personal meaning necessary to art. All these things together spell the death of fiction. So the story goes.

The trouble with most of these arguments is not that they are implausible, but that they are no more true now than during those past times when the novel was supposedly at its heyday. The class structure, for example, is constantly breaking down and regrouping itself. Can anyone contend, for example, that the social hierarchy was not dealt a colossal, and to contemporaries what surely was apparently a mortal, blow by the French Revolution? Yet the very regrouping of the supposedly obsolete class structure provided Stendhal with some of his best subject matter. Besides, to what extent do class and clique help account for, say, Melville? (It will not do to invoke the old distinction between the novel and the romance; if *Moby Dick* is not a novel, then we would gladly settle for the survival of the romance.) It is quite true that modern times seem bewildering, but surely no more bewildering than the early seventeenth century must have seemed to a religious traditionalist like Donne or a religious dissenter such as Milton; alas, the times are *always* chaotic and bewildering. And as always, the apparent lure of nonfiction —naked "truth"—over art is specious; in the eighteenth century everyone used to read another kind of "truth" journals, instead of fiction; in the mid-nineteenth century it was the rise of the daily newspaper. As for television doing the trick, not long ago it was movies that were blamed; a few decades ago the magazines and book clubs were destroying literature. Something is *always* destroying literature, but good books have managed to come along. (The truth is that the only thing that can destroy literature is *bad* books, and surely these are no more common now than in previous eras.) So it will do no good to attribute the alleged death of the novel to our crass times; Hawthorne's times seemed pretty crass to everyone concerned, and so did Proust's. It is not very original to blame the situation on the exploding universe theory and behavioral psychology, either; I would suggest that neither has had anything like the potential for shock that Newtonian physics and the Darwinian hypothesis had in their time; and, anyway, writers are notoriously myopic about such matters. The only really new phenomenon we have to offer to the cataclysmic hypothesis is the atomic bomb; but I suggest that it is probably no more a menace than the Black Death seemed to fourteenth-century Europeans; imaginative literature did not die out then. The truth is that obviously we *do* live in difficult and demanding times, but that the response of novelists to difficult and demanding times will doubtless continue to be what the response of writers to difficult and demanding times always has been: namely, difficult and demanding works of literature.

So I do not accept the theory that the alleged death of the novel is due to the lamentable condition of the cosmos. Times have *changed* some; but they are not necessarily any worse. What I suggest instead is that if the novel is at present in a kind of slump, then in all probability we are roughly in the plight that, say, a devotee of the art of English poetry might have found himself in the year 1790 or so. Pope was dead. Swift was dead. Gray was dead. Dr. Johnson was dead. What more was there to look forward to? The current reigning practitioners seemed competent enough, but were obviously not of the stature of the titans of eighteenth-century verse. How could such a person have heard of the existence of William Blake, or have known that Wordsworth and Coleridge would be growing up in a few years? Surely such a person would have thought that the upheaval of the French Revolution, the swarming confusion of the growing Industrial Revolution in England itself, had killed off all future possibility of poetry for the generations of mankind. Yet the art of poetry managed to survive, and even to take on a new excitement that quite outdid the Augustan achievement.

Or let us think of a devotee of American poetry who looked around him in the year 1890 and perceived such giants of verse as James Russell Lowell, Bliss Carman, Richard Hovey, and Edmund Clarence Stedman. Could anything have convinced him that hope resided in the fact that persons named T. S. Eliot and Robert Frost and John Crowe Ransom and Ezra Pound were growing up?

What I would propose, by inference, is that what we have been experiencing during the past decade or two is a rearrangement and replenishment of literary energies. We have many good and interesting novels, and we apparently have no Faulkners, Hemingways, Fitzgeralds, Prousts, Manns, Joyces, and the like. Is this, after all, odd? Since the post-World War II years, we have lived in a period immediately following one of the richest and most imposing in the history of literature. The first four decades of this century saw the publication of some literary work of almost incredible brilliance. It is no accident that our writers of criticism still devote great attention to this work, that our curricula in colleges and universities are dominated by this work. We are all still trying our best to savor the full flavor of so rich a harvest. This work has dominated our imagination in the way that the drama of Shakespeare, say, dominated the imagination of early seventeenth-century English literature, and that of Milton dominated the imagination of late seventeenth-century literature. The chief impact of this sort of domination, as Eliot remarked of Milton, is on the writers who follow along immediately afterward. A whole way of using language, which is to say, a whole way of giving order to experience, is imposed on the sensibility of the times. This kind of situation is tough on the newer writers, because try as they will, they find themselves writing in other men's modes, which can never be a satisfactory arrangement. They are impeded in the process of self-discovery; try as they may, they see their own experience through Proust's or Joyce's or Faulkner's eyes, which is to say, through the language of those writers, and there is very little they can do except struggle against it. What is produced is work of great technical competence; after all, the immediate problems have been detailed for them already. But what is missing are new perceptions and new discoveries.

We see approximately the same kind of thing going on in France, except that the French have a way of reasoning their problems out in abstract terms that tempts them into all manner of odd extremes of posture and position. The whole business of the *nouveau roman*, it seems to me, is an elaborate and intensive attempt on the part of an entire literary generation to get out from under the massive example of the greatest of twentieth-century novelists, Marcel Proust, and, to a lesser extent, that of Gide and Camus. It would be next to impossible to carry introspective examination and psychological analysis in depth any further than Proust did; very well, said the young Frenchmen, we will move in the opposite direction and write only of what is personally seen and felt.

Over here we have had nothing so determined as the *nouveau roman*. Instead, what we have done is to mark time while a group of very talented writers—Styron, Bellow, Malamud, Barth, others—explores the already mostly discovered ground to see whether anything important has been overlooked. This has, all in all, proved to be a fairly sensible and rewarding thing to do, and there is evidence that several of them have found ample room in which to write well. It is an indication of the capabilities of these four, I think, that while each has published at least three novels—and Bellow has I believe six to his credit—we are quite prepared to believe that each of them may with his very next book produce something more exciting than ever before.

Promise, however, is not fulfillment; and we cannot deal entirely in terms of possibilities. I would instead insist that even if it transpires that not one of these novelists, and not one of their immediate contemporaries, produces fiction worthy to stand alongside that of Faulkner and Hemingway, this would hardly be unexpected. It has been, after all, less than five years since the death of both those writers; apparently there is even now some unpublished Hemingway fiction remaining. Both men were, after all, *our* contemporaries. Their times are still largely *our* times, and it would not be wholly strange if it took the writers who come immediately after them, and so must write in their shadow, a little while longer to disengage themselves from their example. What we are quite likely to have, is seems to me, is a period lasting as long as a full generation or more in which our better writers are more or less engaged, however unintentionally, primarily with learning to see things in their own right again, or at any rate sufficiently their own right so that what they produce is no longer importantly compromised by the version of reality afforded them by their great immediate predecessors. Among the most valuable services that the immediate post-Faulkner and post-Hemingway generation of novelists can perform is that which they are, I think, busily involved in performing, however without their meaning to: searching out the resources at their command, discovering new vantage points, finding where the barriers lie, and so on. They are keeping the spirit of the novel alive and flourishing, and writing some highly excellent books in the process, some few of which, I am convinced, will hold up very well in succeeding years.

To put the matter in this way is, I fear, to put it rather fatuously, for whatever else may be sure, we can say without hesitation that our best contemporary novelists are certainly not writing primarily in order to transmit or rephrase a tradition, and emphatically would not relish being consigned to any such role. And I hasten to add that I am setting forth the notion only in the most long-range and ultimate sense, and with all the hesitation that should rightly accompany such pontification; the truth is that we *cannot* know, and that no time is so poorly qualified as our own time to estimate what its own particular accomplishment, or lack of it, may prove to be. Yet it seems to me that for better or for worse, we tired folk of the 1950's and 1960's may be dwelling, for the time being and until otherwise demonstrated, in a time of transition between one period of major literary accomplishment and the next, a time in which there are many good writers but few great ones, in which there is a great deal to admire but not too much to astound.

If this is so, I might add, then of one thing we can be quite sure: *when* the next outburst of really major literature arrives, most of us who are still around to watch it will probably not be able to recognize it. We will be in the position of the Edinburgh reviewers who could not see what it was that John Keats had to say, or the French men of letters of the age of Chateaubriand who thought Stendhal a clumsy buffoon, or the earnest post-Victorian idealists of the early years of our own century who pronounced James Joyce a crude and offensive obscurantist. We will be like Howells, who could respond to Stephen Crane's work because it had a high style, but who could not perceive that Dreiser was immeasurably more important because he had not. This is doubtless our fate, and we can only try to guard against it. And who knows, what

I am talking about may be going on as I write, and in what I have said and shall say about some of my contemporaries I may be guilty of just this blindness myself. But one thing Transition Folk are is careful; and anyway, that which we are, we are, so we might as well proceed as best we can.

This, then, very likely is a time of transition. If so, one of its signs, I think, is the increasingly articulate role which our national metropolis, New York, seems to be playing in literary affairs. Recently the *Times Literary Supplement* of London called attention to the fact that the American literary fulcrum seems to have shifted to New York City. Now this is a bit misleading, unless one realizes what is meant. Surely the center of good writing in the United States is not now located in New York City, any more than it has ever been—and it never has. A few of our novelists and poets have taken up residence there, but only a few; those who seem to be doing the best work generally continue to reside out in the provinces as they have always done, and any publishing house would soon go into bankruptcy if forced to rely upon the literary provender of the Island of Manhattan for its seasonal fare.

But it is true that no longer does the publishing industry await with drawn breath to see what the mail will bring from Oxford, Mississippi, or from Havana, or Nashville, Tennessee. The big news seems to be what Truman Capote will do next, or who it is that Norman Mailer has trained his critical pop guns upon, or which author is being attacked in the latest issue of the *New York Review of Books*. The metropolis has always been the clearing house for literary doings; of late it has seemed to be the actual scene of the chief goings-on as well.

This is a predictable phenomenon. For when the literary cosmos is not dominated by the presence of great writers, and when the natural excitement that is generated in a period of highly creative productivity is not available, then what results will perforce be a kind of artificial simulated excitement and a frantic attempt at establishing a critical hierarchy among what is available for such purposes.

In a time like this, the center of our literature gets confused with the center for publishing and publicizing our literature, which of course is New York City. For books must continue to be written and sold, and the Book of the Month Club must continue to play its accustomed role in the national culture. Thus no sooner had Faulkner died than there commenced "a literary parlor game to name his and Hemingway's successors"—I quote from the introduction to a volume of essays entitled *The Creative Present: Notes on Contemporary American Fiction,* edited, appropriately enough, by two editors of the *New York Times Book Review.* The claims of this and that writer are bandied about, and everyone gets excited by this or that newest development—everything happens, in short, except the kind of awe, and entrenched resistance as well, that comes when a major writer produces a major work.

The point is that there *is* no successor to Hemingway and Faulkner as such; and merely rearranging the names of writers in a list doesn't make any one, no matter how many votes he gets, into a Hemingway and a Faulkner. But without the presence of a major writer or two to place the work of all the lesser writers into perspective, nobody knows how anyone "ranks"—something which it is very important to know in a literature dominated by the marketplace. Thus the *New York Herald Tribune* book magazine several years ago conducted a poll of a number of so-called experts to determine who were the Leading Writers. And *Esquire Magazine* produced a multi-colored chart of the so-called Literary Establishment to show who was where—writers, critics, reviewers, agents, publishers, teachers—and in which relation to each other. If you haven't any idea of where it is you want to go, in other words, pick out a name at random on the map.

There is also, in the absence of the definitive standards imposed by undeniable literary productivity itself, a constant attempt to manufacture new so-called Major writers out of whatever talent is available. The behavior of a literary marketing center is always predictable in this respect. When major literary talents are available, there is always an uneasy feeling of impatience among the literary journalists and booksellers, a scarcely suppressed desire to find something outmoded or inadequate about what is generally held to be superior work simply by virtue of its obvious literary superiority. Thus the attempt to replace the supposedly "Gothic" Faulkner, a few years back, with the supposed "sanity" of James Gould Cozzens; the famed Lillian Ross profile of Hemingway, in which the author of *A Farewell to Arms* was handled as if he were a visiting French welterweight; there was always, concealed within such activities, and on a month by month, year by year basis in the wayward shiftings of such periodicals as the *Saturday Review—*formerly *of Literature—*and the *New York Times Book Review,* the uneasiness and pique that come of the knowledge that the marketplace is of relatively little importance and influence when great literature is available, since great writers find their own audience.

When the Faulkners and Hemingways are no longer available, the marketplace then aspires to create its own. The most flagrant example of that in recent years has been the gaudy literary career of Truman Capote, a decidedly slight writer with a rare talent for publicity. Ever since *Other Voices, Other Rooms* came out in 1948, with its jacket picture of a cute little fellow in blond bangs reclining moodily upon a divan, Capote has been the favorite Southern writer of the market metropolis. In this role Capote has been admirably suited, for as a writer he had a satisfactory knack for the single quality most admired (and understood) of all the characteristics of twentieth-century Southern literature—flamboyant, thickly-drenched exoticism. The pundits of the metropolis saw little more than this to Faulkner; they could not understand why anyone else might think that there was more to Faulkner than local color. In Capote's instance that *was* all that was there; as a novel *Other Voices, Other Rooms* seemed to offer nothing more than a great deal of lush atmosphere without, finally, any meaning provided for it. Capote's subsequent books have borne out the accuracy of that first impression. *The Grass Harp* was a skillful little exercise in calculated nostalgia and quaintness, in which a slick technique attempted to cover its fundamental sentimentality. *Breakfast at Tiffany's* was hardly more than popular magazine froth; its perception of the depths of human motivation was about on a level with that of the late Joseph Hergesheimer. In each successive work, Capote retreated further and further from doing what a novelist must do if he is to be anything more than a writer of pastiche: finding, through the ordering vision of his imagination, meaning for the human experience he recreates. Now we have had the predictable climax of Truman Capote's journey away from meaningfulness: he has written what he terms a "non-fiction novel," which is to say, a book in which the "techniques" of the novelist are used to re-create a real-life, nonfictional event. But what is meant by "techniques" in this case? For Capote, and for the many reviewers who wrote so ecstatically about *In Cold Blood* when it came out, obviously "techniques" meant skill with adjectives, deft dialogue, slick plot anticipation, and the like. *In Cold Blood* was a skillfully put-together work of nonfiction, but that was all it was: it did not resemble a novel because it lacked what any novel must have, and what any genuine work of imaginative literature has had since Aristotle first observed its presence in tragedy: the ordering of human experience into a meaningful pattern, dependent not on its faithfulness to "real life" but on the validity of its own representation for its impact. Any decent novel does just that. But this is what Capote obviously could not do in his successive works of fiction, and what he abandoned even the attempt to do in his most recent work. The events of *In Cold Blood* simply *happened*; the author did not have to give them the logic and inevitability of imaginative meaning. There was no necessity for him to strive for any *meaning* to what he wrote at all; he could just relate the events. The one thing that *In Cold Blood* was not and could never be, given its author's method, was *fiction*; and neither was it, as its author contended in an interview published in the *New York Times Book Review*, "the story of America." It is the story of a brutal murder in Kansas, and the subsequent capture and execution of the murderers; no more, no less. It cannot be read as saying or meaning anything more than that.

Yet when *In Cold Blood* appeared early in 1966, it was preceded by what was perhaps the most elaborate publicity and promotional campaign in recent publishing history. William Faulkner, Ernest Hemingway, Thomas Mann, Marcel Proust, James Joyce at their zenith had never had a book published with as much public fanfare and shrill blowing of advertising trumpets. And when the occasional skeptical reviewer, such as Stanley Kauffmann in *The New Republic*, ventured to suggest that the book was being perhaps a trifle overestimated ("Capote in Kansas," January 22, 1966), the letter columns in subsequent issues of that magazine were filled with the most shocked, indignant protestations. It was as if Kauffmann had ventured to suggest that the late President Kennedy had kept a mistress in the White House. As I write this, *In Cold Blood* has yet to be reviewed in the better literary quarterlies; my prediction is that in those journals, which are notably unswayed by metropolitan publicity campaigns, Capote's book will be adjudged as something less than a latter-day *Crime and Punishment*. And I also venture to suggest that in ten years the book will be hardly even remembered; all the efforts of the book publishing industry not withstanding, there is nothing about it that re-motely augurs the classic status being claimed for it.

The *In Cold Blood* episode, however fascinating to long-time connoisseurs of American press minstrelry, is but one instance of the attempt to make a lesser talent, and in this instance a decidedly minor one at that, suffice when no major talent is apparently available. It will doubtless be repeated, with appropriate variations, every time that Ca-pote produces a new book, unless a writer turns up in the meantime whose literary stature is such that the so-called "power vacuum" in the literary field is filled. Nor will Capote be the only author thus paraded; there are numer-ous candidates, and numerous promotional organizations available to do a similar job. The *New York Times Book Review* alone can accommodate three or four a year, and *Time* magazine is always on twenty-four-hour alert.

All this, of course, is enacted in the metropolitan mid-dle-brow circuit. The intellectual substratum knows bet-ter and is much more subtle. Its response to the happy notion that "the novel is dead" has been of a different sort. It has been to insist (as Capote himself did, with only somewhat more ingenuousness) that journalism—nonfiction, current politics, and its corollary the topical, "engaged" novel of ideas—has replaced fiction as the chief vehicle of the literary imagination today. The chief prophets of this revelation are Norman Mailer and Miss Susan Sontag, with Norman Podhoretz as high priest, and his magazine *Commentary* and the *New York Review of Books* as the Twin tablets of the Law. (The latter periodi-cal, which started out during the New York newspaper strike of several years ago as an attempt to furnish the country with its first respectable and serious medium of literary journalism, has become almost wholly a political publication now; it is, on a more frequently-published basis, what the *Partisan Review* used to be back in the 1930's and 1940's, before it was overcome by fatigue and moved down to New Brunswick and an academic status.)

Miss Sontag is a very bright young woman who mediates between the more rarified intellectual circles and the less obtuse middlebrows; she is equally at home in *Partisan Review,* the *New York Review, Mademoiselle,* and *Book Week.* She is one of the brightest additions to the literary scene in years; sometimes she goes overboard for trivia, but she is incapable of dullness, and she quickly notices what is really going on. Her book of collected critical pieces, *Against Interpretation,* is an unusually fine sample of the response of intellectual New York to the opportunity presented by the current lull in the American novel. Gleefully Miss Sontag exalts the profundity of foreign movies, plays, works of psychoanalysis, anthropology, and so on. Her most famous essay thus far, "Notes on 'Camp,'" already has an almost historical status as a chronicle of her time and place. It sets out to show why certain things are "camp," which is to say, fashionable among New York intellectuals, and why others aren't. What it finally comes to is that those things are "camp" which are amusing and do not require too much thought, and which scrupulously avoid any serious attempt to discover meaning in human experience. This is quite in line with Miss Sontag's essay "Against Interpretation," which informs us that the act of interpretation is "the revenge of the intellect upon the world. To interpret is to impoverish, to deplete the world—in order to set up a shadow world of 'meaning.' . . . The world, our world, is depleted, impoverished enough. Away with all duplicates of it, until we again experience more immediately what we have."

The similarity to the Capotean concern with the "nonfiction novel" is obvious; in both instances (and I much prefer Miss Sontag's, which has the virtue of freshness and intelligence) one is being told that the second-rate is preferable to the first-rate. It is not necessary, says Capote, to give one's writing any meaning, after the manner of a Faulkner, a Hemingway, a Mann, a Proust; and Miss Sontag says that the insistence upon the function of a work of literature as an ordering image of experience, and the kindred insistence upon reading it as if its author possessed an artistic intellect just as formidable as a philosopher's or an anthropologist's or a scientist's, is now passé. Of course Miss Sontag couldn't get away with that if there were a William Faulkner and a Thomas Mann still around, producing novels which manifestly negated her premises. But since there aren't, she can hold forth in fine style and can declare, in another excellent essay on Nathalie Sarraute and the *nouveau roman,* that "when I reread [*Vanity Fair* and *Buddenbrooks*] recently, however marvellous they still seemed, [they] also made me wince. I could not stand the omnipotent author showing me that's how life is, making me compassionate and tearful; with his obstreperous irony, his confidential air of perfectly knowing his characters and leading me, the reader, to feel I knew them too. I no longer trust novels which fully satisfy my passion to understand." Miss Sontag's proposed remedy for this condition (which I confess I don't find fully satisfies *my* passion to understand) is for the novel to quit trying to *mean* something and to surrender itself to the solving of its own technical problems: "the novel as a form of art has nothing to lose, and everything to gain, by joining the revolution that has already swept over most of the other arts. It is time that the novel became what it is not, in England and America, with rare and unrelated exceptions: a form of art which people with serious and sophisticated taste in the other arts can take seriously."

This is heady talk, but exactly what is Miss Sontag saying? In essence, it is that she doesn't want the novel to make her *think;* she doesn't want the ordering meaning of, say, tragedy to come along and falsify the conditions of life by saying that what certain human beings do and do not do *means* this or that about human experience. She can get away with this demand only because there are not presently available any novelists whose version of what human experience means is so compelling that it is impossible not to see its applicability to our own circumstance. Whatever the merits of Saul Bellow, Bernard Malamud, William Styron, John Barth, and their contemporaries, apparently they can't make Miss Sontag stop long enough to say to herself, "That's *me* and *my* own circumstance that he's writing about. There but for the grace of God goes Susan Sontag."

What does Miss Sontag propose in the place of this novel? At bottom she proposes that which is camp. And what is camp is accessible, apprehensible, and, finally, marketable: "The hallmark of Camp is the spirit of extravagence. Camp is a woman walking around in a dress made of three million feathers. Camp is the paintings of Carlo Crivelli, with their real jewels and *trompe d'oeil* insects and cracks in the masonry. Camp is the outrageous aestheticism of Sternberg's six American movies with Dietrich, all six, but especially the last, *The Devil Is a Woman*. . . ." Camp is what, in a period when major artists are not telling us about ourselves, suffices to amuse us and divert us. And it goes without saying that however much New York City cannot furnish us with the major artists, it can furnish us with all the camp we can afford.

Miss Sontag is a very persuasive young lady, and so is Norman Podhoretz a very persuasive young man. A brilliant editor and a fine essayist, he is one of the most incisive thinkers on the current literary scene, and his magazine *Commentary* is probably the most interesting of all New York periodicals. I first encountered Podhoretz about twelve years ago when, as a Pfc. in the Army, he wrote a review of a book I edited, and proved to the satisfaction of the *Partisan Review* that there wasn't any such thing as Southern literature and what's more there never was. In so doing he was not in the least bothered by the abundant evidence to the contrary. Nowadays his approach to the literary situation is that journalism has replaced fiction, and that the novel form is as obsolete as the epic poem.

Podhoretz's chief disability (though as an editor it serves him well) is that he doesn't *like* fiction. He *prefers* nonfiction, and as is the wont of most of us, he attempts to erect his own preferences into a nationwide consensus. Thus the various hatchet jobs that Norman Mailer attempts to perform on his fellow novelists strike Podhoretz as much more exciting than any novel Mailer might write—which they may well be at that. In any event, Podhoretz is constantly making the point that all is finished with the novel. But when one looks at the novelists that Podhoretz does admire—there are several of them —one can see why he reaches this conclusion. It is indeed unlikely that the novel will survive if its chief bulwarks are Mailer and James Baldwin. But it is just barely possible that we can do better than either.

As for Mailer, he seems to have learned early in his career that if one can't produce a war novel as good as Hemingway's, or a Hollywood novel as good as *The Last Tycoon* or Nathanael West's, or a political novel as good as Dos Passos', then the best thing to do in order to maintain one's sanity is to go around writing articles attacking those of one's contemporaries who are also trying to do those things. Thus *Esquire* magazine comes out with an article featuring Mailer, photographed in a prizefight ring corner, and entitled "Norman Mailer vs. William Styron, James Jones, James Baldwin, Saul Bellow, Joseph Heller, John Updike, William Burroughs, J. D. Salinger, Philip Roth." Great stuff. And true, it *was* infinitely more interesting than Mailer's next novel. But this proves a great deal more about Mailer's fiction than it does about the condition of the contemporary novel.

Thus the leading prophets of doom. Thus the metropolis and its chorus of singers.

CODA

Capote on the "non-fiction novel," Norman Mailer on Viet Nam and the White House, Norman Podhoretz on the greater realism of journalism in our time, Susan Sontag on the jewel-speckled paintings of Carlo Crivelli—what do they have to signify for the state of the novel in our time? What does such counsel mean for the novelist of today, trying to write his *Herzog* and *Sot-Weed Factor* and *Set This House on Fire*? Marcel Proust knew the answer quite well, for he heard many similar pronouncements in his own iron time. It was to look within his own life for signs of the meaning concealed therein:

To read the subjective book of these strange signs (signs standing out boldly, it seemed, which my conscious mind, as it explored my unconscious self, went searching for, stumbled against and passed around, like a diver groping his way), no one could help me with any rule, for the reading of that book is a creative act in which no one can stand in our stead, or even collaborate with us. And therefore how many there are who shrink from writing it; how many tasks are undertaken in order to avoid that one! . . . But in art excuses count for nothing; good intentions are of no avail; the artist must at every instant heed his instinct; so that art is the most real of all things, the sternest school in life and truly the Last Judgment. This book, the most difficult of all to decipher, is also the only one dictated to us by reality, and only one the "imprinting" of which on our consciousness was done by reality itself.

And William Faulkner knew it too: "the young man or woman writing today has forgotten the problems of the human heart in conflict with itself which alone can make good writing because only that is worth writing about, worth the agony and the sweat." And to disagree with Faulkner, I think that the best of our own day's novelists know that, too. They know that there is no substitute in our time for the novel, and that the task of the novelist remains what it has always been: to depict the way that things are, which is an act of the highest intelligence.

Surely there are times when this seems easier to do than at other times, and ours appears not to be such a time, among other reasons because of the existence, right up to the edge of our own day and even into it, of some highly convincing and revealing models of literary perception which however no longer quite illuminate and yet can get in the way of our own attempts to see. But there is only one thing to do about this; it is to write novels, without worrying about the cries and demands of the marketplace, all of which must necessarily grow silent when confronted with the genuine article.

Is the best of today's fiction quite up to that of a generation ago? How can one say, finally? I only know that there are novels being written each year that I find greatly interesting and enjoyable, and I am not disposed to spend much time looking around for what they do not provide, when they so obviously provide so much. I suggest, then, that we stop worrying so much over whether the novel is dead, and spend more time reading living novels. And if, just around the corner, there are coming new novels which will be for our own time what *The Sound and the Fury* and *The Sun Also Rises* and *Ulysses* and *Remembrance of Things Past* were for the generation before ours, one of the ways whereby we will be able to recognize them is that they most assuredly will not start out, "Through the fence, between the curling flower spaces, I could see them hitting," or "Robert Cohn was once middleweight boxing champion of Princeton," or "Stately, plump Buck Mulligan came from the stairhead," or "For a long time I used to go to bed early." They will be their own selves, and because they are, they will speak for all of us as well.

The Search for Lost Innocence:
Karl Shapiro's
The Bourgeois Poet

I

In Baltimore, walking in Victorian-movie snow it occurred to
me: seek for the opposite. I'm for the Faustian super-
market. The opposite enthralls me.

The Bourgeois Poet

It was instructive, and certainly very amusing, to watch
the reaction to Karl Shapiro's most recent book of verse,
The Bourgeois Poet. A few optimistic souls pronounced
it a significant breakthrough, a beacon light by which
young poets may henceforth proceed through the foggy
seas of contemporary verse. Many others have termed it
notes toward a poem, raw material not given meaning, a
kind of unmasticated poetic prose striving toward but not
achieving form. Even the magazine editors who published
portions of it didn't quite know what to do with it; some
artfully contrived a middle position, halfway between the
legitimate poetry in the front and the admitted and declared prose in the back.

The Bourgeois Poet is odd stuff; there is no escaping
that. It consists of ninety-six parts divided into three sec-

tions, the first discursive, the second autobiographical, and the third epigrammatic. In the way it appears on the printed page it doesn't much resemble poetry, though sometimes it sounds very much like what we usually expect when we read a Shapiro poem:

> Wood for the fireplace, wood for the floor, what is the life span? Sometimes before I lay the log on the fire I think: it's sculpture wood, it's walnut. Maybe someone would find a figure in it, as children find faces in the open fire (I never have). Then I lay it on the flames like a heretic, where it pauses a moment, then joins in the singing. . . .

Remove the parenthesis, give or take a few syllables here and there, and one could without too much difficulty read that as verse which scans and otherwise behaves traditionally. But sometimes the condition is much more akin to the conventional notion of prose than of poetry:

> In gold I also use my middle initial but spelled out JAY. J is for Jacob. My father dropped his first name Israel. My son is named Jacob. Upper-class Jews call him Jack. My father-in-law's name was Jack, probably Jacob.

One might be able to figure out a way to present that in regular lines, but that would be the least of it. The tone is conversational, but the conversation is hardly interesting. If, to quote Shapiro, poetry is how ideas feel, then that is surely prose.

The model is at times obviously Whitman, even to the point of conscious parody. More often it is not parody but genuine use of Whitman:

> Quintana lay in the shallow grave of coral. The guns boomed stupidly fifty yards away. The plasma trickled into his arm. Naked and filthy, covered with mosquitoes, he looked at me as I read his white cloth tag. How do you feel, Quintana? He looked away from my gaze. I lie: we'll get you out of here sometime today.

At other times Carl Sandburg seems to be the model, with a little E. E. Cummings thrown in for good savor:

Now both are dead, Dylan and Uncle Saul. Dylan was taken
by the pickling of his beautiful brain. The sacred oxygen
could not reach the convolutions. Uncle Saul was taken
thrice by the heart, thrice by the broken personality.
Uncle Saul joked in the lobby of the plush nuthouse,
wearing a brilliant sportcoat and shined elegant shoes.
The black hair dye had vanished; his hair was snowy
white. They gave him the shock treatment until his heart
exploded. Dylan lay inert with the Moses bumps on his
forehead amidst the screaming of wives and the groans
of lovers and drinkers. And the Beat said—iambic killed
him.

Then at times Ezra Pound gets in a good lick or two:

To the poor (aux pauvres) crime alone (le crime seul) opens
(ouvre) les portes de la vie (the doors of life). Entire
libraries of music are hurled in the gutters: the G.I.'s
are looking for bottles. The Bavarian Venus is snatched
baldheaded.

All we need there is a Chinese ideograph borrowed from
Fenollosa. More importantly the book as a whole seems to
take its cues from Pound's *Cantos*. Shapiro has always
contended that the whole principle of the *Cantos* was dis-
cord, and that only Pound thought otherwise. *The Bourgeois Poet* often appears to be constructed on such a principle.

One could go on in this vein, pointing out this and that
resemblance, but it would not be an especially profitable
thing to do, because *The Bourgeois Poet* is not important
for its borrowings or its adaptations of known style. Shapiro has long since proved himself a craftsman of language
of the first order, and it is no surprise to know that he
can appropriate the distinctive rhythm and style of a number of poets. He always handles what he does very well.
There is only one—and I fear major—criticism of the whole
thing, so far as the style goes. Granted that the language
is varied and not the customary language of poetry,
granted that Shapiro can and does modulate, parody, and

otherwise utilize Whitman, Sandburg, Pound, Crane, Baudelaire, Joyce, Cummings, and other stylists, the question remains, Where is Shapiro? If after reading 113 pages of *The Bourgeois Poet* one were to put it down, pick up a copy of a magazine, and come upon ten similar pages, would there be any way to be able to say with any assurance that they were written by Karl Shapiro and not by someone else? I wish I thought so. Only an occasional metaphor seems distinctive. And that is what is wrong with *The Bourgeois Poet*—not its language as such, not its use of prose rhythms, not even its subject matter. What's wrong is its form. It doesn't have a recognizable form, which is another way of saying that it doesn't add up to anything; the language and content don't fuse together to do something, and the reader has no feeling of its having set things right. One is willing to accept almost any convention that a poet wishes to adopt, including that of saying "to hell with convention," but he needs to justify some convention. Shapiro hasn't.

The question I wish to propound in this essay is, Why? Why has Shapiro done this? Why has he written *The Bourgeois Poet* at all, and what does the fact that he did write it mean about poetry today? Karl Shapiro is no fool; and he has written entirely too much good poetry to be accused of not knowing what a good poem is. When a man of his reputation and character produces a book like this, we had better ask ourselves why he did it and what made him do so.

II

The best book has a bad finality. The best book closes too many rooms. The best poem clicks like a box: you have made yourself a neat little trap, a hideaway with wall-to-wall rhyme. . . .

The Bourgeois Poet

Some fifteen years ago, in a lecture he gave at the Johns Hopkins University, Shapiro discussed the work of several

British poets of the First World War. He quoted from a review he had written of their work some years before, in which he had said something to the effect that the experience of these poets stopped with the war, and he went on to remark that when he had written that statement he had not quite understood what it meant, but that now he had a much better idea. Shapiro was of course referring to his own work and his own career. For like those poets, he was a "war poet." It was while he was in uniform during the years from 1941 to 1945, when the United States was at war with the Axis Powers, that Shapiro first began to attract attention. Actually his first book was published privately some time before that, but it was youthful work and he has properly collected none of it. Several more years were to elapse before the work on which his reputation depends began appearing in literary magazines. In 1941 New Directions collected some of it in *Five Young American Poets,* and the following year there appeared *Person, Place and Thing,* published when Shapiro was already on military service in the South Pacific. This book attracted attention everywhere; it contained many of his most characteristic poems, such as "Nostalgia," "Haircut," "Buick," and "Auto Wreck." It was followed, in 1944, by *V-Letter and Other Poems,* which won him the Pulitzer Prize the following year and included such work as "The Leg," and "Troop Train," and what is probably the finest poem written about the Second World War, "Elegy for a Dead Soldier." The year after that, Shapiro brought out *Essay on Rime,* a nonscholarly study of the art of verse, composed in a loose blank-verse form, which was so fresh and so original that it attracted widespread notice and sold an astonishing number of copies.

Whatever the personal discomforts of serving in the Pacific, it should be noted that so far as his status and reputation as a poet were concerned, Shapiro's military service conferred at least two distinct advantages. For one thing, it isolated him from the American literary establishment, allowing his reputation to grow and flourish without his getting involved in whatever politics, personalities, and the like go along with making one's professional way in the hierarchy. More importantly, at a time when in technique and status both he was moving from strength to strength, it kept him in a situation whereby he remained an "amateur" rather than a "professional" poet. By this I mean that in the army his experience was of necessity primarily nonintellectual and nonliterary, was shared by millions of others who were in no way intellectuals and literary men, and thus did not cut him off from what as a poet was peculiarly the source of his strength—his ability to give form and meaning to common, everyday experience. Very few poets have been able to articulate such experience for us. But when Shapiro describes the red light of an ambulance arriving at the scene of an automobile accident as

> one ruby flare
> Pulsing out red light like an artery

he takes a visual image of something mechanical and inanimate, unites it with the human life and death with which it is connected, and creates a metaphor of the associations of terror and fear that overwhelm us at such a moment. When he refers to "the ambulance with its terrible cargo" leaving the scene, the sense of the cold helplessness of our utter dependence on the physical body is re-created; mangled, the human being at that moment is flesh, "cargo." The whole scene is explored in the images of shock, disbelief, and awareness that accompany us at such times. One policeman "with a bucket douches ponds of blood / Into the street and gutter," while another "hangs lanterns on the wrecks that cling, / Empty husks of locusts, to iron poles." Then, after reminding us of the way in which we seek desperately to accommodate the vision of the horror of death on such an occasion to the everyday routine of our lives ("The grim joke and the banal resolution"), he proceeds to do what we cannot ourselves do at such a time: isolate what our reactions really signify.

> For death in war is done by hands;
> Suicide has cause and stillbirth, logic
> And cancer, simple as a flower, blooms.
> But this invites the occult mind,
> Cancels our physics with a sneer,
> And spatters all we know of denouement
> Across the expedient and wicked stones.

We cannot, in other words, accommodate the violence of sudden death into our cherished systems of cause and effect, meaning and justice, and so the auto wreck is terrible because it reminds us of our helplessness, our inability to understand what life and death really are, and our human and social condition of being at the mercy of blind chance.

Another important quality of his poetry is that not only the experience but the *attitudes* toward it, however heightened and intensified, are true to everyday life. There is not that dissociation from everyday experience and attitudes that marks so much twentieth-century poetry. There are no housemaids with damp souls, as in Eliot. Consider, for instance, the vast difference between, say, Eliot's sarcastic reference to "the sound of horns and motors which shall bring / Sweeney to Mrs. Porter in the spring," in which the use of an automobile is portrayed as a sign of modern degeneracy and middle-class crudeness, and Shapiro's (I almost wrote "the American poet's," which I suppose is part of what I am getting at) "Buick":

> And not as the ignorant beast do you squat and
>   watch me depart,
> But with exquisite breathing you smile, with
>   satisfaction of love,
> And I touch you again as you tick in the silence
>   and settle in sleep.

The same holds true for the poet in the emporium, the barber shop, the drugstore, and so on; and in wartime the troop train, the induction camp, the troop ship, and other such experiences. Again, the poet's attitude is not one of sophisticated detachment; it is not that of an intellectual looking down self-consciously at the artifacts of a middle-class civilization. The poet does not need to make a distinction between his experience as a citizen or a soldier and his attitude as a poet. In this sense Shapiro isn't really a "soldier"; he is a civilian in the army who doesn't like it very much but who makes the best of it. It is this ability to articulate the common experience of his generation that made possible his fine "Elegy for a Dead Soldier." There is not the slightest bit of ironic qualification of the subject, and no self-consciousness at voicing the ideals for which Americans generally went to war in 1941–45. They are the poet's as well, and he differs from others who hold them primarily in his ability to articulate them. Again, thoroughly "bourgeois" poetry, by a member of a thoroughly middle-class society.

I want to make one more observation about Shapiro's earlier work, which is that though essentially social, it is a very personal, autobiographical kind of poetry. This I think is not always realized about Shapiro. The fact is that almost all of Shapiro's earlier poems are drawn directly out of his own experience; they are not conceptual in their thought, which is to say that they do not attempt to impose a philosophical or social system on experience. They consist of the poet's keen and unashamed exploration of the social meaning of his own attitudes; ideas are important, but not ideological systems. The limitation of such work, scarcely apparent at this stage, lies precisely there: it begins with the poet's own experience, it ends with it, and it explores what the experience means, not as tested against a larger system of value judgment but with a pragmatic, no-holds-barred, subjective strategy that can change with each experience and each poem. Everything, in short, depends on the poet's state of mind.

III

The bourgeois poet closes the door of his study and lights his pipe. Why am I in this box, he says to himself (although it is exactly as he planned). . . .

The Bourgeois Poet

What happens, though, to the "war poet" who comes out of uniform and back into civilian life? No longer is he a soldier who writes poetry; he is a Man of Letters. In Shapiro's case he was appointed Consultant in Poetry to the Library of Congress, where he served for two years, following which he became Associate Professor of English Writing at the Johns Hopkins University. He became, that is, a member of what some like to call the Establishment. He served on prize committees, was a Fellow in Poetry of the Library of Congress, gave the Phi Beta Kappa poem at Harvard, and in 1950 accepted the editorship of that most influential and important of all American magazines of verse, *Poetry* of Chicago.

In 1947 Shapiro brought out a third collection of his poems, *Trial of a Poet*. This time the hosannas were few; the new book was roundly panned. Save for a few poems, it had much less of the excitement and distinction that had characterized the two earlier collections.

The explanation, I think, was simply that Shapiro had, by the very nature of his intelligence and craft, lost that "innocence" of perception, that familiar and sympathetic identification with the artifacts and attitudes of ordinary middle-class life which had been the mainstay of his art. The Bourgeois Poet now "knew too much." The intense exploration of immediate impressions, the pragmatic strategy of expanding the social meaning of the everyday occurrence, no longer sufficed. He had said all he could say about Buicks and barber shops and auto wrecks, and the common experience of the civilian soldier far from home no longer existed for him. He had become an Intellectual. When he thought of terror now, for example, he thought, not of an automobile wreck so much as of Hieronymus Bosch. And to make poetry out of that kind of experience required a very different strategy. It is interesting that the chief poem he wrote during this period of not too much poetry was at first entitled "Eden Retold," though later changed to "Adam and Eve." For the territory he was now working was no longer largely unexplored and virgin; it was material that was all too familiar to the modern poet, one largely dissociated in language and attitude from that of ordinary middle-class American society. Few good poets before Shapiro had thought to make a poem out of a barber shop, but writers from earliest times down through Milton, Blake, Wordsworth, and Mark Twain to the present have been dealing with the Garden of Eden.

What does a good poet such as Shapiro do in such a case? He looks around for an absolute. It is in this light that I see the strategy, in 1958, of collecting some of his best poems, including many of the older ones and a few recent pieces, under the title *Poems of a Jew*. He asked himself, that is, what he is that he can be sure of, and he decides that whatever else he is, he is a Jew, and that this means, in his own words, "a certain state of consciousness which is inescapable." The Jew, whatever else he may or may not be, is someone absolutely committed to this world, someone who "represents the primitive ego of the human race," and the Jews as a people are "beyond philosophy, beyond art, virtually beyond religion, a stranger even to mysticism . . . at the very center of the divine manifestation—man." Which is another way of saying, I think, that if one thinks of himself in this way he can put aside the search for a cultural system and trust to the concrete cultural identity thus afforded him.

Alas, it doesn't work. Whatever being a Jew might have meant in times past, nowadays it doesn't provide one with a ready-made identity that can answer any cultural problem and evaluate any experience—any more so than Roman Catholicism could for Allen Tate, or Zen Buddhism (Shapiro has flirted with that a little, too) for Allen Ginsberg. Shapiro's Jewish identity has served from time to time to give him material and meaning for several good poems (I like especially "University," "Travelogue for Exiles," and "The Crucifix in the Filing Cabinet," though I am not convinced that either of the first two is indebted more to Judaism than to several other aspects of Shapiro's identity).

IV

The molasses of lecturing is sweet and the rum of polemic is good for the stomach. I write prose to find out what I think. Then it is printed. The whole business is irresponsible. . . .

The Bourgeois Poet

Another thing that a poet does, if he has got the kind of fine analytical intelligence that Karl Shapiro has, is to write criticism. Now Shapiro in recent years has become very much a professional anti-critic; his book of essays, *In Defense of Ignorance*, was an attack on all literary criticism and all critics, and all poets who like to write criticism. "It has taken me twenty years," he wrote then, "to break away completely from modern poetry and modern criticism, which I consider to be one and the same thing. Being a teacher has helped me immeasurably to know how pernicious this poetry and criticism really are and how destructive they have been to poetry and the faculty of judging poetry." He even accuses criticism of creating made-to-order poetry.

But the truth is that good poets write criticism not to "capture poetry," as Shapiro has accused Eliot and Pound of doing, but to find out what they think, as he himself admits elsewhere. And Shapiro has always written criticism; the *Essay on Rime* was criticism, even though it was written in blank verse. Shapiro wrote criticism all during the 1940's and 1950's, first on the side of the "Culture Poetry" (his own term) and then against it. When he was Consultant in Poetry at the Library of Congress, he even wrote an essay on prosody and threw in a bibliography to boot. He wrote a dialogue on dramatic poetry and a number of pronouncements about the state of poetry in the years when he first took over the editorship of *Poetry*. When he decided to break loose from the Establishment, about the time he gave up the editorship of *Poetry*, he published a series of lectures entitled *Beyond Criticism*. His 1960 collection, *In Defense of Ignorance*, contained only a small portion of his critical prose; he declared in it that "the present essays are intended to be the last criticism I shall ever write." But four years later *The Carleton Miscellany* turns up with "A Malebolge of 1400 Books," being six lectures by Shapiro amounting to some 50,000 additional words of criticism. So it is highly unlikely that he really intends to stop writing criticism, and one hopes he will not.

Shapiro wrote and writes criticism in order to write poetry; it is as simple as that. If poetry is the mansion, then criticism is entrusted with clearing out the woods and the fields so that the foundations can be laid. If we look at Shapiro's criticism from the *Essay on Rime* up through "A Malebolge of 1400 Books," we will see that it has at all times really been intended not as an effort to dictate taste or to reform the literary world, but as a way of working out the principles by which he can write his verse. In this respect the *Essay on Rime* is interesting. On the one hand it is a statement of the need for a poetry which does not depend on conceptual systems, upon involvement in and close familiarity with the intellectual life, and which is drawn not out of books but out of everyday experience. Yet at the same time and by its very nature the *Essay on Rime* is an ingenious way of providing just such interpretation, analysis, and criticism without actually writing it in prose—as if the poet were getting himself ready for his entry into the intellectual world as Man of Letters, but by doing the book in verse he was avoiding taking the final step just yet (and the verse is at most points very, very close to straightforward prose).

It may be recalled that in 1948 the Fellows in Poetry of the Library of Congress, who constituted many of our most distinguished poets, voted to award the Bollingen Prize for Poetry to Ezra Pound, then a patient at a Washington mental hospital and under indictment for treason because of his pro-Axis broadcasts from Italy during the war. Shapiro was, I believe, the lone dissenter from the vote. In the furore that followed, the *Saturday Review of Literature* asked Shapiro to write an essay attacking the decision. He refused, whereupon Robert Hillyer was commissioned to do it, and he produced a series of articles which all but accused the Fellows of a Fascist plot against American democracy and linked the so-called obscurity of Modern Poetry (which the fuss was really about, when one comes down to it) to an anti-democratic plot. Public outcry was such that the Library of Congress dissociated itself from the Bollingen Prize, and the incident soon became a kind of Dreyfus Case in which all members of the profession of poetry had to choose sides. If you were for the award to Pound, you were for the practice of poetry as promulgated by its leading poets, and you were also in favor of the New Criticism in particular and the practice of criticism of poetry in general. If you were against the award, you were against modern poetry, and you objected to the New Criticism and generally to "culture poetry" and the primacy of the intellect in modern letters. Either you were on one side or the other. The only poet of reputation I can recall who genuinely attempted to play it down the middle was Peter Viereck, who only succeeded in angering both sides.

As for Shapiro, he felt he had to choose, and he did. He wrote an essay, entitled "What is Anti-Criticism," in which he reversed his decision, and while he was at it he went all the way: he defended the New Criticism, he defended Culture Poetry, and he attacked all those who were against it. Why did Shapiro do this? Again I think the answer is to be found not in his cultural or literary convictions, but in his poetry. The kind of poetry Shapiro defended (and in so doing, explained) was the kind of poetry he was attempting to write at the time. It was "Culture Poetry," to use his term again, the poetry of "Adam and Eve," and of "A Calder," and "Going to School," and "The Alphabet." Whatever the merits of this poetry, it was not a poetry based on the discovery and analysis of the meaning of everyday middle-class experience. It is meditative, reflective poetry, which, as in "Going to School," seeks to resolve the physical world of science and the occult imagination of the poet in a metaphor, or as in "The Alphabet" would sum up moral history in the authority of the Old Testament.

Shapiro's editorship of *Poetry*, his new-found legitimate critical status, his willingness to accept his role as Man of Letters in the Cultural Establishment were all very nice, but they involved one drawback: he wrote very little poetry in these years, and what he did write was not conspicuously outstanding. As a poet he wore his new identity very uneasily. And if, as I believe, a poet's critical position, his place in the hierarchy, his livelihood itself are all ultimately subservient, in his own scale of values, to his success in writing the verse he wishes to write, then Karl Shapiro's next mutation was entirely predictable.

V

What interests me is that Sandburg, a long time ago, made an intellectual decision to abdicate from intellectualism. . . .
                              "A Malebolge of 1400 Books"

He resigned. He quit. He left *Poetry* and he went to California, and finally he wound up in the state of Nebraska, editing a literary magazine and teaching at the university, and he decided to have a try at pulling down the pillars on which the whole edifice of modern poetry rested. His strident assertion of his identity as a Jew, through his choice of title for his 1958 collection of verse, was one way of asserting his independence. Eliot the Anglican, Pound the anti-Semite, Auden the Anglo-Catholic "convert" became the villains who had ensnared all of modern poetry in a conspiracy designed to make it intellectual, effete, highbrow, anti-scientific, sexless, ivory-towerish, and so on. The New Criticism was part of the plot; by removing moral and social judgment from the act of criticism it allowed Eliot and Pound to introduce all manner of un-American doctrines into modern poetry. Even his onetime idol William Butler Yeats was no longer safe; a good poet, Yeats had been spoiled by being seduced into composing "Culture Poetry."

Having gone this far, Shapiro next began to extend the logic of his position, and he began doing, I fear, what he criticizes Eliot and Pound for doing. When Pound decried the poetry of Shakespeare because it did not fit into his system, and Eliot did the same with Milton and others, Shapiro said that both knew perfectly well how good the poetry was that they were thus castigating, but they criticized it anyway. "It is my contention," Shapiro wrote in *In Defense of Ignorance*, "that modern criticism is not honest, though it may be sincere. Its dishonesty results from its undying loyalty to generalities. . . . Pound knows as well as you do that Shakespeare is the finest of all English poets, but he must remain sincere to the system he has blocked out. He thus engages in a fantastic act of dishonesty. . . . Sincerity to the idea always takes precedence in the mental life of the intellectual, whether the idea comprises a total system or is some offshoot of one of the *isms*."

But Shapiro, I think, proceeded to do precisely the same thing. Eliot was now "a poet of religion, hence a poet of the second or third rank." Pound's *Mauberly* is "a very bad poem." Yeats "will always remain pretty much of a

poet of his time, because of his commitment to the historical role" (a qualification worthy of Eliot at his best!). A
poem entitled "Hot Afternoons Have Been In Montana"
by Eli Siegel is "one of the last authentically American
poems . . . before the final triumph of Eliot's culture
poetry." William Carlos Williams is, along with D. H.
Lawrence, "the leader of what authentic American poetry
is being written today." Wallace Stevens is "a beautiful
poet who is really devoid of imagination." Henry Miller
is "the greatest living author." James Joyce is "that master
manufacturer of literary cuckoo clocks." Wilhelm Reich
is one of our "true leaders and visionaries." "John Bun-
yan knew more about the uses of literature than [John]
Donne." Robert W. Service is "a superlative poet on the
lowest possible level." And so on. Now no more than
Pound on Shakespeare or Eliot on Milton, I surmise, did
Shapiro really believe all that, but it fitted his own current posture, and so he said it. He knows that as poetry
the work of Robert W. Service isn't worth the paper it is
printed on, and that by contending that Service's doggerel
is "as much poetry as *Hamlet* or *The Rape of the Lock* or
The Ballad of Reading Gaol" he is guilty of the most
blatant kind of casuistry. Shapiro said all that because he
thought it "needed to be said," whether or not it happened to be true.

VI

I seek the entrance of the rabbit hole. Maybe it's the door
that has no name.

The Bourgeois Poet

I write this not in dispraise of Shapiro, but with a kind
of genuine admiration, however much I disagree with
him. For to repeat, Shapiro is a *poet,* and an honest poet,
and in order to deal honestly with himself as a poet he is
quite willing to adopt any posture or critical position he
finds useful, and to burn every other book of poetry or
criticism ever written.

Now manifestly he could not go back to writing poems about Buicks and haircuts; he had left that kind of poetry for good. On the other hand, there was the distinct feeling that in trying to write Culture Poetry he was trying to be what he wasn't, to falsify, through overinhibiting, his own experience. The old kind of direct statement, the pleasure of showing things as they are without having to take account of various kinds of cultural cross references, literary, social, and cultural associations, the comfort of not having to be aware of his own consciousness in the act of expressing himself, were being denied him. Very well. What he must do was to find a method of recovering that immediacy and freshness, that "lost innocence."

If he could create poetry free of the kind of formal pattering that conventional rhyme and meter demanded, sufficiently pliable in structure to permit him to work into the poem what he knew about things without having to fit them into the artificial unity of a rigid structure, flexible enough in language and diction to let him qualify his thoughts without falsifying them by making them too ponderous and clumsy, unified by no more severe a logic than that of casual association, a poetry which in its pattern of imagery and its rhetorical structure led the reader ahead toward the next thought without encouraging him to examine each new image in relation to what had preceded it—if he could do this, it would again be possible for him to do what almost since *V-Letter* he had found it so very difficult to do: *get himself down on paper*, in words. For with Shapiro that was the all-important thing; he didn't want to erect a system of culture and belief, he wanted to say what he knew. And what he knew was Karl Shapiro.

The obvious model was Whitman, the poet of *Song of Myself*. The equation, the paradox if one will, whereby Whitman had constructed *Song of Myself* was the dual existence of the individual as a solitary being, and as the perceiver and therefore possessor of his society and his culture. Whitman set forth the duality in the first two lines:

> I celebrate myself, and sing myself,
> And what I assume you shall assume

The resulting paradox Whitman pursued through a division of body and spirit, society and self, pitting one against the other to show how each contained the other, so that one human being constituted within himself history, biology, politics, science, the arts, commerce, geography, and so on, while at the same time he was *not* any of these things, but a private, solitary soul with its own consciousness and integrity. In many, one—in one, many.

Whitman made this believable in two ways. One was through a mystic identification of flesh and spirit, form and substance, in a transcendental unity. The other was through a cumulative rhetoric which brought together rather than set apart, which dealt with a various and numerous experience and made it one by alliteration, repetition, restatement, and copula. Thus Whitman's long lines, his catalogues, his repetition; they were a structure designed to make the reader move along with him, not stand back and examine everything separately. The unifying factor, to repeat, was the individual, the person, to whom all things related and came back, and this person was, through an act of mystical poetic transcendence, the poet himself.

If, therefore, Shapiro could like Whitman write a poem of this kind, in many parts, structured primarily by association of ideas and by rhetoric, in format loose enough and flexible enough to permit anything and everything to be expressed that seemed appropriate, he might at last achieve what he had been looking for: a way to get himself and what he knew into a poem. He needed a way that would enable him to show, without on every occasion having to link up, what he saw. What way would this be? The answer was *The Bourgeois Poet*.

It was a very good idea. The only drawback was that it didn't work.

VII

O pickpock moon, subject of all lost poems, birthplace of tides et cetera, true bottom of the sea et cetera, O wallsocket.
The Bourgeois Poet

The Bourgeois Poet doesn't work because the basic metaphor, the principle of structural oneness by which Whitman was able to make *Song of Myself* a cohesive and unified work of art, and thus control and direct the role of all the parts, is impossible to Shapiro. I am many, Whitman said, therefore I am one; in place of Whitman's mystical transcendental assertion of oneness with the universe, Shapiro attempts to use the principle of solipsism, the notion that one creates the world in the act of comprehending it:

> The world is my dream, says the wild child, ever so wise, not stepping on lines. I am the world, says the wise-eyed child. I made you, mother. I made you, sky. Take care or I'll put you back in my dream.

But at once irony must be trained on such an assertion, or else it will collapse into fragments:

> If I look at the sun the sun will explode, says the wicked boy. If I look at the moon I'll drain away. Where I stay I hold them in their places. Don't ask me what I am doing.

And when the first section ends, it is with a reminder of the peril involved in being one with nature, and of the potentially disastrous relationship of disembodied, pure thought to the blood-reality of people and events:

> De Sade looks down through the bars of the Bastille. They have stepped up the slaughter of nobles.

De Sade, the "Divine Marquis," who in another context is said by Shapiro to have known only two varieties of relationship of men to men, "abstract morality and crime," was like Whitman and Emerson willing to look at man purely as a creature of nature, but unlike them De Sade saw nature as evil instead of good. Shapiro's one-in-many, many-in-one world will thus contain what Walt Whitman's didn't in *Song of Myself*—the possibility that the world within one man's consciousness is an evil world.

But to acknowledge this possibility, to look at the negative side of the metaphor, is to undercut the principle of structural unity, because if the fact that one contains the world in one's perceptions may equally mean that one contains everything or nothing, then nothing is no-unity, no-oneness, no-coherence. The whole scheme flies apart. The resultant training of irony onto the confident assertions throws the reader, as Whitman's verse does not, into an awareness of separateness, of dis-unity, which instead of making the poem develop as a unit splits it apart.

Tactically it also works the wrong way. The success in *Song of Myself* of the loose, flowing construction of cumulative detail and succeeding emotions depends rhetorically on the reader's being always propelled forward, without stopping to speculate critically on the appropriateness and conviction of the similes and metaphors. Shapiro, by postulating disunity as well as oneness, draws attention to just such separation, and when the reader sees that things don't go together, the poem becomes a disjointed collection of images and ideas.

The real difficulty is that Shapiro isn't a mystic, however much he tries to be one by dabbling in Zen Buddhism, Wilhelm Reich, Jung, Ouspensky, and "cosmic consciousness." He is essentially a rationalist, and whenever his imagination begins wondering away from the logical his sense of irony comes charging in to rectify the situation. However much Shapiro denounces "Culture Poetry" and intellectual systems, however much he complains that from Dante through Eliot a poem which is philosophical is to that extent weakened as a poem, he can't help putting things together himself. It is amusing, in *In Defense of Ignorance,* after watching him complain because Pound and Eliot try to make everything into a rational system, to see him turn right around and declare that Yeats's preoccupation with magic "weakened his whole structure of thought."

We have in *The Bourgeois Poet,* therefore, the example of a poem which, written by a poet whose art consists in perceiving the relationship between things and social ideas, is structured nevertheless according to the theory that at least half the time things do *not* add up. The result is that often they don't—in his poem; and yet every instinct in the poet, which means every metaphor and every simile, continually works toward making the reader look for relationships. In the end the only unifying principle of *The Bourgeois Poet,* which is another way of saying the only principle designed to keep us reading on, is the personality of the poet. And that isn't nearly enough, because that personality itself isn't naturally unified and whole. So what we get are random thoughts, this idea of that, this memory and that judgment, this reference to an event and that comparison, and so on, for 113 pages, some of them brilliant and intense, some indifferent and flat.

Why does the book end on page 120, at the end of part No. 96? I have read it three times, and I don't know. Shapiro has modeled his final section on that of Whitman's *Song of Myself.* But the irony undercuts it. It is left hanging. Life may be like that, but poetry can't be; the way for a poet to show that nothing adds up is to make a poem add up to a statement of that. Otherwise there is chaos. And chaos itself is a very different matter from the depiction of chaos.

VIII

The antithesis of the closed poem is not necessarily the open poem, the freedom of Whitman or surrealism or just plain spillover of feeling, anger or illumination.

"A Malebolge of 1400 Books"

The Bourgeois Poet is, I think, a brave attempt by an honest poet, and to the extent that it can give order and coherence to that poet's personality, it is a successful work. But its design is such that nothing in the structure or presentation can help very much to give it that coherence; it is deliberately constructed not to help. The poet's personality, not the poem, must do the job. And it won't do it. All of which goes to show that the traditional machinery of poetry—rhyme, rhythm, metrics, verse forms— are not arbitrary restrictions, however much their overly rigid application may sometimes give that impression. Rather, they are methods of ordering experience through intensifying and controlling language. And if for Karl Shapiro all traditional and known forms are too confining and artificial to allow him to discover such order, then given his uncompromising intelligence there would seem to be but one alternative; to find the form. It will not be enough to pretend that one is not needed. No-form is not the answer, and however attractive it might be to do so, Shapiro no more than anyone else can will himself back to a condition of ignorance and innocence.

Meanwhile there are straws in the wind. In "A Malebolge of 1400 Books" Shapiro shows signs of backtracking in his attitude toward Eliot and Pound. He is "beginning after a decade of swatting the Tse-tse and subverting Pound to appreciate their gift to us," and also "to give in to the *Four Quartets* as a model from which to go into production." He hedges the bet by prefacing it with the statement that the principle of both Eliot's and Pound's work is disorganization, "a new definition of the organization of life." But Shapiro knows better than that; whatever else may be true of Eliot, the *Four Quartets* are no one's disorganized poem. So it may be that Karl Shapiro is once again ready to move in another direction.

However much he may fence himself in with this or that system, he always manages at the proper moment to leap over the railing and get on with the business of writing new poems. He says of Pound, in "A Malebolge of 1400 Books," that "I am not concerned about making these remarks consistent with any I have made in the past —in the event that anyone should go to the trouble of comparing them." No one is finally going to worry how much or how often Shapiro contradicts himself in his critical writings, providing that in his poetry he uses his discoveries and his insights to good advantage. I suggest that we view *The Bourgeois Poet* as an attempt to do that, and if as I think he has failed to do it, let us hope that it in its turn will help him on the next try. That Karl Shapiro will keep trying there is not the slightest doubt.

Edgar Allan Poe:
A Study
in Heroism

What shall we make of Poe? What is his place today?*

All who must deal with the literature of nineteenth-century America have to confront that question at one time or another. For there is his poetry: "The Raven," "Ulalume," and the others, which we have all known since childhood, and which seems, once we have learned to read other and less immediately obvious poets, so very much overwrought and labored. And there is his fiction: ingenious, not without its considerable appeal—and yet, place it next to *Moby Dick* and *The Scarlet Letter*, not to mention *Huckleberry Finn* and *The Ambassadors*, and does it not seem pretty thin stuff, altogether too gaudy and contrived? Finally, there is his criticism: written with much verve, surely, and historically quite important, quite valuable when one considers that no American, absolutely no one, was dealing so decisively with literature *as* literature at the time it was written. But compared to Coleridge, to Hazlitt, even next to the Edinburgh reviewers,

* This paper was originally written for the Poe Society of Baltimore, Maryland, for its annual observance of Poe's death, in October of 1965.

its incompleteness, its crudeness are perforce made all too evident.

Then, if this all be true, or mostly true, what after all *is left*? Is Poe only of historical interest? Is he of importance only because Baudelaire and Mallarmé and Rimbaud found him useful, because he "invented" the short story genre (if indeed he did, which is doubtful), because he proposed formalistic critical standards in place of the moralistic criticism of his day and therefore is a legitimate ancestor of the New Criticism?

One is not willing to concede so much, so easily. For such a formulation misrepresents, or at any rate misinterprets, the true problem involved here. That problem is, Why does Poe the Writer seem of so much more consequence than the actual writings themselves? As indeed he does; he is, not only in the history of our culture but in the totality of our literary achievement today, nothing more or less than a Hero, and a highly authentic one at that.

As one of his Baltimore kin wrote upon publication of *Al Aaraaf, Tamerlane and Minor Poems*, "Edgar Poe has published a volume of Poems one of which is dedicated to John Neal the great autocrat of critics—Neal has accordingly published Edgar as a Poet of great genius etc.—Our name will be a great one *yet*." Which it is indeed, and certainly so in the city where he resided for a time and where, as Baltimore's other great author has remarked, "he rests: thrust among Presbyterians by a Methodist and formally damned by a Baptist."

The Baptist in the case, of course, was the Reverend Rufus Griswold, whose calumnies and forgeries as Poe's literary executor served to discolor and discredit Poe's reputation among right-thinking people for many years, and which still tend to make Poe something less than an entirely honorable man in many people's eyes, for all that Arthur Hobson Quinn and others have long since exposed Griswold's claims for the lies and half-truths that they were. Indeed, we do sometimes tend to think of Poe's writings as summed up by the title of one of his short stories: "Ms. Found in a Bottle." Now of course Poe did drink—and while that was not itself disgraceful in his day, he could not hold his liquor, which is almost always considered disgraceful. But actually Poe apparently drank relatively little, and, if one considers the conditions under which the man labored for most of his life, one is inclined not to censure him too much for doing it.

Very well, then—he was a hero who sometimes drank. Or if you prefer the Reverend Mr. Griswold's way of putting it, he was a drinker who wrote "The Raven" and "The Murders in the Rue Morgue," which makes us recall Abraham Lincoln's famous retort to the delegation of ministers which came calling on him to protest General Grant's drinking—the President told them that he wished he could find out the General's brand, so that he could send some to his other generals. In any event, the name of Reverend Rufus Griswold, who did not drink, comes down to us today solely because he knew and defamed Edgar Allan Poe.

It is difficult to assess Edgar Allan Poe's stature in American letters. He was poet, short story writer, literary critic. Was he a major poet, in the way that, say, Walt Whitman, Emily Dickinson, T. S. Eliot, and Robert Frost are major poets? How, as a writer of fiction, are we to think of him in comparison with Herman Melville, Nathaniel Hawthorne, Mark Twain, Henry James, Theodore Dreiser, Ernest Hemingway, William Faulkner? Were his critical writings about literature of the same order as those of, say, Mencken, or Eliot, James, Ransom, Blackmur, Edmund Wilson? It is a ticklish problem. Even in his own day he was a puzzle, and the critical estimates by his nineteenth-century contemporaries reflect the same kind of hesitation. "Three-fifths of him genius, and two-fifths sheer fudge," said Lowell. "The jingle man" was Emerson's contemptuous dismissal. For Alfred Tennyson he was the most original of all American poets. Henry James declared that an enthusiasm for Poe was "the mark of a decidedly primitive stage of reflection," while Walt Whitman thought he belonged "among the electric lights of imaginative literature, brilliant and dazzling, but with no heat." "The extraordinary genius of Edgar A. Poe is now acknowledged the world over," wrote John Greenleaf Whittier, and part of the proof is the lofty estimate of a Russian novelist very unlike Whittier in taste and outlook, Fyodor Dostoyevsky, who found that "there exists one characteristic that is singularly peculiar to Poe and which distinguishes him from every other writer, and that is the vigor of his imagination."

If the nineteenth century could not agree on the merits of its own contemporary, the twentieth century has been even less certain. The Irishman George Moore reprinted six Poe poems in his famous *Anthology of Pure Poetry*. The Englishman D. H. Lawrence found Poe "an adventurer into vaults and cellars and horrible underground passages of the human soul. He sounded the horror and warning of his own doom." Norman Douglas declared Poe's influence on literature "a civilizing and purifying agency. Poe is a great anti-vulgarian," a somewhat different verdict from Aldous Huxley's statement that Poe was "unhappily cursed with incorrigible bad taste" and that "a taint of vulgarity spoils, for the English reader, all but two or three of his poems. . . ."

Among Americans of our own time, William Carlos Williams has asserted that on Poe "is FOUNDED A LITERATURE—typical; an anger to sweep out the unoriginal . . . to annihilate the copied, the slavish, the FALSE literature about him. . . ." Yvor Winters, on the other hand, thinks Poe is "a bad writer accidentally and temporarily popular," whose poems are "an art to delight the soul of a servant girl." Allen Tate, in a distinguished essay, paid Poe this moving tribute: "I confess that his voice is so near that I recoil a little, lest he, Montressor, lead me into the cellar, address me as Fortunato, and wall me up alive. I should join his melancholy troupe of the undead, whose voices are surely as low and harsh as the grating teeth of storks. He is so close to me that I am sometimes tempted to enter the mists of pre-American genealogy to find out whether he may not actually be my cousin."

Confusing? Perhaps the great William Butler Yeats himself best illustrates the difficulty of placing Poe in his proper niche. For in 1899 he writes to an artist, "I do not know why you or indeed anybody should want to illustrate Poe however. His fame always puzzles me. . . . I admire a few lyrics of his extremely and a few pages of his prose, chiefly in his critical essays, which are sometimes profound. The rest of him seems to me vulgar and commonplace and the Pit and the Pendulum and the Raven do not seem to me to have literary value of any kind." But not very many years later we find Yeats asserting quite positively that Poe is "always and for all lands a great lyric poet." Which of Yeats's estimates of Poe are we to believe?

Perhaps we had better trust to the French. They at least seem unconfused and unwavering in their high estimate of Poe. Charles Baudelaire, certainly the greatest French poet of the nineteenth century, described his experience on first reading Poe as follows:

I can tell you something even more strange and almost unbelievable. In 1846 or 1847 I happened to see some stories by Edgar Poe. I experienced a peculiar emotion. His complete works not having been collected in a single edition until after his death, I patiently set about making the acquaintance of Americans living in Paris, in order to borrow copies of the magazines which Edgar Poe had edited. And then, believe me if you will, I found poems and short stories which I had conceived, but vaguely and in a confused and disorderly way, and which Poe had been able to organize and finish perfectly. Such was the origin of my enthusiasm and of my perseverence.

Baudelaire collected a file of the *Southern Literary Messenger*, ordered the new edition of Poe's works from New York and London, and ultimately translated five full volumes of Poe's writings. Indeed, it was his first two volumes of translations, preceding as they did the *Fleurs du Mal*, that first established Baudelaire's position in the French literary world. Since Baudelaire, almost every leading French writer has paid his tribute to Poe. For the Goncourts, in 1856, "reading Edgar Allan Poe is a revelation of something that criticism does not seem to suspect the existence of. Poe, a new literature, the literature of the twentieth century. . . ." For Mallarmé Poe was *the* poet, and he spoke of "those severe ideas which I owe to my great master Edgar Poe." When Rimbaud fled Paris before the oncoming Prussian armies in 1870, he carried with him only two books, and one of them was a copy of Poe. For Paul Valéry, "Poe is the only impeccable writer. He was never mistaken." And again, writing to Mallarmé, Valéry declared, "I prize the theories of Poe, so profound and so insidiously learned; I believe in the omnipotence of rhythm, and especially in the suggestive phrase." Villiers de l'Isle Adam, Verlaine, Huysmans, Claudel, Gide, Jaloux, Jules Lemaître: all these and many other Frenchmen have revered Poe, and have expressed scorn for the failure of the Americans and the English to recognize his genius. "Let us not fail to observe here," wrote Valéry, "that Poe's universal glory is weak or contested only in his native country and England. This Anglo-Saxon poet is strangely neglected by his own race."

How do we account for this consistently high French estimate of Edgar Poe? What is it that the French seem to find in him that so many of our own English and American writers fail to discern? Aldous Huxley had a simple explanation. "Not being English," he said, "they are incapable of appreciating those finer shades of vulgarity that ruin Poe for us." Poe, in brief, gains merit when a Frenchman reads his poetry because to one unfamiliar with English, Poe's language seems exotic rather than trite and overwrought. Huxley says that Baudelaire, for example, did not grasp the fact that where in French verse the stresses are equal, in English verse they are consistently uneven: ". . . such verses as

> It was down by the dark tarn of Auber
> In the Ghoul-haunted woodland of Weir

must have taken on," says Huxley, "for Baudelaire, heaven knows what exotic subtlety of rhythm. We can never hope to guess what that ghoul-haunted woodland means to a Frenchman possessing only a distant and theoretical knowledge of our language."

I must confess to a certain sympathy for Huxley's attitude here. I have never been able to read "Ulalume" without writhing a little at the excess of Poeticism:

> And now, as the night was senescent
> And star-dials pointed to morn—
> As the star-dials hinted of morn—
> At the end of our path a liquescent
> And nebulous lustre was born. . . .

"Senescent" / "Liquescent"; did Poe possess a rhyming dictionary? Did he use it? He seems to have used it there, and to have sacrificed meaning and credibility to rhythm and rhyme. I find it difficult to believe fully in that poem; I would find it difficult to do so in any poem that ends:

> Said we, then—the two, then: "Ah, can it
>   Have been that the woodlandish ghouls—
>   The pitiful, the merciful ghouls—
> To bar up our way and to ban it
>   From the secret that lies in these wolds—
>   From the thing that lies hidden in these wolds—
>   Have drawn up the spectre of a planet
>   From the limbo of lunary souls—
>   This sinfully scintillant planet
>   From the Hell of the planetary souls?"

A little "sinfully scintillant planet" goes a long way, and so do rhymes of "can it" and "ban it." Poe, Arthur Hobson Quinn soberly informs us, commonly followed "a basic law of English versification, which poets have always followed," which "bids poets make their metrical form a servant to their thought, and never permit their metrical scheme to limit the free play of their ideas." Poe violated this supposed basic rule, so far as I am concerned, more often and more disastrously than any other poet of comparable stature. He would do anything to fill out a rhyme scheme, use any word to effect an internal rhyme or make his metres regular. "The Raven" may be a great poem, but it is difficult to sympathize with the plight of a man who can write this stanza and expect one to feel terror instead of amusement?

> But the Raven still beguiling my sad fancy
>   into smiling,
> Straight I wheeled a cushioned seat in front
>   of bird and bust and door;
> Then, upon the velvet sinking, I betook my-
>   self to linking
> Fancy unto fancy, thinking what this ominous
>   bird of yore—
> What this grim, ungainly, ghastly, gaunt, and
>   ominous bird of yore
>   Meant in croaking "Nevermore."

One could multiply examples; the man who could write that was capable also of "Annabel Lee"—"For the moon never beams without bringing me dreams / of the beautiful Annabel Lee / And the stars never rise but I see the bright eyes / of the beautiful Annabel Lee . . ." and "The Bells," with its last three lines: "Of the bells, bells, bells, bells, / Bells, bells, bells— / To the moaning and the groaning of the bells." And more besides. It is the kind of poetry that appeals to persons who seldom read poetry. It is the kind of poetry my father-in-law recites.

(I do not think we dishonor Poe, or commit sacrilege

to his memory, when we consider what he has written in this way. For when we look at Poe's writings without fear or favor, we are only doing what he wanted done to literature in his own day.)

Is, then, the French appreciation of Edgar Poe no more than a matter of failing to appreciate the vulgarity of the language, as Huxley says? Of course not—and it behooves us, I think, to examine our own consciences on occasions like this, when we find an American writer who to us seems to have glaring defects so honored by the French. For the French in our own time detected the genius of William Faulkner when our leading magazinists considered him no more than a prurient sensationalist, and the French have always taken literature very seriously, with none of the contempt that our "practical minded" society customarily displays toward "mere" writers.

What is it, then, that the French saw in, say, "The Raven," which we may not see? To put it simply, perhaps overly so, here was a poem, and here was a poet, who saw, and was not afraid to point out, the dark, irrational, sinister side of the human condition. What, after all, is the situation in "The Raven"? A man, an intelligent, learned man, is reading and nodding in his room, bereaved over the loss of a woman, and he hears a tapping on the door. What is it? he wonders, and his thoughts wander off in various idle and gloomy directions, and he wishes that it were tomorrow so that he could be engaged in his everyday pursuits again, and then the tapping continues. So he goes to the door, and a raven, of all things, comes in and perches in the room, on a bust of Pallas Athene. The man speaks to the raven, asks it what its name is, and the raven answers only, "Nevermore." So he thinks, well, the raven will leave on the morrow, just as his friends and his hopes of the past have all left him, but again the raven says, "Nevermore." So he wonders what the bird means, and he continues to stare at it, until he grows frenzied. Will there be respite from his grief? he shrieks. "Nevermore." Will he be reunited with his dead lover in heaven? "Nevermore." Then depart, leave me, "leave my loneliness unbroken, take thy beak from out my heart. . . ." "Nevermore." And the bird is there, and its presence remains there forever, and "shall be lifted—nevermore!" To each question—and implied in each is an assertion of purpose, of meaning, of the reality of human love, affection, intelligence, thought, religion even—only that one word. Even the manner of the repetition itself questions all these things by which the nineteenth century, and ourselves as well, govern and justify our lives; for is it a word, an answer to the questions, or only the automatic, senseless, memorized glottal response of a mindless, dumb organism? And if the latter, by implication is not the man asking the questions, the learned, feeling, bereaved lover, only a somewhat more complex, more highly developed, but still essentially animal organism? Then what of all the hopes, aspirations, ideals of society, what of all its brave assertions of divine purpose and meaning, its quest for greater knowledge, its belief in a logical and God-ordered universe, its faith in a society of progress, of men of good will, of institutions for perfection? Are these cherished goals too only mirages? Are the strength and comfort they have afforded men for thousands of years still available today? "Nevermore"?

Not only that, but is the raven real, or but a figment of a despondent, disintegrating mind? That too is involved in this poem. Why, after all, a raven? Poe tells us only that he chose the raven to speak his refrain because he wanted a monotonous effect, which a human being's words would not credibly provide, so that "here, then, immediately arose the idea of a *non*-reasoning creature capable of speech, and very naturally, a parrot, in the first instance, suggested itself, but was superseded forthwith by a raven as equally capable of speech, and infinitely more in keeping with the intended tone." But why? Because the black, sinister-looking carrion raven, with its connotations of death, was an apt symbol of unreason, of fear, of the morbid, unenlightened depths of the human mind. (In this respect it was much more suitable, perhaps, than Poe's favorite poet Coleridge's albatross.) Scholars, notably Harry Levin, have devoted much attention to the fascination of blackness for nineteenth-century American writers, and the matter is indeed worthy of note. For it represents an aspect of American life that oddly comports with the optimistic, hope-bringing, transcendental daylight sunshine of the nineteenth century as it commonly viewed itself. It is foreign and alien to the image of the human condition that one finds in, for example, Wordsworth and Whitman (both of whom, I should say, I consider superior to Poe as poets). But it is not foreign and alien to the poetry of Charles Baudelaire, nor is it foreign and alien to the insights of Sigmund Freud, Søren Kierkegaard, and certain other great European thinkers.

Patrick Quinn, in his excellent study, *The French Face of Edgar Poe*, points out that Baudelaire recognized in Poe the kindred seer who helped him transform French poetry. Romanticism had until Baudelaire been a fairly jejune, superficial affair in France; it was Baudelaire who brought it to its fruition, and who triggered the great poetry of French symbolism which has so profoundly explored the depths of the human psyche. Suffice it to say that through the enthusiastic propagandizing of Baudelaire the example of Poe helped French literature to resume that great exploration of the limits of human consciousness that had characterized it during the seventeenth and eighteenth centuries, and which had been largely absent in the writers of post-Napoleonic France. We get it, to be sure, in Stendhal, who however was ignored during his lifetime, but it was with Baudelaire that the searching spirit of Voltaire was, however changed, reasserted, and has continued to dominate French literature on through Mallarmé, Rimbaud, Flaubert, Laforgue, Verlaine, in our own time Valéry, Gide, Sartre, Camus, Sarraute—and of course the greatest Frenchman of all, Marcel Proust, whose Baron de Charlus might at times almost have walked out of a short story by Edgar Allan Poe.

And as Enid Starkie and others have shown so well, from the Symbolists have come much of the insights and techniques of our modern poets. In his essay "From Poe to Valéry" T. S. Eliot has traced quite brilliantly the influence of Poe on Baudelaire, Mallarmé, and Valéry. What these poets have in turn meant to him he has elsewhere confessed. Presumably, therefore, Poe has meant something to the author of *The Waste Land*, and what it is, one might just possibly be able to glimpse if one thinks, for example, of these lines from that most influential of twentieth-century poems in English:

A woman drew her long black hair out tight
And fiddled whisper music on those strings
And bats with baby faces in the violet light
Whistled, and beat their wings
And crawled head downward down a blackened wall
And upside down in air were towers
Tolling reminiscent bells, that kept the hours
And voices singing out of empty cisterns and exhausted wells.

The hand is the sure hand of Eliot, but the apocalyptic motif is that of "The Fall of the House of Usher."

And what of that other great master of poetry in English in the twentieth century? What of Yeats?

The Second Coming! Hardly are those words out
When a vast image out of *Spiritus Mundi*
Troubles my sight: somewhere in sands of the desert
A shape with lion body and the head of a man,
A gaze blank and pitiless as the sun,
Is moving its slow thighs, while all about it
Reel shadows of the indignant desert birds.

There again is the Satanic vision, the cataclysmic breakdown of the façade of nineteenth-century optimism and faith in scientific progress that had so fascinated Charles

Baudelaire and that he found expressed so eloquently and for almost the first time in the tales and poems of Edgar Allan Poe.

In our country, Poe was far ahead of his time. The leading authors of his own day were Bryant, Longfellow, Emerson, Lowell—and in nothing that any of them wrote is to be found any recognizable amount of that "dark night of the soul" that Poe saw and described. It is present in Hawthorne and Melville, to be sure, but even there it is different. The universe in which Hawthorne's creatures exist is theological—lighted with luridly sensuous flames to be sure, but the flames are those of the old Calvinistic sinfulness and depravity, which is sullen and unregenerate. Poe's hell is psychological, and it is not eternal damnation, but irrational destructiveness and sickness of the psyche that he recognizes and fears. As for Melville, Captain Ahab dares to oppose his raging and blasphemous will to know the truth against the ghastly whiteness of the unknown, and his duel with the whale is epic and heroic; whereas Poe's typical protagonist is too sophisticated to be heroic, too wrapped in introspection to look outside of himself for the sources of his spleen. He is the underground man ahead of his time, the morbid, splenetic, abstractly logical, emotionally perverse "moyen sensuel" who peered behind the glittering vision of nineteenth-century materialistic achievement and foresaw the concentration camps.

It was this that Baudelaire and the French saw in him. ". . . we shall see that this author," wrote Baudelaire, "product of a century infatuated with itself, child of a nation more infatuated with itself than all others, has clearly seen, has imperturbably affirmed the natural wickedness of man. There is in man, he says, a mysterious force which modern philosophy does not wish to take into consideration; nevertheless, without this nameless force, without this primordial bent, a host of human actions will remain unexplained, inexplicable. These actions are attractive only *because* they are bad, dangerous; they possess the fascination of the abyss."

It is no accident that Poe virtually invented the modern detective story—or rather, that he virtually invented the detective hero of the modern detective story. For C. Auguste Dupin, who reasons logically and is not swayed by emotions or appearances, lives in his Paris apartment while all about him there are intrigue, confusion, evil, passion; and here and there, when he is consulted on this or that case, he imposes the momentary order of the single solved crime on what was and continues to be the chaos of the metropolis.

I have thus far said little about Poe's prose, when in fact it is his prose that reads most freshly and convincingly nowadays. Baudelaire, in truth, was even more taken with the stories than with the poems. He did not write fiction himself, he said, because Poe had already taken care of that well enough. Poe's stories fall into several categories, which complement each other most appropriately. One kind is given over wholly and passionately to horror: human beings in the grip of passion, at the mercy of irrational emotions, driven beyond the boundaries of sanity by overwhelming fears, hatreds, desires. The other kind portrays human beings with extraordinary powers of analysis, who in their coldly objective cerebration are neither moral nor immoral, but only ruthlessly efficient. Seldom in Poe's fiction is human intelligence wedded to human passion. Emotion and logic are separate and hostile qualities. The result of intelligence applied to a human problem is sometimes material success, sometimes a solved crime—but it is never happiness. When there *is* passion, it is destructive to all concerned, for it is incapable of being regulated or directed by intelligence. The alternatives, as propounded by Poe, would seem to be: feel, and one is lost; think, and one cannot then feel.

One senses the same kind of dichotomy in Poe's literary criticism, and in its relationship to his writing. As critic,

Poe is the craftsman, the great advocate of technique, of the absolute mastery of form. The act of composition for him was ideally that of the cold, objective arrangement of material; one need not believe in the literal truth of his account of the writing of "The Raven" to recognize that Poe's way was not that of a fervent outpouring of unmediated emotion in language. Yet he imposed his technique on some of the wildest, most passionate subject matter in all poetry, and when we object to his work it is because the technique is sometimes too calculated, too artificial, and the subject matter too lurid, too crammed full of atmosphere, emotion, states of feeling. Not always do they come together in formal marriage. It is this that Huxley and others call Poe's "vulgarity": in the highly conscious technique and the too-blatant sensationalism of the material is a crudeness that is sometimes offensive:

> These were days when my heart was volcanic
> As the scoriac rivers that roll—
> As the lavas that restlessly roll
> Their sulphurous currents down Yaanek
>   In the ultimate climes of the Pole—
> That groan as they roll down Mount Yaanek
>   In the realms of the Boreal Pole.

Too much self-conscious alliteration, too much consonance and assonance, and also too much and too blatant atmosphere of heat and suffocation, so that we believe neither in the emotion nor the artistry. But is not that division, in its own way, quite the same as the malady of which Baudelaire adjudged the nineteenth century sick, the destructiveness that comes of the admixture of abstract logic and uncontrollable passion?

It is true, I think, that even in Poe's most overwrought, most self-consciously labored poetry, there remains a kind of dignity, a certain core of integrity, that commands our respect. He is not bad in the way that, for example, Wordsworth can be bad. The second-rate Wordsworth

poems are pompous, ridiculous; as in these lines, so justly
cited by D. B. Wyndham Lewis in his eminent anthology
The Stuffed Owl:

> —Hast thou then survived—
> Mild offspring of infirm humanity,
> Meek infant! among all forlornest things
> The most forlorn—one life of that bright star,
> The second glory of the Heavens?—Thou hast.

Poe seldom seems merely silly; he overdoes matters again
and again, but the effect appears always that of the show-
man who is laboring his art, and not that of a boor or a
fool thinking. Even the poorest poem of Poe's possesses
dignity; we do not laugh at it, or at him for writing it.
Why is this?

It seems to me that N. Bryllion Fagin gives us a clue in
his book *The Histrionic Mr. Poe*, when he interprets
Poe as always performing as an actor, in whatever he
writes. We sometimes forget, I think, that lyric poetry is
by definition very much a first-person utterance, and it
implies the presence, and the voice, of a speaker. In our
insistence nowadays on the integrity of the poem, the need
for reading it for its own sake and not as a facet of the
poet's biography, we tend to neglect that speaker's necessary presence. But the speaker, whether he uses the pro-
noun "I" or not, is always there, and we are always conscious of him, for he is a formal part of our experience of
the poem. The personality of Poe in particular is part of
our exposure to his poems, and we hear him—not bio-
graphically, but artistically and formally—speaking to us.
Poe does indeed dramatize himself in his poems, and that
is why, however much he may overdo his effects, we retain
our respect for his poetry. The speaker may overextend
himself in his striving for artifice, but he never makes
himself ridiculous. The same, I think, is true of his tales;
however lurid and garish the atmosphere as evoked by the
narrator, we take him for what he is, and do not laugh at

him. We may not especially admire him, but he is not to be treated with contempt. I suggest that the experience of being told a story by this author, or listening to him recite a poem to us, is essentially a *dramatic* experience, which we accept as monologue. The personality who is Edgar Poe may sometimes say outlandish things, but we respect him and we take him seriously for all his excess.

I view Edgar Allan Poe as a hero, both in his career, in what he stands for in American literary history, and in the courage of his vision. We know his story very well: the orphan, sent to college by a wealthy spendthrift who gave him insufficient funds, then disowned him when he gambled for money to pay his debts. The would-be Byronic poet who knew mostly futility and failure as a writer, the ambitious young editor whose slashing criticism alienated his friends and made powerful enemies, the devoted husband whose young wife burst a blood-vessel and died a lingering death, the tormented visionary who sometimes drank to forget his misery, the pathetic and not always respectable man of letters who was found dying in the streets of Baltimore under mysterious circumstances and who left his literary reputation in the hands of a jealous charlatan—the image is familiar.

He was our first true man of letters, the first American writer of uncompromising literary standards who sought to earn a living in a society that was unwilling to pay for good literature, and yet he would not and could not give up his unwavering devotion to his art. Against the prevailing moralistic literature and didactic criticism of the time, he engaged in almost single-handed combat, insisting that literature must first of all be judged as literature, that not the ideas it stood for, but what it was and what it accomplished, were what mattered. Craftsmanship: that is the word we associate with Poe. "A skillful literary artist has constructed a tale"—this is the statement that Poe used to discuss the writings of his only peer among contemporary American writers, Hawthorne. Savage he could be in his criticism; and he could also be gentle, too gentle perhaps, if he thought that the work being reviewed was not to be taken seriously. But when his standards were involved, he said what he thought, in a way that no other American critic dared. Who is to say, now, that he was wrong in his principal judgments? When he ripped into Longfellow for shallowness and imitativeness when that poet was the toast of his countrymen, was he not generally correct, and were his strictures really too severe? When he opposed his own literary criteria to those of New England's cozy, optimistic didacticism, can anyone now say he was presumptuous? He was a professional writer; he meant business; he insisted that in literature, good intentions were not enough, and nothing could ever substitute for craft. In early nineteenth-century America there was no place for that kind of critical integrity. But it was not until American writers began adhering to the uncompromising standards he advocated that our national letters can be said to have come of age. The Richmond editor John W. Daniel's prediction on the occasion of Poe's death has proved accurate: "While the people of this day run after such authors as Prescott and Willis, speak with reverence of the Channings and Adamses and Irvings, their children, in referring back to our time in literary history, will say, 'this was the time of Poe.' "

But more than that, he was a hero in what his imagination confronted. Not for Poe the easy optimism of Emerson, the indulgent escape into nature of Thoreau; he saw what was going on in his time. He glimpsed the horror and the desolation of a humanity deeply at war with itself, complacently and even criminally ignoring the terrible emptiness and irrationality underlying its comfortable optimism; he sensed the false security and pious materialism of a privileged western society adrift in the powerful flow of unseen currents. What do we know now, with the experience of civil and world war, mass slaughters, concentration camps, barbaric crimes against human dignity, worldwide hunger, hatred and fear, that is not prefigured in "The Tell-Tale Heart," "The Pit and the Pendulum," "The Black Cat," "William Wilson," "The Mystery of Marie Roget," "The Masque of the Red Death," "The Descent into the Maelstrom," "The Conqueror Worm," "The Haunted Palace," "The Raven"? What do prophets of holocaust envision that was not anticipated in "The Fall of the House of Usher"? No wonder that a Baudelaire could recognize his kinship with Edgar Poe, and a Mallarmé write one of his greatest poems to Poe's memory.

Let no one take Poe for granted. There is that about him that could not and cannot be dismissed with easy generalizations. In 1833 he went calling, an unknown writer, on three distinguished gentlemen of Baltimore who had awarded him a prize for a story. Many years later one of them, John H. B. Latrobe, recalled his appearance:

His figure was remarkably good, and he carried himself erect and well, as one who had been trained to it. He was dressed in black, and his frockcoat was buttoned to the throat, where it met the black stock, then almost universally worn. Not a particle of white was visible. Coat, hat, boots, and gloves had very evidently seen their best days, but so far as mending and brushing go, everything had been done, apparently, to make them presentable. On most men his clothes would have looked shabby and seedy, but there was something about this man that prevented one from criticizing his garments, and the details I have mentioned were only recalled afterwards.

These three men—Latrobe, John Pendleton Kennedy, and James H. Miller; two lawyers who wrote, and a physician —were looking for the first time at the man who was Edgar Allan Poe.

In 1875 a tomb was finally dedicated to Poe's memory. Walt Whitman was the only important American writer who thought the occasion worthy of his presence. But in France Stéphane Mallarmé composed a sonnet for the occasion, which was read at the graveside. It reads as follows, and it seems as pertinent today as when it was first written:

THE TOMB OF EDGAR POE

Himself alone, the way eternity makes him,
The poet arouses with a naked sword
His frightened age for having failed to hear
That death conquered in that alien voice!

As vile hydras writhing to hear an angel
Come to purify the language of their tribe
His countrymen proclaim his magic drunken
From the black brew of a witches' potion

O grief! if from the hostile soil and clouds
Our thought can carve no bas-relief
To ornament the shining tomb of Poe

Calm stone, fallen from a dark disaster,
May this granite ever mark the boundaries
To black flights of Blasphemy scattered in the future.

One More Turn
of the Screw

There must be almost as many critical studies of *The Turn of the Screw* as there are pages in Henry James's brilliant little novel. An "amusette," James called it, designed "to catch those not easily caught (the 'fun' of the capture of the merely witless being ever but small), the jaded, the disillusioned, the fastidious," and since its first publication in successive installments of *Collier's* in 1898, it has set off a dispute that has gone on without abatement. During his own lifetime James had frequently to fend off queries about the "true" meaning of his famous ghost story, and in the almost half a century since James died, the interpretations have only multiplied.

The plot of *The Turn of the Screw* is well-known. A young woman is sent to a country estate as governess, charged with the responsibility of looking after two little children. She begins to see apparitions, which are identified as those of a former governess and a valet, both dead. To fend off these evil spirits, which have corrupted the children, she interposes herself, with the result that eventually the soul of one of the children is saved, though the child dies in her arms, while the other child is taken back to London in a state of delirium.

But the plot is only the point of departure. What exactly did it mean? Were the ghosts real? If they were not, why did the governess think they were? What were the governess' real actions and motives, as compared with what she declared in her narrative? What was James trying to do in the novel? What did he actually do? We have had theory after theory proposed as the answer to those questions, and there is still no single explanation which satisfies everyone.

I propose still another theory. I want to show, not that my reading of the novel *must* be true, but that it *could* be true. I want to suggest what it might mean if it were true, and then I want to use the fact that it could be true to make some observations about the way that I think every reader, whatever his own theory of the novel's meaning may be, ought to approach *The Turn of the Screw*.

My notion about James's novel, previously suggested by Carvel Collins, is based on the prologue. It requires that one take with the utmost seriousness certain things said and done in that prologue, and that one apply them to the narrative proper, as told by the governess. What I have to say is based on the supposition that when Henry James placed details and people in a story, he usually did so by deliberate intention. This I believe is a fair assumption to make about Henry James. I agree with T. S. Eliot's remark that, compared with James's fictional characters, those of most other novelists "seem to be only accidentally in the same book."

Very well. How does the prologue to *The Turn of the Screw* begin? In an old house in the country, a group of men and women have been telling ghost stories by the fireside. One of them, the authorial voice, is the narrator. Someone had been describing an apparition that had appeared to a child. The host, whose name is Douglas, is at length compelled to say that he knows a ghost story involving not one but two children. No one else, he declares, has ever heard the story, which is written out in a manuscript at his London apartments. He could, he suggests, send for the manuscript.

The narrator of the prologue notices at once that his host is peculiarly concerned about the story: "It was to me that he appeared to propound this—appeared almost to appeal for aid not to hesitate." The host "had broken a thickness of ice, the formation of many a winter; he had his reasons for a long silence"(2).* Whatever the story is about, it is obviously very important to the host.

The narrator thereupon asked the host whether it had happened to him. "Oh, thank God, no!" Douglas replies (2). Then did Douglas transcribe it? "Nothing but the impression. I took that *here*"—he tapped his heart. "I've never lost it" (3). Douglas goes on to say that the manuscript is "in old, faded ink, and in the most beautiful hand" (3). He hesitates, then continues. "A woman's. She's been dead these twenty years. She sent me the pages in question before she died" (3).

At this point "there was someone to be arch" (3), to draw the inference that Douglas had once been in love with the woman. Douglas does not smile at the suggestion, but he does speak without irritation. "She was a most charming person, but she was ten years older than I. She was my sister's governess. . . . She was the most agreeable woman I've ever known in her position; she would have been worthy of any whatever. It was long ago, and this episode was long before. I was at Trinity, and I had found her at home on my coming down the second summer" (3).

What has James said there? The syntax is ambiguous. He appears to be making Douglas say that the episode in question took place long before Douglas knew the gover-

* Page references throughout are to the Modern Library edition of *The Turn of the Screw* (New York, 1930).

ness. But grammatically at least there is also the possibility that "it was long ago" could refer to the time when the woman sent the manuscript to Douglas, or perhaps when she died, so that "this episode was long before" may be the time when the story itself took place.

The possibility may not at first seem either very likely or very important. But soon we learn some other details. We learn that the situation described in the governess' manuscript also involves the governess and a boy who was ten years younger than herself, that in both instances she had been sent to a country place to take charge of a young girl, that both times the girl's brother had come down from school for the summer. Thus in each case the situation is interestingly similar.

Douglas tells his guests more about his experience with the governess. "I was much there that year," he says. He and the governess "had, in her off-hours, some strolls and talks in the garden—talks in which she struck me as awfully clever and nice. Oh yes; don't grin: I liked her extremely and am glad to this day to think she liked me too. If she hadn't she wouldn't have told me. She had never told anyone. It wasn't simply that she said so, but that I knew she hadn't. I was sure; I could see. You'll easily judge why when you hear" (3).

Why does James make Douglas say all this? Why is it still important to Douglas that the governess had liked him?

Later in the novel we learn that, like Douglas, Miles, the ten-year-old boy in the narrative, was very fond of the governess, and she of him. Once they are talking outside a church, and the governess asks Miles whether he does not love his sister, "our sweet Flora." To which Miles replies, "If I didn't—and you too; if I didn't—!" (85). Miles's fondness for the governess grows as the story progresses, despite his continuing wish to go back to school. In the final scene Miles and the governess are left at Bly, the estate, after a housekeeper and the little girl have gone off to London, and the situation becomes strikingly erotic in its implications. In the governess's words, "we continued silent while the maid was with us—as silent, it whimsically occurred to me, as some young couple who, on their wedding journey, at the inn, feel shy in the presence of the waiter" (123).

"Well—so we're alone!" Miles says (123), and the governess is embarrassed. "Of course," Miles adds hastily, "we have the others," and the governess agrees. "Yet even though we have them," Miles continues, "they don't count much, do they?" To this the governess' reaction is very revealing: "I made the best of it, but I felt wan. 'It depends on what you call "much"'" (124). Whereupon the scene moves to its climax. The governess attempts to persuade Miles to make some intimate revelations. At that point an apparition appears at the window, the governess grasps the terrified Miles to her to protect him, Miles cries out, and, as the governess tells us, dies in her arms.

To return to the prologue, this motif is foreshadowed in the course of a dialogue which follows Douglas' description of his feelings toward the governess. He has told the others that he knows the governess' story has never been revealed before to anyone else. Was that, someone asks, "because the thing had been such a scare?" In other words, was the governess' long silence about the episode due to the horror of it? This explanation Douglas turns aside. "You'll easily judge; *you* will" (3).

The narrator understands then. "I see. She was in love." At which Douglas laughs, "You *are* acute. Yes, she was in love. That is, she had been. That came out— she couldn't tell her story without its coming out. I saw it, and she saw it; but neither of us spoke of it" (3).

In other words, the reason that the governess had not told the story to anyone else was not that it was so horrifying, but that the story revealed the fact that she was, or had been, in love.

The customary interpretation is that the governess had indeed been in love, with her employer, Miles's uncle. But in what way has *that* been concealed? Far from not speaking of it, the governess refers to it again and again in her narrative. Almost as soon as she arrives at Bly she tells the housekeeper, Mrs. Grose, that "I'm rather easily carried away. I was carried away in London!" To which the housekeeper replies, "Well, Miss, you're not the first—and you won't be the last" (13).

So if the governess is not reticent about revealing her infatuation with her employer, then what is the love story that comes out in the narrative, that both she and Douglas are aware of, but of which they never speak? What else can it be other than the governess' love for Miles? That *does* come out only in the telling, and neither Miles nor the governess ever directly concedes it. Indeed, from her very first meeting with Miles, the governess had been drawn to him: "What I then and there took him to my heart for was something divine that I have never found to the same degree in any child—his indescribable little air of knowing nothing in the world but love" (20).

Surely Douglas' guests suspect the truth, even before they hear the narrative. A Mrs. Griffin asks, "Who was it she was in love with?" The narrator of the prologue comes to Douglas' aid: "The story will tell." "Oh, I can't wait for the story!" Mrs. Griffin says. Whereupon Douglas replies that "the story *won't* tell; not in any literal, vulgar way." Mrs. Griffin is disappointed. "More's the pity, then. That's the only way I ever understand" (4). (Mrs. Griffin is evidently one of those "merely witless" readers whom James says he finds no fun in tricking.) And Douglas is quite right; the story does not "tell" who it was that the governess was in love with, "in any literal, vulgar way."

At this juncture Douglas leaves for bed, and after he is out of earshot, Mrs. Griffin gets right to the point:

"Well, if I don't know who she was in love with, I know who he was."

"She was ten years older," said her husband.

"*Raison de plus*—at that age! But it's rather nice, his long reticence."

"Forty years!" Griffin put it.

"With this outbreak at last" (4).

What I am suggesting, of course, is the distinct possibility, a possibility that I think James wishes us to entertain, that Douglas *is* Miles, and that the story Douglas reads, supposedly about another little boy and the governess, is in fact about *him*.* If this were so, then the scarcely disguised erotic implications of the narrative are of importance. They would mean that not only did Miles not die at the close, but that the whole basis for believing in the governess' narrative is seriously undercut.

To recapitulate: we possess the following bits of information. Douglas was in love with a governess ten years older than himself. So was Miles. Douglas had a younger sister. So did Miles. The governess had been very fond of Douglas. The governess was very probably in love with Miles. Douglas kept the secret of his love for the governess for forty years. If the governess was in love with

---

* Note the way in which James seems to be making a point about how Douglas and Miles act when dealing with an awkward situation. In the introduction he describes Douglas preparing to speak about his "ghost story": "I can see Douglas there before the fire, to which he had got up to present his back, looking down at his interlocutor with his hands in his pockets" (2); and, "He turned around to the fire, gave a kick to a log, watched it an instant. Then as he faced us again . . ." (2); and, "He got up and, as he had done the night before, went to the fire, gave a stir to a log with his foot, then stood a moment with his back to us" (8); and "A little to my surprise, Douglas turned round to me" (8). Now, the climatic scene in which the governess and Miles are alone in the house, and are preparing to take dinner together: "Miles, before he sat down, stood a moment with his hands in his pockets . . ." (122); and, "While this was done Miles stood again with his hands in his little pockets and his back to me . . ." (123); and, "'Yet even though we have them,' he returned, still with his hands in his pockets and planted there in front of me . . ." (124); and "When he at last turned round to meet me . . ." (125). Nowhere else in the novel does anyone behave in just this fashion.

Miles, Douglas kept that story to himself for many years as well, revealing it only after "a long silence."

Could Douglas and Miles, then, have been one and the same person, so that the story that Douglas read to his guests, having "broken a thickness of ice, the formation of many a winter," (2) was the governess' account, revealed to him shortly before her death, of her love for him?

It all depends on how one interprets the facts. Leon Edel's explanation is that Douglas' acquaintance with the governess dates from a period of from eight to ten years after the events described in the narrative, and that James carefully worked this out to give the governess more time to learn the ways of the world, so that her narrative could reflect this greater wisdom. He bases this on the reasonable assumption that Douglas must have been eighteen or twenty years old, since he was down for his second summer after beginning Trinity College. Since the governess was ten years his senior, and was thus twenty-eight or thirty, Douglas' visit must have taken place eight or ten years after the events at Bly, at which time the governess was only twenty years old herself.* This is I think a plausible explanation, but it does not sufficiently account for the obvious truth that Henry James went out of his way to draw striking parallels between Douglas' relationship with the governess and that of Miles. Why did he do it? Why was it necessary to have Douglas also home from school, to give him a younger sister, to dwell so arch-

* Leon Edel, *The Modern Psychological Novel* (New York, 1955). In point of strict fact "Trinity" need not be Trinity College, Cambridge, or that in Dublin, either. Douglas is obviously a Scotch name, and there is a well-known grammar school, also called Trinity College, at Perth, Glenalmond, Scotland. This seems hardly likely, however. The point is that Douglas is a fictional character, and just as in the case of the governess, his comments must be evaluated. If he *were* the Miles of the story, he would have every reason for wanting to throw his companions off the track. I do not recall who it was who once said that one can never properly understand a James novel until he realizes that all the characters are liars, but it is a very perceptive remark, provided that one realizes that there are various kinds of liars.

ly on the possibility of his having been in love with the governess, and she with him? We can usually assume that when Henry James does something in a novel, he has a reason for doing so.

The only explanation that I can see for James's having done this, and I think it a very logical explanation, is that he very much wanted us to consider the possibility that Douglas was Miles, and therefore that Miles did not die at the end of the narrative, because the impact of this possibility would render still further suspect the reliability of the governess as objective narrator of the uncanny events she chronicles in her manuscript. For if, to repeat, the governess had been in love with Miles, and if Miles had not died in her arms at the end, then not only the final scene of *The Turn of the Screw* but the entire narrative takes on another level of meaning, and, for the purposes of fiction, of ambiguity.

The possibility is then much greater that the governess' narrative is not a truthful rendition of events at all, but a story which an unmarried, middle-aged woman sent to a man shortly before her death, a man with whom she had once been in love when he was still a boy, in order to tell him about that love. It would then be, in short, an allegory of love, as it were, the application of which the governess intended for her now-grown lover to guess. This would indeed go far toward accounting for Douglas' extreme concern over the whole thing in the prologue.

As Gerald Willen, who has also noticed the odd resemblance between the circumstances of Douglas and Miles, notes in the Introduction to *A Casebook on Henry James's "The Turn of the Screw"*, "the essential fact remains that the story told by the governess needs to be read at varying levels. This is all the more true if we say that her story is, in effect, a fiction."*

* But what then, one might ask, of Douglas' remark that "I liked her extremely and am glad to this day to think she liked me too"? The obvious objection to Douglas' having been Miles is that Douglas would

Mr. Willen's observation, I believe, gets directly at the matter. Whether Douglas was indeed Miles, or whether he was not and learned the story at a later date, the fact remains that the possibility exists, and that the import of its existence is to remind us of the need at all times to examine very closely what the governess is saying throughout the story. She is *not* an unbiased observer. An observation made by Leon Edel in 1955 still essentially holds true, I believe, even though at least a half-dozen interpretations of James's novel have been published since he said it: "The governess's account of her stay at Bly is riddled with inconsistencies which the many critics who have discussed the story have never sufficiently perceived." In their zeal to "prove" that *The Turn of the Screw* is this or that kind of novel, whether Christian, Freudian, hallucinatory, old-fashioned supernatural, social commentary, and so on, James's critics have again and again seized upon certain statements made by the governess in the course of relating her story, without always remembering that *almost every remark* that the woman makes is subject to suspicion. (I except Mr. John Lydenberg, whose essay, "The Governess Turns the Screws," is very subtly worked out.)

James's every hint is that the governess tells lies. Whether her lies are the result of deliberate calculation,

---

hardly have felt kindly disposed toward a woman who had subjected him and his sister to such an ordeal as that described in the narrative. Remember, however, that Douglas received the governess's manuscript many years later. It was, as he says, "beyond everything. Nothing at all that I knew touches it." "For sheer terror"? someone asked. "For dreadful—dreadfulness. . . . For general uncanny ugliness and horror and pain," Douglas replies (2). In other words, looking back on the memory of that year at Bly, and having realized from reading the governess' manuscript what had been going on in her mind that summer, Douglas is overwhelmed by pity for the unhappy woman, and what is horrible to him is not the terror of the ghosts, but what was happening to the governess. He is even disposed to admire her pluck in the face of her obsession, and is comforted to think that, for all her bizarre way of showing it, she did feel genuine affection for him. Was not that affection, which he in his ten-year-old innocence had even returned, the root cause of the governess' hallucinations?

or whether they come to her spontaneously and without premeditation in the heat of her passionate obsession, is not as important as the supremely evident truth that her explanations simply do not add up. To show this, I can cite three examples, all taken from crucial scenes in the novel.

The first is the episode in which the governess is seated by the pond at Bly while little Flora plays nearby, and is overcome by the sensation, first that someone is coming toward them, and then that an apparition is standing cross the pond observing them. Here is how she describes it:

I transferred my eyes straight to little Flora, who, at the moment, was about ten yards away. My heart had stood still for an instant with the wonder and terror of the question whether she too would see; and I held my breath while I waited for what a cry from her, what some sudden innocent sign either of interest or of alarm, would tell me. I waited, but nothing came; then, in the first place—and there is something more dire in this, I feel, than in anything I have to relate—I was determined by a sense that, within a minute, all sounds from her had previously dropped; and, in the second, by the circumstance that, also within the minute, she had, in her play, turned her back to the water. This was her attitude when I at last looked at her—looked with the confirmed conviction that we were still, together, under direct personal notice. She had picked up a small flat piece of wood, which happened to have in it a little hole that had evidently suggested to her the idea of sticking in another fragment that might figure as a mast and make the thing a boat. This second morsel, as I watched her, she was very markedly and intently attempting to tighten in its place. My apprehension of what she was doing sustained me so that after some seconds I felt I was ready for more. Then I again shifted my eyes—I faced what I had to face (44).

Later the governess relates the incident to Mrs. Grose as positive evidence that "they *know*—it's too monstrous:

they know, they know!" "She has told you?" the housekeeper asks. To which the governess replies, "not a word
—that's the horror. She kept it to herself! The child of
eight, *that* child!" (45).

On the face of it, this seems very suspicious, because
there was nothing in what the little girl was doing which
necessarily indicated any awareness on her part of the apparition's presence. The little girl had evidently become
quiet, had turned her back to the pond, and had intently,
and in a markedly Freudian fashion, occupied herself with
a piece of wood and a stick.* But if this were not reason

* Mr. John W. Aldridge has suggested to me that the governess' conviction that Flora "knew" is based on her unconscious assimilation of
the meaning of the sexual symbolism of Flora's play, and its tie-in with
the kind of perversion hinted at in Flora's relationship with the dead
governess, Miss Jessel. Thus the governess, in reporting to Mrs. Grose,
is unconsciously describing her *interpretation* of Flora's actions.

The question arises of just how conscious was Henry James's use of what
we would today call Freudian symbolism. Mr. Aldridge has called my
attention to James's first novel, *Watch and Ward*, in which, most surely
unconsciously, James's symbolism is in several instances almost embarrass-
ingly Freudian. Leon Edel comments on this in his introduction to the
1959 reprinting of that book, which was first published in 1871. But *The
Turn of the Screw* was written twenty-eight years later. Oscar Cargill, in
an essay entitled "Henry James as Freudian Pioneer," asserts that James
must have been familiar with Freud's early work. The case he presented
was rather tenuous. More recently, however, in an essay published in
PMLA and entitled "'The Turn of the Screw' and Alice James," Mr.
Cargill has documented his case much more thoroughly and convincingly.
He also makes several observations on the governess' veracity as narrator
which are similar to those in this essay, and recognizes that if Freudian
fixation is in the novel, it is the governess' frustrated desire for Miles,
not for her employer, that is involved. Unfortunately for my purposes,
Mr. Cargill's essay was published long after the present essay had been
accepted for publication.

Until Mr. Cargill's most recent interpretation, the two chief Freudian
readings of James's novel, Cargill's earlier essay and that by Edmund
Wilson, had both assumed that the governess' frustrated desire for her
employer was the root cause of her hallucinations. Perhaps this was
true at the outset of her stay at Bly, but it seems far more likely that
her desires were soon transferred to Miles. If so, this would certainly
give another and more appalling dimension to the governess' thought,
as she waited at dinner for Miles that final evening, that "I felt afresh—
for I had felt it again and again—how my equilibrium depended on the
success of my rigid will, the will to shut my eyes as tight as possible to

enough already to doubt the governess' veracity, shortly afterwards she gives another account of what Flora had been doing when the apparition was there: "It was a pity that I needed once more to describe the portentous little activity by which she sought to divert my attention—the perceptible increase of movement, the greater intensity of play, the singing, the gabbling of nonsense, and the invitation to romp" (51–52). Nothing like that had taken place at all, if we are to believe the governess' own account of what was going on by the lake. It is clearly in direct contradiction to the governess' earlier description. The two versions of the episode cannot be reconciled. Either Flora was playing silently, with her back to the pond, intently working away at twisting the stick into the hole, or else she was romping, gabbling, singing, dancing about. It does seem likely that the governess is not telling the truth.

The only explanation that seems to me even remotely possible for the governess' contradictory accounts is that Flora's dancing about and romping took place *after* her activity with the stick and the block of wood, and *after* the governess had summoned the courage to look up at the apparition—after, that is to say, the governess' description of the event is concluded. But if we once admit the possibility of actions taking place which the governess does not describe in her narrative, almost anything becomes possible. The governess might then, as some critics have suggested, have found out on another occasion what Peter Quint, the dead valet, looked like before describing him to the housekeeper, so that Mrs. Grose's ability to identify that apparition as the dead valet would in no way consti-

---

the truth that what I had to deal with was, revoltingly, against nature" (122).

I am still not quite convinced that James was familiar with Freudian theory in the late 1890's, but I do feel that he must have had some idea of what he was dealing with along this line. Here, of course, we get into the whole question of just what the creative imagination is and how it functions. Whichever way one decides, one marvels at the uncanny appropriateness of James's symbolism.

tute a verification of the reality of the governess' hallucinations.

This brings us to what I think is the second clear hint that the governess tells lies. One of the chief arguments in favor of the governess' story has been the fact that Mrs. Grose was able, through the governess' description of the apparition she saw first on the tower and then peering through her window, to identify Quint, when there was no way at that stage of the narrative for the governess to have known what he looked like. Freudian theories of the novel have attempted to show that the governess could have known it. When the housekeeper asks the governess whether the apparition she saw might not have been someone from the village, or one of the employees at Bly, the governess replies, "Nobody—nobody. I didn't tell you, but I made sure" (33). This would mean, writes John Silver in his essay, "A Note on the Freudian Reading of *The Turn of the Screw*," that the governess had obviously been asking people about the identity of the apparition, and could well have received a description of Peter Quint.

The whole question appears irrelevant to me. If we examine the accounts of the two occasions on which the governess saw the apparition, we will discover, I think, that the governess could *not* in any event have seen what she describes to Mrs. Grose. When early in the novel she sees a stranger in the tower, she reports that they were "too far apart to call to each other" (25). When she next sees him peering through the window, she remarks that "he appeared thus again with I won't say greater distinctness, for that was impossible, but with a nearness that represented a forward stride in our intercourse and made me, as I met him, catch my breath and turn cold" (30). Shortly afterward, however, she proceeds to describe his face in great detail, even to the shape and shading of his eyebrows and the cast of his eyes! (35). To have made out such details when standing at a distance "too far apart to call to each other" would indeed have been a remarkable feat—too remarkable for anyone to believe. Obviously the governess did not see what she tells the housekeeper that she saw. If Mrs. Grose was able to identify Peter Quint from the governess' description, then either the governess already knew what Quint looked like, or the housekeeper is leaping to conclusions not warranted by the evidence.

My final instance of the governess's glaring unreliability is the scene in which she returns to her room to find her dead predecessor, Miss Jessel, seated at her table. This occurs immediately after the governess' interview with Miles in the churchyard, when Miles tells her that he wants to return to school, and that if the governess will not write to his uncle about it, he will do so.* Here is the governess' description of the confrontation with Miss Jessel:

There was an effort in the way that, while her arms rested on the table, her hands with evident weariness supported her head; but at the moment I took this in I had already become

---

* It is odd, I think, that Miles at no time betrays any sure knowledge that he *has* been expelled from school, and not merely sent home for the summer vacation. His conversation about it with the governess in the final episode is very ambiguously worded. How then do we know that he was expelled from school? Only by taking the governess' word for it. It is the governess who places all the sinister meanings on the expulsion. She does affect to show the headmaster's letter to Mrs. Grose, only to find that the housekeeper cannot read. But this might have been only a shrewd gesture, based on the guess that Mrs. Grose would not in any event have presumed to read the letter. It is after she finds that Mrs. Grose cannot in any case read that she begins hinting at the possibility of really serious misconduct on Miles's part while at school. The letter she eventually wrote to the employer, and which Miles stole and read, obviously said nothing, as Miles agrees. All that we know (if indeed we know that) is that Miles cannot return to the school. The employer had earlier told the governess that Miles was really too young to be at boarding school. If he was not being permitted to return, could not that have been the reason? Miles does admit to minor offenses while there, but he appears quite surprised that they would have been considered important enough to be reported to his uncle. To repeat, the sinister meanings are, it should be emphasized, entirely those supplied by the governess.

aware that, in spite of my entrance, her attitude strangely persisted. Then it was—with the very act of its announcing itself—that her identity flared up in a change of posture. She rose, not as if she had heard me, but with an indescribable grand melancholy of indifference and detachment, and, within a dozen feet of me, stood there as my vile predecessor. Dishonored and tragic, she was all before me; but even as I fixed and, for memory, secured it, the awful image passed away. Dark as midnight in her black dress, her haggard beauty and her unutterable woe, she had looked at me long enough to appear to say that her right to sit at my table was as good as mine to sit at hers. While these instants lasted indeed I had the extraordinary chill of a feeling that it was I who was the intruder. It was a wild protest against it that, actually addressing her—"You terrible, miserable woman!"—I heard myself break into a sound that, by the open door, rang through the long passage and the empty house. She looked at me as if she heard me, but I had recovered myself and cleared the air. There was nothing in the room the next minute but the sunshine and a sense that I must stay (89–90).

The governess waits until tea time to inform Mrs. Grose about it: "I just came home, my dear, for a talk with Miss Jessel." The housekeeper, not surprisingly, is incredulous: "A talk! Do you mean she spoke?" (92).

Whereupon, in a beautifully equivocal reply, the governess says, "It came to that" (92). And she proceeds to tell the housekeeper what Miss Jessel told her.

But we were there. We saw what happened when the governess saw the apparition. It was present only for a moment. It said nothing at all like that to her. So either the governess is lying when she tells Mrs. Grose about the conversation, or else we are supposed to accept the governess' interpretation of the incident as having been "implied." This is hardly anything we can accept on such flimsy evidence as that, not when she had already told us what the former governess *did* appear to say, and did not mention any other communication. "It came to that" is too obviously an evasion of the issue.

In the face of such evidence, how is it possible to take the governess at her own word at any point in the narrative? Obviously we must regard everything she wrote, everything she says that she has done, every conversation she reports, with entire skepticism. We must, among other things, attempt to visualize what might have been going on at Bly as it would have appeared to the other persons involved. What did it seem like to Miles? Note, for example, the conversation that Miles and the governess have concerning Flora's leaving for London with the housekeeper (123). Does Miles really have any idea of what has been going on? Does he think anything more about it than that his sister has been taken ill? Has his concern ever been anything more than his wish to return to school? Does he show any awareness of something unusual going on at Bly? Has not all the portentous "meaning" of events been assigned to them by the governess? From Miles's standpoint, has anything really out of the ordinary been happening that summer?

What this signifies about the meaning of *The Turn of the Screw* is clear. It means that any interpretation of the narrative in which the governess is made into the heroine must be examined very closely. For a heroine who makes up her facts as she goes along, tells half-truths and whole lies to the housekeeper and others in order to persuade them of the existence of apparitions which no one but herself ever actually sees or admits to seeing, who proudly envisions herself as the sole protectress of two children against the forces of evil, and yet who immediately threatens to quit on the spot if the housekeeper should try to summon her employer, is a very odd sort of heroine.

I find it very difficult to see her, as Robert Heilman has done, as occupying the role of "savior, not only in a general sense, but with certain Christian associations." Nor does the summation of Alexander E. Jones's essay on the novel seem appropriate: "Granted, the governess is not perfect; but her all-too-human frailty should not blind the reader to her great accomplishment. Standing resolutely at her own little Armageddon, she has routed the forces of evil." This is beyond doubt what the governess *thought* she was doing, but that it was what Henry James thought she was doing is doubtful.*

Instead there is every likelihood that the governess saw not apparitions, but hallucinations, that she was possessed of a talent for martyrology of staggering proportions, that she was an out-and-out psychotic, that her sublimated desire for Miles was strongly sexual in nature, and that the result of her obsession was to drive an eight-year-old out of her mind and to frighten a ten-year-old boy to death.†

If, that is, Miles did indeed die at the end of the novel. But if the suggestions that James seemed to be making about Douglas' identity in the prologue are true, Miles did *not* die in the governess' arms after uttering the name of the dead valet. And if that is the case, then the whole story is to be doubted, and we can be certain of nothing. What do we have then?

I suggest that what we have is a fascinating ghost story by Henry James, who with consummate mastery has led us along first one trail and then another, until finally we have doubled back upon ourselves and we are just where we started. In short, true to his announced intention of tricking "those not easily caught," Henry James tells his tale of a governess and her two charges so very convincingly that he first makes us believe that we have read a

---

* Indeed, if Christianity is what is involved in the novel, then John Lydenberg's contention that the governess, "hysterical, compulsive, sado-masochistic," is nothing less than a religious fanatic who "alienates the children so completely that they have no alternative but to go the devil," seems much much more likely. James once told Raymond Blathwayt that "intolerance is of the devil, and yet, contradictorily enough, it often appears to me to be the outstanding characteristic of the Church and the priestly mind."

† In this connection James's letter to Dr. Louis Waldstein in response to a query about *The Turn of the Screw* is interesting: "But ah, the exposure indeed, the helpless plasticity of childhood that isn't dear or sacred to somebody! That *was* my little tragedy—"

true ghost story, in the traditional vein. Then when we begin thinking back on the events of the story, he makes us see that the whole narrative has been significantly qualified, so that there is every reason to doubt the existence of the ghosts at all. And the consequence of that is that we look closely at the description of the circumstances in which the story has been told, only to have it hinted that it isn't a factual account at all.

One can imagine him chuckling at the whole thing. A triumph of craft indeed, of precisely the sort that he most enjoyed.* For had he not accomplished just what he said he wanted to do: renovate a supposedly outmoded story form, the tale of horror? First he had proved it was not true that "the good, the really effective and heartshaking ghost stories (roughly so to term them) appeared all to have been told. . . ." For he had held our undivided attention with just such a story himself. Then he had triumphed as well over "the new type . . . the *mere* mod-

---

* What a master James was at the deliberate creation of ambiguity! Not only does he realize it through the artful manipulation of facts, but with the very syntax of his prose as well. Examine a speech such as one that I have already quoted in part: "You *are* acute. Yes, she was in love. That is, she had been. That came out—she couldn't tell her story without its coming out. I saw it, and she saw I saw it; but neither of us spoke of it. I remember the time and the place—the corner of the lawn, the shade of the great beeches and the long, hot summer afternoon. It wasn't a scene for a shudder; but oh—!" (3–4). At first reading it seems fairly simple. A paraphrase would be: "the governess had been in love that year at Bly, and when she later told the story to me, this came out, though we pretended not to notice it. I remember how lovely it was the summer when she told me about it, and how much in contrast the surroundings were with the horror of the story she told." But if one inspects the sentences closely, they can as easily be made to state quite another situation: "The governess had been in love that year at Bly, though she wasn't when she wrote the story down. It was obvious at the time it happened, and in the manuscript it was also obvious. As a child at Bly I knew that she was in love with me, and she realized that I did, though of course we never spoke of it then. I remember how lovely it was that summer at Bly, and how much in contrast the surroundings were with the horror of the governess' story." Which is the correct reading? Either could be; it depends on whether Douglas was or was not Miles. Such is James's remarkable technique.

ern 'psychical' case, washed clean of all queerness as by exposure to a flowing laboratory tap, and equipped with credentials vouching for this." He had transformed the psychotic hallucinations of an obsessed woman into a drama of the supernatural, made us believe both in the ghosts and the obsession, until we could not be sure which was true. How thorough the ambiguity he attained! The further we try to extend the meanings of a passage, a scene, the more elusive the answer. How often one finds oneself, after weighing all the evidence, coming to the same conclusion: "It could be either."

Ambiguity? To the last. Examine the dialogue in the final scene, in which Miles supposedly utters the name of the dead valet, and is thus saved even as he dies. *Does* Miles actually pronounce the name? Remember that the governess has been striving to force the child to admit his knowledge of the apparition's identity. How can we be sure that it is Miles, and not she, who asks, "It's he?" If the question is hers, then Miles, not the governess, answers, "Whom do you mean by 'he'?" And in that event, it would not be Miles, but the governess herself, who speaks the next sentence: "Peter Quint—you devil!" (134).

Not once does James write, "I said," or "he asked." Direct identification of the speakers is missing. I cannot think that in those crucial sentences of dialogue, he did this unintentionally.

It is the governess who tells us that "they are in my ears still, his supreme surrender of the name and his tribute to my devotion" (134). But have we not seen the governess make similar deductions before? Recall her words about Miss Jessel: "It came to that." This time, however, there was no housekeeper present to ask for clarification. The only response to the naming of the name is one word: "*Where?*" If Miles asks that (and why, after all, should the governess ask it? she *sees* the apparition), it would be enough to permit the governess to believe that he had capitulated. All we have is her word for what happened. But then, if we don't take the governess' word, where are we? *We are back where we started.*

As James phrased it, "the thing was to aim at absolute singleness, clearness and roundness, and yet to draw on an imagination working freely, working (call it) with extravagance; by which law it wouldn't be thinkable except as free and wouldn't be amusing except as controlled." Note the words: "aim at." To make it seem that a simple, literal tale of ghosts was being revealed, but to play the literalness against our controlled reaction to the tale, to set our minds to speculating endlessly, finally turning the story back into itself—never once will he say *yes, that is it,* or *no, you are wrong; that is not it at all.*

How tempting, and how inconceivable, to work out a single theory about this novel, to "prove" that it must be one thing and therefore not something else, when the whole point about the puzzle is its ultimate insolubility. How skillfully he managed it, and with what exquisite ambiguity of language and image! The Master indeed. Carefully, stroke by stroke, he built his riddle, spread his hints, told and denied, held us. The evening's entertainment he prepared for those fortunate readers of *Collier's* magazine sixty-five years ago remains as fresh as on the day it was written. "The art of the romancer," James once wrote, "is, 'for the fun of it,' insidiously to cut the cable, to cut it without our detecting him." We are still trying to determine where it was that he did it.

Tom Sawyer
and the
Use of Novels

Because Mark Twain is so important a figure in American literary history, and because *The Adventures of Tom Sawyer* (1876) is his first work of fiction, there is the temptation to dwell on the historical aspects of the novel. Like *The Adventures of Huckleberry Finn* (1884), it can be approached as a guide to what life was like along the Mississippi in the years before the Civil War, as a mirror of the pivotal position the Missouri region occupied in the slavery controversy, as a species of "frontier humor," and so on.

Such investigations are often extremely interesting. Yet when one is finished, this question remains: what can *Tom Sawyer* tell us about American life that any of a half-dozen almost forgotten but "representative" novels could not do better? Or that diaries, letters, memoirs, newspaper accounts could not do with much greater authenticity? And does not the frontier humor approach place an American classic such as *Tom Sawyer* on exactly the same plane as a much less accomplished work such as the *Flush Times in Alabama and Mississippi*?

In other words, if we use literature as history, then the more imaginative the work of literature, the less "accurate" it seems to be as history. So that if history is our subject, might it not be wiser to eschew Mark Twain's novels in favor of those by men less imaginative and more literal in their writings?

All that is literary in one very naturally rebels against such a conclusion. Our major writers *should* be able to tell us more about our country's life than their less perceptive contemporaries, and if it seems to work out the other way, then perhaps the fault may lie not with our major writers but in the way we try to use their work. It may be that, in attempting to study American life as portrayed in *Tom Sawyer*, we fail to consider it as a novel at all, but as a document. We treat it as a compendium of raw material for research, as an accumulation of facts, when the truth is that the chief reason for paying any attention at all to *Tom Sawyer* is that it is *not* merely an accumulation of facts. It is a story; it is a unit. It is a work of art.

It may be, then, that in using *Tom Sawyer* as a factual guide to life on the big river, we neglect it as literature, when it is precisely the literary considerations that give the novel its excellence. The one question we should be asking about it first of all might well be, What happens? What is the plot of the novel? Who are the characters, in particular who is the protagonist, and what happens to them and to him? What, in short, is this novel about *as a novel*?

A small boy grows up a little during one summer in a town on the Mississippi. He is a romantic, highly imaginative little fellow, who enjoys playing at pirates, outlaws, and other fanciful pursuits. He lives with his Aunt Polly, a long-suffering lady whose prosaic outlook on things causes him no little inconvenience. His closest friend is a devil-may-care lad named Huckleberry Finn, who accompanies him on his adventures. Tom has a girl, too, whom he wants mightily to impress.

In the course of his summer's activities he searches for buried treasure, sees a dastardly murder perpetrated by a half-breed named Injun Joe, testifies in court as to what he saw, discovers a real treasure, goes off on a picnic with Becky Thatcher, is lost in a cave, finally makes his way to safety, and returns in triumph to claim his share of the treasure.

At the beginning of the novel, Tom is just another boy, distinguished chiefly perhaps for the quality of the devilment he can plan. In the eyes of the townsfolk—those who notice him at all—he is a child, with absurd, romantic dreams of success and grandeur, and one whose conduct is not beyond reproach.

Yet when the summer is over and the novel closes, what is Tom's station in life? He has won the eternal fealty of his girl friend. He is exceedingly wealthy. He has solved a murder mystery. He is the town hero. From being just another boy, he has risen to be someone quite important in community affairs.

This is what happens in *Tom Sawyer*, then. In effect Tom has *changed his world*. He has made reality conform to his conception of what it should be. No longer does reality consist of life in a humdrum river town, in which he must grow up obscurely and insignificantly, being made to be good, attending church, studying tedious lessons at school. Rather, reality for Tom Sawyer has come to mean pirates, treasure, heroism, and glory.

It is toward that end that the events of *Tom Sawyer* have been directed, and if one will look over the various episodes comprising the novel, he will find that nothing happens therein which does not directly or indirectly contribute toward the impact of that result. This is the form of the novel. The plot structure of the novel is directed toward that end.

So much, for the moment at least, for plot development. Plot structure is the framework on which words, scenes, and episodes are arranged. What of these constituent parts: the style, the conversations, the description, the events? The novelist made his book out of them; they are the texture of his story, the flesh on the bones, giving the novel its content and meaning. We know the plot of the story that Mark Twain told, but how did he tell it?

First of all, the story of *Tom Sawyer* is not presented in a vacuum. It is told in a very specific place, and the place is a part of the novel. All novels take place somewhere, of course, but in this instance the *somewhere* is very important. So let us look at it. How does Mark Twain depict the scene of *Tom Sawyer's* exploits?

Notice how carefully Twain sets a scene before he allows Tom and the other characters to appear. Here is the beginning of Chapter II, the renowned fence whitewashing episode:

Saturday morning was come, and all the summer world was bright and fresh, and brimming with life. There was a song in every heart; and if the heart was young the music issued at the lips. There was cheer in every face and a spring in every step. The locust trees were in bloom and the fragrance of the blossoms filled the air. Cardiff Hill, beyond the village and above it, was green with vegetation, and it lay just far away enough to seem a Delectable Land, dreamy, reposeful, and inviting.

It is against this backdrop that Tom Sawyer will conduct his celebrated feat of getting the board fence whitewashed by his friends and becoming rich in worldly goods in the process, in utter defiance of the customary attitudes toward fence-painting prevalent among the young of St. Petersburg. Tom is not himself conscious of the natural beauties of a summer day along the Mississippi for very long or very often, but the reader is, and for the reader Mark Twain has placed the episode in its tranquil, summery context so that Tom's manipulations can take place in the warm light of that lovely Saturday morning, with the green, dreamy backdrop of Cardiff Hill overlooking the children's activities.

Cardiff Hill—how often do we catch sight of it in the novel. Here is another typical scene, that which opens Chapter VII and precedes Tom's courtship of Becky Thatcher:

> The harder Tom tried to fasten his mind on his book, the more his ideas wandered. So at last, with a sigh and a yawn, he gave it up. It seemed to him that the noon recess would never come. The air was utterly dead. There was not a breath stirring. It was the sleepiest of sleepy days. The drowsing murmur of the five and twenty studying scholars soothed the soul like the spell that is in the murmur of bees. Away off in the flaming sunshine, Cardiff Hill lifted its soft green sides through a shimmering veil of heat, tinted with the purple of distance; a few birds floated on lazy wing high in the air; no other living thing was visible but some cows, and they were asleep.

There we have the same image as before: summer, somnolence, nature drowsing, for all the world as if the author had read the opening lines of *Piers Plowman*, 'In a summer's season, when soft was the sun,' and had merely substituted Cardiff for Malvern Hill. It is extraordinary how often Mark Twain does this sort of thing in *The Adventures of Tom Sawyer*, so we might very well pay some attention to the function of this kind of composition of place in the total effect of the story. It cannot be a mere accident that Twain has chosen to tell his story against a background of nature, and has interspersed in his narrative so much gentle but persistent scene setting and good-natured humor.

Before we examine this any further, however, we should consider the other part of the picture, too: the human action and events that take place against the background. Here we get something quite different. There is a great deal of action throughout the book, and a great deal of dialogue. These contrast directly with the background.

Take for example the scene in Chapter X, after Injun Joe and Muff Potter have attacked and killed the doctor in the previous chapter, while Tom and Huck watched aghast. The two boys raced back toward town, and finally fell panting inside the old tannery, where at last they caught their breath:

"Huckleberry, what do you reckon 'll come of this?"
"If Dr. Robinson dies, I reckon hanging 'll come of it."
"Do you though?"
"Why, I *know* it, Tom."
Tom thought awhile, then he said:
"Who'll tell? We?"
"What are you talking about? S'pose something happened and Injun Joe *didn't* hang? Why he'd kill us some time or other, just as dead sure as we're a-laying here."
"That's just what I was thinking to myself, Huck."
"If anybody tells, let Muff Potter do it, if he's fool enough. He's generally drunk enough."

The language is sharp, alive, unadorned. It is the speech of everyday life, spoken the way children would speak it. The dialogue—and Mark Twain uses it to a greater extent than almost any previous American novelist—is completely realistic. Unlike that in Longstreet's *Georgia Scenes,* there is no feeling of condescension, of strained exaggeration for humorous effect. Though the sentences are short, not complex, the language is in no sense lifeless or monotonous, either. Twain the literary artist has managed to make the dialogue both lively and appropriate. In other words, Mark Twain does not treat these young Missouri boys primarily as quaint local color types. For Twain, life in St. Petersburg is real, not merely picturesque.

So, from what we have seen so far, we might attempt to summarize the novel this way. It is an essentially realistic novel, describing the process by which a youngster changes the community and his life to suit his tastes. However, the realistic action is placed in a rich, timeless context in which the natural world seems to lie in the sun

forever, back of the activities of the characters. The mat-
ter-of-factness of action and dialogue are thus contrasted
with an underlying sense of never-never-land fable. The
image of Cardiff Hill in the background, green in the sun,
is of complete inaction, of timelessness. We leave *Tom
Sawyer* with Tom and Huck talking of how they will
eventually go off for good and be outlaws; Tom's dreaming, which has turned into the everyday plot of the novel,
is once again the romance and fantasy of a child.

Thus *The Adventures of Tom Sawyer* is a kind of dual-
istic work. It is an action story, in a definite situation
with a definite plot, and it is also a fable of boys in childhood. Tom is the practical young man, and he is also
dreamer in the sun.

Is there any one scene that exemplifies this dual nature
of the book and of its protagonist? Some lines at the outset of Chapter VIII, when Tom is rebuffed by Becky
Thatcher and steals out of town to meditate, will do:

Half an hour later he was disappearing behind the Douglas
mansion on the summit of Cardiff Hill, and the schoolhouse
was hardly distinguishable away off in the valley behind him.
He entered a dense wood, picked his pathless way to the
center of it, and sat down on a mossy spot under a spreading
oak. There was not even a zephyr stirring; the dead noon-day
heat had even stilled the song of the birds; nature lay in a
trance that was broken by no sound but the occasional far-off
hammering of a woodpecker, and this seemed to render the
pervading silence and sense of loneliness the more profound.
The boy's soul was steeped in melancholy; his feelings were
in happy accord with his surroundings. He sat long with
his elbows on his knees and his chin in his hands, meditating.

It seems to me that this image is the heart of the novel,
as Mark Twain wrote it. Here is Tom, reflecting upon
his earthly woes, very much concerned with the situation
that comprises the plot of the book, and at the same time
Tom is also outside the immediate action, there in the
wood near Cardiff Hill where nature lay in a trance all

about him, and he is outside, too, of the community and its immediate concerns. This is the essential Tom as the author created him. Mark Twain seemed to see young people such as Tom as both caught up in the worldly time and place and events, and part too of that timeless world of sun and summer and Cardiff Hill.

Which world is real: the daily life of St. Petersburg and of Tom Sawyer, or the natural world of Cardiff Hill? Both are real, and the boy Tom is a part of both. Here in that passage Tom is aware of both worlds. An adult would not have been, could not have been. Adults in St. Petersburg are prosaic creatures, very much occupied with their mundane pursuits. Tom can look to no adult in the town for help in the matters which most concern him.

What Mark Twain really does in the novel is to defy adulthood, defy the world of practicality, by proving that Tom Sawyer's child's world, with its pirates, robber bands, buried treasure, and Cardiff Hill green and still in the sunlight, is valid too. In a very real sense, Tom Sawyer arrests the progression of time, holds onto childhood instead of conforming to the values and habits of adults.

Actually, however, it is only a delaying action. It is over when the novel is over, and the eventual victor is the mundane world, for Tom will of course grow up. "So endeth this chronicle," Mark Twain writes in concluding the novel; "it being strictly a history of a *boy*, it must stop here; the story could not go on much further without becoming the history of a *man*." The ultimate triumph will be the community's, the adult's; Tom will cease retreating to the woods beyond Cardiff Hill, and cease hunting for buried treasure. Yet while the novel lasts, Tom Sawyer holds on to life on a child's terms, and forces the community to accept it.

Thus a brief thematic and textual analysis of *The Adventures of Tom Sawyer*, read not as a document, but as a story, in order to see what the story means. What, then, of the use of the novel as a help in understanding American life?

For such a purpose, I think that what we have found in the course of this literary analysis offers rich material. Take, for instance, the idea of success. For Tom Sawyer, life on the Mississippi has indeed been a place where all things are possible, where a man can change the world. Tom Sawyer adjusts the conditions of life to suit his tastes. He looks on the world not as a settled, fixed community, but as a place of boundless possibilities. Is not this novel a very good interpretation of a typically American attitude? Tom is not merely lucky. He *makes* his opportunities. Far more so than with the shallow, stereotyped novels of Horatio Alger, this story is an American success story. Individualism, the will to succeed, the cult of success even, are exemplified in the theme of this novel. It is built around and it explores on many planes an idea that we accept as entirely appropriate to nineteenth-century America.

Yet compare *The Adventures of Tom Sawyer* to a European novel of childhood, and note the difference. When we analyze novels about young boys growing up in Germany, England, France, what do we get? *Wilhelm Meister,* with its heavy intellectual adventure toward maturity and adjustment with the world. *Tom Brown's School Days,* with all its cruelty and reforming intentions. *The Red and the Black* or *The Charterhouse of Parma,* with their cynical, preoccupied attitude toward achieving success in a given jaded situation, and their notion of an almost Nietzschean superman-like approach to destiny. Where in any of these novels is there room for that happy serenity of Tom Sawyer, for gazing out of the window and observing the sun and the shadows and the sleeping cattle on Cardiff Hill? In these European novels, it seems to me, there is a basic feeling of the world being what it is, and the young man's growth a process of becoming adjusted to its essential limitations. By contrast, Tom Sawyer changes his world, and that was possible because the author was able to conceive of the world as a place of boundless possibilities.

Yet as we have noted, it has been only a temporary victory that Tom has been able to achieve. He will grow up; he will have to conform; he will make his way on adult terms, in a community. The triumph has been bittersweet. Tom has gained renown and riches and romance, he has become somebody, yet he is in the process of losing as well as gaining. He is losing that moment in the woods beyond Cardiff Hill; he is steadily growing away from the world of childhood, of timeless nature and sun and green hillside, that "Delectable Land, dreamy, reposeful, and inviting." It is most reminiscent of a passage in Thomas Wolfe's *Of Time and the River*, in which the protagonist is seated at a restaurant in a French town and hears the sound of workmen going home after the day's labor. Instantly it makes him think of another sound, "a suddenly living and intolerable memory, instant and familiar as all this life around him, of a life that he had lost, and that could never die." And Wolfe goes on to describe that memory:

It was the life of twenty years ago in the quiet, leafy streets and little towns of lost America—of an America that had been lost beneath the savage roar of its machinery, the brutal stupefaction of its days, the huge disease of its furious, ever-quickening and incurable unrest, its flood-tide horror of gray, driven faces, starved, brutal eyes and dull, dead flesh.

The memory of that lost America—the America of twenty years ago, of quiet streets, the time-enchanted spell and magic of full June, the solid, liquid, lonely shuffle of men in shirtsleeves coming home, the leafy fragrance of the cooling turnip-greens, and screens that slammed, and sudden silence—had long since died, had been drowned beneath the brutal flood-tide, the fierce stupefaction of that roaring surge and mechanic life which had succeeded it.

Wolfe was writing of childhood in Asheville, North Carolina, while Mark Twain was describing childhood in Hannibal, Missouri, seventy years before. Yet in both passages there is what Wolfe called "the time-enchanted spell and magic of full June," and in Wolfe's first novel, *Look Homeward, Angel*, there are numerous passages that remind one of those scenes in *Tom Sawyer*.

When we think of Mark Twain, that practical man, popular lecturer, eager businessman, who chided the South for its improvident romanticism, and we think of his practical, eager country of booming business and material prosperity, well on its way to becoming the richest nation on earth, does not this sense of spiritual loss in the very act of practical, adult achievement seem important? In the moment of attaining success and renown, Tom Sawyer is losing contact with the natural world of Cardiff Hill. There is achievement—and there is paradoxically the denial of achievement. Just as in Robert Penn Warren's poem, "The Ballad of Billie Potts," young Billie goes west and achieves success, something is yet lost in the very act, and he must come back east to find it. As Warren described it,

Though your luck held and the market was always satisfactory,
Though the letter always came and your lovers were always
        true,
Though you always received the respect due to your position,
Though your hand never failed of its cunning and your glands
        always thoroughly knew their business,
Though your conscience was easy and you were assured of
        your innocence,
You became gradually aware that something was missing from
        the picture,
And upon closer inspection exclaimed, "Why, I'm not in it
        at all!"
Which was perfectly true.

We see this theme in Warren, in Wolfe, and we have found it in Mark Twain. Not the repudiation of success and practicality, but the achievement of it. Tom has succeeded. He has changed his world. He is rich, and famous, and heroic. He would not have it differently, and neither would his creator. Yet along with it there is the sense of something impractical and spiritual lost in the doing.

If this theme has any relevance for understanding American life, and of course it does, then it follows that its presence at the heart of a great nineteenth-century American novel has some significance for for us. It shows us something that we did not perhaps see so well before. It is not documentation, but *analysis*. It tells us what to look for.

A great novel creates its art by synthesis, not by fragmentation. It is in the novelist's ability to fuse complex experience into a single artistic entity, to make a whole out of parts, that his art achieves its goals. It took a Mark Twain to show us how the meaning of success, and of loss, lies at the heart of American experience. To deny ourselves the insights of our major writers in our search for knowledge of our country's life, is needlessly to impoverish and weaken the quality of our understanding. Documentation can tell us *what*, but fiction tells us *why*. It may not provide us with all the facts we want about American life, but it can do something at least equally as useful. It can draw multitudinous experience together into one coherent artistic image, and tell us what American life means.

H. L. Mencken
and the National Letters

Whenever anyone mentions H. L. Mencken's name nowadays, we tend to think of the 1920's. We think of the *American Mercury*, Prohibition, the Scopes Trial, the banning of *Jurgen*, the smiting of the booboisie. It is Mencken the idol-shatterer that we think of, Mencken the irreverent, the apostle of the Good Life—by which is meant the kind of life in which Beethoven and the belles-lettres play equally conspicuous parts with pilsener and crab cakes Maryland. Beyond doubt the twenties were his heyday, the era when he was, as the New York *Times* editorialized, the most powerful private citizen in the United States. Yet when the literary history of our century comes to be written definitively, it is doubtful, I think, that it will be the Mencken of the allegedly Roaring Twenties who will be most noticed. Rather, the phase of Mencken's career that will be adjudged of most significance and usefulness will be the 1910's, when he was composing his monthly literary essays for the old *Smart Set*. In the 1920's Mencken was a symbol and a symptom; in the 1910's he was a maker and a finder. He will figure in our national letters as the leading dismantler of the genteel tradition, the chief crusader against certain venerated nineteenth-century literary attitudes which had long since outlived their usefulness and had to be destroyed if future American writers were to do their best work. This is what Mencken accomplished, and he did his job masterfully, and in the 1910's for the most part, not the 1920's—though it was not until the 1920's that most people began realizing what had happened.

Mr. Huntington Cairns recently edited an anthology, *The American Scene: A Reader*, in which he put together his own choice of the best of Mencken's writings. By my count it was the tenth such major item of Menckeniana to come forth in recent years. Mencken himself put together his *Chrestomathy* in 1948, shortly before his stroke; Alistair Cooke edited *The Vintage Mencken*; James T. Farrell put together a selection from the *Prejudices*; Malcolm Moos edited some of Mencken's political reportage; Robert McHugh collected his Chicago *Tribune* pieces; Mencken's own *Minority Report* was found among his posthumous papers; Louis Cheslock has made up a volume of Mencken's writings on music; the *Letters* have been edited by Guy J. Forgue; a new edition of *The American Language* has been abridged and brought out by Raven I. McDavid, Jr.; and now Mr. Cairns has assembled, ultimately for enshrinement in the Modern Library I am told, a large volume containing samples from almost the whole range of Mencken's writings. Each of these collections has its virtues; that of Mr. Cairns is that it contains some excellent Menckeniana in its entirety, such as his delightful dissection of Thorstein Veblen, and also a fine introduction by Mr. Cairns. It is not precisely the selection I would have made had I been editing such a book, but that is a quibble based on personal taste. Mr. Cairns is a legal philosopher and thus tends to go in for Mencken's longer, more conceptually developed essays. I prefer Mencken in rebuttal; his best work, I think, appears in the short demolitions of his *Prejudices* volumes. But what of that? There is plenty to go around.

It is obviously, then, a figure of still widespread interest and appeal that we are dealing with in H. L. Mencken, one who is important not only because of his historical role but also because he is an interesting writer in his own right, whose prose shows every sign of surviving. But in what form will it survive? As an increasingly quaint period specimen? As a species of American humor, after the manner of *Innocents Abroad* and *Archy and Mehitabel*? As documentation—that is, as source material for historians to compile excerpts and footnotes from? There is no way of knowing, of course. My own guess is that Mencken's best writing will survive as genuinely imaginative literature—literature which was also highly influential in the development of the national letters. His social and descriptive commentary is witty, his political thinking often amusing, but his writings about literature were and are of lasting interest and influence.

When Mencken began writing in the 1900's, he confronted the platitudes and stock ethical responses of a once flourishing intellectual and cultural establishment that had long since lost most of its capacity for dealing with reality and was simply waiting around to be removed. Whitman, Melville, Emerson, Dickinson were dead; Hawthorne and Poe had perished long ago. Clemens was still alive, but was confining his literary activities for the most part to after-dinner speeches. Nobody paid any attention anymore to Henry James, who was across the ocean in England and had long since moved into new and different artistic territory. Only William Dean Howells was left, and Howells' day was done. The most influential literati were Henry Van Dyke, O. Henry, Hamilton Wright Mabie, William Vaughan Moody, Emerson Hough, Hamlin Garland, James Lane Allen, F. Hopkinson Smith, Brander Matthews, Walter Hines Page, Owen Wister, Booth Tarkington, and so forth. The leading literary magazines were still the old monthlies—*Harper's, The Century, The Atlantic, Scribner's*—which were edited by respectable gentlemen such as Henry Mills Alden, Bliss Perry, Robert Underwood Johnson, Richard Watson Gilder, and the like. Our literature, in short, was thoroughly institutionalized and the institution was decrepit. New writers were waiting in the wings, but few knew they were there.

Such was the literary situation when Henry Louis Mencken took on the job of writing a monthly literary essay for *The Smart Set* in 1908. What had to be done was obvious, or so it seems in retrospect, and the man to take the lead in doing it would have to possess certain qualifications. He ought not to have much of a stake in the reigning cultural establishment—in what Henry F. May has described as "the Anglo-Saxon monopoly of American culture"—because he would have to deal quite heavy-handedly with most of its heroes and its beliefs. He ought not to be overly protective toward the national tradition, because his job would consist most importantly of happily cutting away at its excrescences. He ought not to be very much of a chauvinist, because what American writing most needed was a strong exposure to the ideas and techniques which were common enough in France, Germany, and even England, but which had so far failed importantly to come across the ocean and clear through the customs. He ought also to have a thorough grounding in everyday urban middle-class American life, because the big task was to get our literature involved in that life again. Finally, he ought to have both a strong set of lungs, because it was going to be difficult at first to make himself heard at all, and a plentiful share of combativeness, because the dismantling job was not for the faint-hearted or the meek.

The extent to which Mencken possessed those qualifications, and certain additional qualifications as well, is abundantly evident. To begin with, Mencken was of German descent, and not part of the old Maryland social elite;

gentility was a threat to his self-esteem, and he delighted in bringing it low. All his life he was an Anglophobe; I suspect that a great deal of the impetus for *The American Language* lay in his desire to show that American speech was no longer dependent on its English origins. He was not a college-educated man; he learned his lessons in a newspaper city room, and his reading was accomplished on his own. He was not very much interested in the past. Perhaps because his family's roots did not extend very far back into American history, he was not inclined to measure present conditions by past yardsticks, and almost his entire concern was for what was currently going on— in literature, in politics, in thought. He was strongly drawn to European writers and continental ways of thinking and feeling, and unlike Howells, his attitude was not that they were exotic imports. Quite without any condescension he considered it his mission to propagandize for them, and in so doing to castigate the American establishment for its failure to adopt them. His extensive journalistic experience necessarily involved longtime immersion in everyday goings-on, and the exposure there was not as a literary man but as a working newspaperman. He had a muscular and vivid writing style; hyperbole was his habitual mode of expression. Finally, there was a chip on his shoulder most of the time, a grudge against those in positions of cultural and intellectual authority, and he took endless joy in cutting the philistines down to size. To all this, add a magnificent, sardonic sense of humor, and the right man had arrived to take advantage of the opportunity that presented itself.

We can get an idea of the kind of role Mencken played from his remarkable essay entitled "The National Letters," published in book form in the second of the *Prejudices* series, in 1920. This is about as good a statement of Mencken's position as was ever put forward. He reviews the century-long history of demands for a truly American literature, then takes up the essential shallow-

ness of American writing in the early years of the twentieth century: "American thinking, when it concerns itself with beautiful letters as when it concerns itself with
religious dogma or political theory, is extraordinarily
timid and superficial— . . . It evades the serious problems
of life and art as if they were stringently taboo—and the
outward virtues it undoubtedly shows are always the virtues, not of profundity, not of courage, not of originality,
but merely those of an emasculated and often very trashy
dilettantism." Next he proceeds to the day's chief littera-
teurs, of whom he instances Henry Van Dyke, who while
he has a knack for rhetoric and shows, "in discreet moments," some imagination, "all the while he remains a
sound Presbyterian, with one eye on the devil. He is a
Presbyterian first and an artist second, which is just as
comfortable as being a Presbyterian first and a chorus girl
second. To such a man it must inevitably appear that a
Molière, a Wagner, a Goethe or a Shakespeare was more
than a little bawdy."

As for the literary criticism that "supports this decaying
caste of literary Brahmins," it is moralistic rather than
artistic: "You will spend a long while going through the
works of such typical professors as More, Phelps, Boynton,
Burton, Perry, Brownell and Babbitt before ever you en-
counter a purely aesthetic judgment upon an aesthetic
question. It is almost as if a man estimating daffodils
should do it in terms of artichokes." He ticks them off,
concentrating on Stuart Sherman, Babbitt, and More ("To
More or Babbitt only death can atone for the primary
offense of the artist"). Then he asks a crucial question,
one which by implication describes his own role as opposed to theirs:

I often wonder what sort of picture of these States is conjured
up by foreigners who read, say, Crothers, Van Dyke, Babbitt,
the later Winston Churchill, and the old maids of the Freudian suppression school. How can such a foreigner, moving in
those damp, asthmatic mists, imagine such phenomena as

Roosevelt, Billy Sunday, Bryan, the Becker case, the I.W.W., Newport, Palm Beach, the University of Chicago, Chicago itself—the whole gross, glittering, excessively dynamic, infinitely grotesque, incredibly stupendous drama of American life?

There, of course, we have it: whatever the merits of American literature of the late genteel tradition, it was by virtue of convention and attitude quite unable to come to grips with the kind of life that Americans, being human beings living in the early years of the twentieth century, knew—which is to say, with reality, whether in America or elsewhere. Even Howells couldn't manage it, for all his valiant efforts to do so; as Marcus Cunliffe says, Howells could deal with the lack of culture only as a deprivation, and not as a fact. Mencken put the general problem this way, discussing a now forgotten figure named Clayton Hamilton, then vice-president of the National Institute of Arts and Letters:

Here are the tests he proposes for dramatic critics, i.e., for gentlemen chiefly employed in reviewing such characteristic American compositions as the Ziegfeld Follies, "Up in Mabel's Room," "Ben-Hur," and "The Witching Hour":
1. Have you ever stood bareheaded in the nave of Amiens?
2. Have you ever climbed to the Acropolis by moonlight?
3. Have you ever walked with whispers into the hushed presence of the Frari Madonna of Bellini?
What could more brilliantly evoke an image of the eternal Miss Birch, blue veil flying and Baedeker in hand, plodding along faithfully through the interminable corridors and catacombs of the Louvre, while the bands are playing across the river, and young bucks in three-gallon hats are sparking the gals, and the Jews and harlots uphold the traditions of French *hig leef* at Longchamps, and American deacons are frisked and debauched up on martyrs' hill?

Having disposed of the apparent titans of American literature of the day, Mencken gets to work on what he terms "the bottom layer," by which he means Greenwich Village and the churning literature of rebellion. He doesn't think that the Village produces very much literature worth reading, but even so he is for it, because it constitutes the beginnings of "a challenge to the accepted canons in letters and to the accepted canon lawyers. . . . The Village, in brief, is an earnest that somewhere or other new seeds are germinating." He follows this with a brief castigation of what he terms the "middle layer," which is the popular commercial literature that fills the mass magazines of the day. Of these the *Saturday Evening Post* is the best, but in general American popular magazines are "gaudily romantic, furtively sexual, and full of rubber-stamp situations and personages—a sort of amalgam of the worst drivel of Marie Corelli, Elinor Glyn, E. Phillips Oppenheim, William Le Quex and Hall Caine. This is the literature of the middle layer—the product of the national Rockefellers and Duponts of letters. This is the sort of thing that the young author of facile pen is encouraged to manufacture. This is the material of the bestsellers and the movies."

When Mencken gets around to diagnosing the reasons for this national literary barrenness and superficiality, his prognosis is fairly close to that which a writer he was never able to understand had earlier put forth. Revisiting his native land in 1904, Henry James had found that its literature consisted for the most part of "a vast homegrown provision for entertainment, rapidly superseding any that may be borrowed or imported," prepared for a "public so placidly uncritical that the whitest thread of the deceptive stitch never makes it blink." Mencken echoes James's sentiments, adding some further complaints of his own. American literature, he declared, "habitually exhibits, not a man of delicate organization in revolt against the inexplicable tragedy of existence, but a man of low sensibilities and elemental desires yielding himself gladly to his environment, and so achieving what, under a third-rate civilization, passes for success. To get on: this is the aim. To weigh and reflect, to doubt and rebel: this is the thing to be avoided." What happens therefore is that the American artist who cannot swallow the American success story, whose viewpoint encompasses "the far more poignant and significant conflict between a salient individual and the harsh and meaningless fiats of destiny, the unintelligible mandates and vagaries of God," instinctively turns from American scenes and looks abroad for his models, and thus the better American writing "takes on a subtle but unmistakable air of foreignness. . . . The native author of any genuine force and originality," he says, "is almost invariably to be found to be under strong foreign influences, either English or Continental." This bohemianism in turn separates the writer from his culture, makes him an object of suspicion and distrust among his fellow citizens, and creates what Mencken calls "the lonesome artist," neglected by his countrymen, attacked by the Puritans in control of the national arts, and quite isolated in the American cultural wilderness.

This is a not altogether unfamiliar indictment; several years before Mencken, Van Wyck Brooks had said as much. What distinguishes Mencken from Brooks, I think, and makes him a considerably more important figure in our literary history, is his wholehearted commitment to the life of his own time. Where Brooks looked at American experience and found it deplorably distasteful, Mencken did not propose to approach it in such fashion. Here it is, he said in effect: now let our writers start dealing with it, and let our critics recognize that it exists. Brooks was, I think, every bit as idealistic and unworldly as the writers and critics he rebuked for their lack of vitality. He demanded nothing less than that our culture be changed entirely, so that we could have good writers. His famous division of American culture into Highbrow and Lowbrow wings was in essence a programatic formulation: on the one side was effeteness, on the other vulgarity. Let us, he proposed, get rid of both, and in their place substitute the emancipated American artist—something not so different from the liberated American Scholar of Emerson.

It is hardly surprising that before too long Brooks was to be found attempting to set up a genteel tradition of his own— for the literature that came along to replace that existing when he composed *America's Coming-of-Age* was hardly free from either the devotion to craftsmanship he saw among the Highbrows or the acceptance of the reality of vulgarity that he detected in the Lowbrow attitudes. Brooks's ideal was Emerson, and he subsequently devoted most of his life to proving that Emerson and his contemporaries were what American writers ought to be. Those who see in Brooks's later work a precipitous retreat from his earlier radicalism miss the fact that Brooks was never really sympathetic to modernism. His interests stopped at the Atlantic Ocean, and he held the line as surely as did Howells when Howells defended realism in its more smiling aspects only; Brooks was not greatly sympathetic with Joyce, Mann, Proust, Lawrence, Kafka—with, that is, many of the most vital currents of modern literary thought. He termed James an "immortal symbol"—of what he later decided was cultural treason. Calling though he did for less prudery and more bloodiness in American literature, his ideal exemplars of those qualities were Emerson, who defended them theoretically but contained neither, and Whitman, who constantly invoked them but as spectator rather than participant.

By contrast, Mencken, though not I think as discriminating a critic as Brooks, went in for no such utopianism. He did not propose either to shore up the genteel tradition by making it less precious, or to infuse the dominant vulgarity of the day with more European spirituality. He wanted to get rid of the genteel tradition entirely, and to substitute more realistic and worldly-wise literary standards in its place. As for popular vulgarity, he entertained no hopes of ever reforming it. He wanted rather to have our writers admit its existence, as the European writers had been doing for some time. Nor was Mencken a chauvinist in literature; he read widely in the European authors, and did not worry lest their version of reality corrupt American life. Like his favorite critic, James G. Huneker, his approach to the arts was aesthetic, not moralistic, and he saw the predominant moralistic approach of American literature as working to exclude much significant human experience from its spectrum. Mencken's long vendetta against puritanism in American life is well known. Less well understood, perhaps, is the reason for it: he wanted our writers to deal with the significant phases of human experience, and any system which tabooed important aspects of that experience he considered unduly repressive. The Brooksian division of culture into Highbrow and Lowbrow—however much Mencken may have approved some of Brooks's bill of grievances—was utterly foreign to Mencken's way of viewing the matter; Mencken was an elitist all the way, in the sense that he considered literature as being properly written only for a cultural minority. The writers whom Brooks called Highbrows he considered timid souls. So-called Highbrow literature, he thought, wasn't nearly Highbrow enough; it didn't address itself to the best intelligences. As for preserving the tradition of Emerson and the Classic American writers, Mencken was not very much interested. From time to time he invoked the spirit of Poe and Whitman (he rather preferred Poe), but his commitment and his allegiance were squarely with the moderns, and the past could look after itself.

Whatever one might think now of the ultimate merits of Mencken's basically anarchic position as compared with Brooks's dream of a revitalized tradition, it can hardly be disputed that Mencken's was the far more effective and useful approach for his time, so far as the immediate well-being of the serious American writer was concerned. To create an intellectual climate that would provide a hearing for a Dreiser and an O'Neill, not to speak of the host of better writers who came along after the First World War, far harder knocks than Van Wyck Brooks was prepared or equipped to administer were needed. The provincial narrowness of the American literary scene had to be expanded, and the complacent moralism that had made literature its bloodlessly virtuous handmaiden must be divested of power. Nowadays we are hardly prepared to concede that the great writers of the early twentieth century—Proust, Joyce, Eliot, Shaw, Dreiser, and so forth—are lacking in morality; Mencken's notion of good literature as being essentially amoral is not ours. But so long as morality was being conceived of exclusively in terms of the thin puritanism of the late genteel tradition, then most of what is worth reading in modern literature had perforce to seem not merely amoral but immoral, and Mencken's great virtue was that he refused to accept morality on any such impoverishing terms.

It ought to be pointed out that in one sense Mencken's adventurousness and his receptivity to modern literature was more a matter of theory than of practice; as a critic Mencken apparently possessed only a limited understanding of or sympathy with the kind of literature that he championed. Typically he was on much firmer ground while high-heartedly denouncing the second-rate moralistic writers of the dying genteel tradition than when discussing the books of the writers with whom he wanted to displace them. In poetry, for example, his tastes were quite conventional; writing about the new poetry of the 1910's, we find him declaring that "there is no poet in the movement who had produced anything even remotely approaching the fine lyrics of Miss [Lizette Woodworth] Reese, Miss Teasdale and John McClure. . . ." With fiction he was more at home, but even there he showed no astounding critical insight; his strong praise of Dreiser is primarily for that writer's agnosticism, his lack of didacticism, his "wondering and half-terrified sort of representation of what passes understanding." Mencken's technique was essentially that of the Impressionist; he discussed the merits of works of literature by telling how he felt about them. He insisted that the act of literary criticism was an act of self-expression, and that the critic's role was essentially the same as the novelist's or the poet's: "the simple desire to function freely and beautifully, to give outward and objective form to ideas that bubble inwardly and have a fascinating lure in them, to get rid of them dramatically and make an articulate noise in the world."

Mencken's was not, obviously, a critical art involving fine discriminations of meaning, nor was it one of constructiveness. "I have described the disease. Let me say at once that I have no remedy to offer," he begins the concluding section of his essay on "The National Letters." And in another essay, "I cannot recall a case in which any suggestion offered by a constructive critic has helped me in the slightest, or even actively interested me . . . constructive criticism irritates me. I do not object to being denounced, but I can't abide being schoolmastered, especially by men I regard as imbeciles." It has always seemed to me that Mencken's gradual retirement from the field of literary criticism during the 1920's, and his increasing involvement in social and political rather than literary commentary, is due primarily to the fact that Mencken was indeed not a so-called "constructive" critic, but an artist in destruction. In the 1900's and 1910's such a role suited his talents and the national need exactly; by the 1920's, however, the ruins of the genteel tradition had pretty much been cleared away, and the task that confronted the intelligent critic was no longer one of destruction so much as of discriminating recognition and evaluation. That was not Mencken's forte, and apparently he had the good sense to realize it; he was not vitally interested in evaluating Hemingway, Fitzgerald, Dos Passos, Eliot, Joyce, Proust, Mann, Kafka, and the other major writers who came into prominence after the First World War. This was a task for a man such as Edmund Wilson, who proceeded to perform it wonderfully well. In *Axel's Castle, The Triple Thinkers,* and *The Wound and the Bow,* as well as in his numerous magazine reviews, Wilson took on the job of training the reading public to read the literature of the day intelligently. One cannot imagine Mencken filling such a function.

Prejudiced as most of us are in favor of the builder rather than the destroyer, we sometimes tend therefore to undervalue Mencken's contribution. The party line on Mencken today appears to run something like this: He was an amusing but not very discerning champion of Dreiser and belaborer of puritans, whose work is interesting historically because he had considerable influence as a popular iconoclast during the 1920's, but which has long since become very "dated," so that any lasting importance he possesses probably rests with his pioneering work in the American language—as (I echo one American Literature professor's wording) "Baltimore's amateur philologist."

Such a verdict strikes me as being largely nonsense. No doubt *The American Language* and its several *Supplements* are important work for etymologists and other students of language change and usage, but to say that H. L. Mencken's principal importance today must rest on his contributions to that highly specialized and peripheral branch of literary endeavor is to damn an exceedingly good writer with very faint praise. One frequently reads that Mencken's writings are "dated." Some of it without doubt is: much of his political journalism, for example, and book reviews of now forgotten novels and studies. But Mencken at his best is no more "dated" than Boswell's *Life of Johnson* is dated. One need not, for example, know precisely who and what the late Nicholas Murray Butler was to savor Mencken's remark that "The President of Columbia, Nicholas Murray Butler, is a realist. Moreover, he is a member of the American Academy himself, elected as a wet to succeed Edgar Allan Poe." To be sure, the humor depends in part upon one's recognition of the term "wet" as Mencken used it, but even the most casual student of the 1920's would know that, and there seems little likelihood that future generations will lose interest in the folklore of the Jazz Age. Mencken's humor is no more spoiled by the presence within his prose of such references than the humor of Boswell's description of Samuel Johnson dining with John Wilkes is spoiled because the issues that divided Whig and Tory in the 1760's are no longer of general knowledge. What has happened to Mencken in that respect is that some of his wit is no longer available to a mass audience—something which is equally true of many of our best writers, and is hardly a disqualification of much importance. Is Samuel Pepys dated?

As for Mencken's shortcomings in critical finesse, which is to say, his failure to provide the kind of discriminating criticism of the best writers of his day that an Edmund Wilson so amply provided, one ought to keep in mind that this failure was in itself rather more an aid than a hindrance for the kind of task he had to perform. Would our national letters, would the history of American literary criticism be better off today if H. L. Mencken had spent more time explaining just what it was that Emerson Hough, or James Lane Allen, or Booth Tarkington, or O. Henry, was attempting to do? That is what a critic of Wilson's temperament would undoubtedly have done had he been writing in the 1900's and the 1910's instead of the 1920's. He would have done it well, and he would have wasted a great deal of time doing it. Surely each of those writers of the fading genteel tradition had *something* to offer, if one would but take the trouble to discover it. But what they had to offer was not as important as what they stood in the way of, and what they represented. By helping to consign their work to oblivion, by making discriminating readers aware of what such writers were *not* providing, Mencken helped to create a demand and an audience for better writers. This was no mean accomplishment.

It is an error, therefore, to think of Mencken's contribution as being purely a negative one. His tactics, true, were those of demolition, but what he was accomplishing —quite apart from the very genuine worth of his own writings as literature—was something quite constructive and positive: he was pointing out, educating the reading public (and the writers as well) to demand, what American fiction and poetry ought to be providing, which was, a much broader and more authentic report on human experience than was being offered at the time. You have a right, he said to his fellow readers, to insist that the literature of your time deal with experience in terms which are meaningful to you, and not in those appropriate for your grandparents. Any work of literature which represents your experience as consisting of something less complex and less important than you have found it should not be tolerated.

That is what Mencken managed to get across. I do not of course mean by this that all readers of *The Smart Set* immediately went out and demanded refunds on their copies of Henry Sydnor Harrison's *Queed*. The influence of a good critic does not work that way. Rather, when Harper's reissued *Sister Carrie*, and brought out *Jennie Gerhardt*, and when F. Scott Fitzgerald published *This Side of Paradise*, there was an audience ready to read and understand those books.

I seem to be assigning to Mencken an importance that is primarily historical; and this is true enough, provided that what one means by historical importance is understood. The literary writings of Thomas Warton possess "historical importance," in that students of the eighteenth century read them to find out what was being said about literature in the eighteenth century, but no one reads Warton today for his own sake. Samuel Johnson's criticism is also "historically important," not merely for eighteenth-century scholars but for anyone interested in English literature. Is this because Johnson was in his own time a more influential critic than Warton? I assume that he was, but either way it makes no difference. Rather, Johnson is read today because Johnson reads well today—because, that is, a first-rate literary intelligence composed the *Lives of the Poets,* and a first-rate intelligence is always worth reading. The fact that Johnson wrote the criticism, in other words, constitutes a large part of its importance. The same is true of the criticism of H. L. Mencken: Mencken and Huneker, for example, shared many similar ideas, but today Mencken is read much more widely than is Huneker. This is because Mencken was a better writer and thinker than Huneker (who was no inconsiderable figure himself), and that such a mind as Mencken's was at work in his time is of itself intrinsically important to American letters.

He was—we should never forget it—so very fine a craftsman! Huntington Cairns rightly insists that Mencken's prose style possessed "a vividness and a vitality, a discipline and a rollicksomeness that mark it as distinctly his own." This in part accounts for his superiority to Brooks, I think. Brooks's writing is vivid enough, but it often has a kind of breathless earnestness, a striving for emphasis, that makes it seem quite sophomorish now. Mencken's rhetoric is never breathless, never urgent; in the great tradition of American humor, his customary method is to deliver his often highly shocking pronouncements in a calm, matter-of-fact voice. Consider these sentences, in the famous essay "The Sahara of the Bozart," a prose masterpiece which all commentators on the South seem still obliged to cite whenever setting out to discuss the region's literary output. Mencken is holding forth on the shortcomings of the South, so in quite moderate and measured language he advances the outrageous proposition that the average white Southerner is the intellectual nonentity he is because the males of the old Southern aristocracy preferred to commit their adultery with Negroes. "As a result of this preference of the Southern gentry for mulatto mistresses," he says, "there was created a series of mixed strains containing the best white blood of the South, and perhaps of the whole country. As another result the poor whites went unfertilized from above, and so missed the improvement that so constantly shows itself in the peasant stocks of other countries." Mencken is writing about Southerners as if they were stallions and brood mares, and since this in itself implies a critical judgment on the pretensions of such people, it delightfully belies the calm, factual tone of an apparently dispassionate sociological observation. The sentiment expressed is also sweepingly without regard for all cherished notions of democratic equality, it flies in the face of the purported Southern belief in racial purity, and it accuses the white gentlefolk of the Old South of practicing habitual adultery along with habitual miscegenation. Thus in two comic sentences Mencken has attacked democracy, Southern aristocrats, Southern lower-class whites, segregation, and the rest of the people of the Republic as well. Yet it is all done so dispassionately, so pseudo-scientifically and pseudo-sociologically, as if Mencken were writing an essay for a scholarly journal! This is the finest kind of satire, infinitely more amusing and therefore more effective than either shrill invective or virtuoso imagery.

No one, I think, has ever surpassed Mencken in the use of the concrete reference for purposes of sarcasm. A typical Mencken rhetorical device is to compose an insult, advanced as if it were a statement of fact, and then to "prove" it through an analogy which is likewise an insult. Consider the following sentence from "The National Letters." Mencken is discussing the manner in which moralistic puritan standards as applied by leading literary critics of the day serve to hamstring American literature: "[William Crary] Brownell argues eloquently for standards that would bind an imaginative author as tightly as a Sunday-

school superintendent is bound by the Ten Commandments and the Mann Act." Again, the tone is not
flamboyant; the ostensible analogy is between moralistic
critical principles and theology. The *implied* premises are
(1) that Brownell has the mentality of a Sunday-school superintendent, (2) that Sunday-school superintendents are
hypocrites, (3) that they are lechers, (4) that literary puritanism is the product less of moral conviction than of
sublimated concupiscence, and (5) that good writers are
not puritans, and vice versa. The charges he makes about
literary puritanism, apparently only metaphorical, are actually set forth quite precisely and devastatingly. And the
humor resides not only in the choice of analogy, but in
the concrete juxtaposition, made without any apparent
editorial comment on Mencken's part, of the hallowed
sacrosanctity of the Ten Commandments and the blunt
worldliness of the specific act of legislation.

Has there been, in our time, any more enjoyable writer
of critical prose than H. L. Mencken? I doubt it. He
had a fine, eighteenth-century kind of style, about as far
removed from poetry as good prose can be, endowed with
the specifically prose virtues, deftly concrete but never
cluttered, and playing off elevated discourse against the
choicest of colloquial vulgarity in fine good humor. Consider yet another typical sentence: "Miss Amy Lowell is
herself a fully-equipped and automobile Greenwich Village, domiciled in Boston amid the crumbling gravestones
of the New England *intelligentsia*, but often in waspish
joy-ride through the hinterland." It is the "joy-ride" that
does it, with its hilarious implication of Amy Lowell out
careening on a lark. The choice of words reinforces the
contrast and the shock.

Yet it should be remembered that however humorous
the manner of Mencken's prose, and however piquant the
irony, he is making a serious literary observation, and not
merely being funny. Wittily gay though his approach may
be, Mencken is no trifler. His assembled essays and other

writings constitute a wealth of discerning commentary on the American literary scene. No one can read him without laughing, and also without thinking.

He happened along at just the right time. Had he come earlier, he would have seemed too shocking and irreverent to have had any impact; had he come later, the critical stance that he assumed would have seemed too frivolous, and the literature of the day would have required of his criticism a discrimination he was unprepared to offer. As it was, he could deal in large distinctions, without an excess of fine shadings of meaning. He confronted the literature and the criticism of a period in which the customary moral formulations were no longer adequate, and had to undergo extensive reshaping and readjustment before they could again permit the American writer to discover an aesthetic order for his experience. Occasionally in the United States there were writers who ventured beyond the day's conventions and forms, but whose acceptance was being hampered by a critical literature based on those outmoded formulations. Mencken's role was to assert the primacy of aesthetic over moralistic criteria such as those then in general use. It was a threefold assignment. He had to demonstrate the aesthetic inadequacy of the prevailing critical standards. He had to apply aesthetic standards to the literature which the established moralistic criticism most valued, and to point out any shortcomings thereby revealed. Finally, he had to champion the literature which satisfied aesthetic standards, but which the moralistic criticism deemed unworthy. He was admirably equipped to undertake the assignment, and he fulfilled it splendidly. It is not given to many men to enter upon a literary scene designed to accommodate Maurice Thompson, Richard Harding Davis, and Jack London, and to leave it readied for *The Waste Land, The Sun Also Rises,* and *The Great Gatsby.*

Edmund Wilson
and the Despot's Heel

Whenever a new book by Edmund Wilson arrives, I think of what the Duke of Gloucester said to Edward Gibbon upon being presented with a copy of the second volume of *The Decline and Fall of the Roman Empire*: "Another damn'd thick, square book! Always scribble, scribble, scribble! Eh? Mr. Gibbon?" For as long as I can remember Wilson's books have always appeared in the same uniquely thick, squat little format, too big to fit into the pocket, too small to be held open properly, bound so that it seesaws back and forth along its spine, with margins too small for annotation. But it always *looks* interesting, looks like a real book. And that is the way that any book by Edmund Wilson ought to look, because its author is just about the most *interesting* literary critic in the business. He has an unexcelled talent, when he writes about a work of literature, to make one want to read the book. Not all good critics write about literature in a way that causes one to do that. Wilson almost always does. If part of the task of a critic is to open doors to the library, Wilson fills this function altogether admirably.

His study of the literature of the Civil War is a typical Wilson product.* It isn't particularly well-organized, it is cranky and arbitrary, it is filled with marvelous insights, and is greatly informative. All the customary Wilson mannerisms are present. He has a way of seeming to be discovering everything for the first time, of assuming that until he, Edmund Wilson, has read a book, it hasn't really been properly evaluated. "We discover," he explains, "that [General John Bell] Hood has written his own memoirs," as if any serious student of the Civil War hasn't long since read Hood's *Advance and Retreat*. It is as if the Civil War and all the books about it had been lying in utter obscurity these many years, until Wilson came on the scene. He is obviously very conscious of his role; he is an explorer describing his adventures. Where in the 1920's he was discovering Joyce, Proust, Eliot, Fitzgerald, now he is discovering nineteenth-century American literature and history.

That is part of the charm. For here is one of the most original minds of the twentieth century, setting out systematically now to examine a whole new province of literature and life. As always he is eclectic, open-minded in the way he goes about approaching a book. He chooses the most convenient method of entry, whether it be biographical, historical, psychological, philosophical, textural, even anecdotal. What this book does is to examine the way in which the coming and going of the Civil War affected a number of interesting people. He is concerned with the manner in which individuals responded to the war, which is to say, with how a massive social disaster is confronted by the people involved in it. He wants to show the kind of person, and the kind of thinking, *responsible* for the coming of the war and the way in which it was fought; or rather, the kind of person who would acquiesce in the onset of war, and the response to it, since he de-

* Edmund Wilson, *Patriotic Gore: Studies in the Literature of the American Civil War* (New York, 1962).

clares very bluntly that no one knows why wars start. The war is seen as a kind of magnetizing force entering into a static field, which catches up the energies of various people, carries them along, and when concluded leaves them rearranged forever afterward. Of all the persons whom Wilson discusses, only the younger Oliver Wendell Holmes, he says, was "never corrupted, never discouraged and broken, by the alien conditions that the war had prepared."

It is a mixed gallery of people that he gives us—heroes such as Lincoln, Grant, Lee, Sherman; minor writers such as Harriet Beecher Stowe, Sidney Lanier, George W. Cable, Albion Tourgee, Ambrose Bierce, John W. DeForest; several major writers such as Whitman and Melville, about whom he has little to say, however; journalists, pamphleteers, and apologists such as Frederick L. Olmstead, John T. Trowbridge, Hinton Rowan Helper, George Fitzhugh, Thomas Wentworth Higginson; a political theorist, Alexander H. Stephens; several Confederate diarists; and various other figures.

He is best, I think, on Mrs. Stowe, on Lincoln, Grant, and Sherman, and on Ambrose Bierce. He is least convincing with Holmes and DeForest. His interpretation of Lincoln is remarkable, and if not startlingly original (which would be difficult with one so much written about as Lincoln), is nonetheless sharp and illuminating in its outline. He sees Lincoln as one born with a great sense of destiny, feeling himself created for a crisis and helping, as it were, to bring it on with a sure sense of his own epic and even tragic role. He is not sentimental about Lincoln —"there are moments," he writes, "when one is tempted to feel that the cruellest thing that has happened to Lincoln since he was shot by Booth has been to fall into the hands of Carl Sandburg"—but he sees him as far more than an opportunistic politician. He isn't sure, ultimately, what *does* account for Lincoln; given Wilson's views on the eventual absurdity of the Civil War, the Union

President would almost seem to be an evil genius by Wilson's lights. But that isn't what Wilson thinks; he admires Lincoln greatly.

The only Confederate leaders about whom Wilson has much to say are Richard S. Taylor and John S. Mosby, both of whom wrote memoirs recently reissued, and Alexander H. Stephens, the Southern vice-president. What little he has to tell us about Lee is based almost exclusively on the *Recollections and Letters of General Robert E. Lee,* by the Confederate general's son. I wondered whether Wilson had read through all of Douglas Freeman's four-volume life of Lee, even though he does quote from it. If Wilson didn't, surely it was not because of the length of the Freeman study; incredibly he seems to have ploughed all the way through Alexander Stephens's drearily-argued *Constitutional View of the Late War Between the States!* Though what he has to say about Stephens's mind is quite informative, I cannot but feel that this chapter is a labor of supererogation. Wilson might have done just as well with any of a number of shorter sources. (Occasionally one gets the impression that Wilson *enjoys* plodding through notably boring and long-winded material, just to be able to show that he has done it.)

Wilson's choice of subject matter is haphazard and random; this is part of the fun of his book. Many of these essays seem to have been occasioned by the publication of new editions of certain volumes, such as Grant's and Sherman's memoirs, Brom Weber's edition of *Sut Lovingood,* Arlin Turner's biography of George W. Cable, and so forth. Wilson comes upon such a book, reads it, gets interested in the subject, saturates himself in it, and produces an essay. One can easily point to certain works which Wilson should have read, but did not. But this doesn't really matter; of course he overlooks works which a trained scholar in nineteenth-century American literature would never have overlooked. But he is worth ten such scholars, I think, because of his great ability to breathe life into his subject, to rescue forgotten books and revitalize stereotypes—almost, though not quite, including Stephens's *Constitutional View*. And also, because of his contagious excitement about books, his approach to literature as something alive and important, he can relate books to society and history and thus provide a compelling picture of a nation made up of men who were neither particularly stupid nor more than ordinarily innocent, and who yet blundered into a terrible war.

The Sherman essay is perhaps the most satisfactory in this respect. Wilson understands Sherman, because he respects his intelligence even while recognizing the cruel contradictions in the man's thoughts and his deeds. He recognizes that Sherman fought in the fashion he did because of some deep need within him, so that "we can catch from the pages of Sherman the strong throb of the lust to dominate and the ecstasy of its satisfaction which in the past has made people believe that they were fighting as instruments of God and in our own time as instruments of 'History.' "

For a man who was at one time an acknowledged Marxist, Wilson often seems very unconcerned with economics. The Civil War for him was the product of a lust for power, which was cloaked in slogans having to do with freeing the slaves and saving the Union. As a Southerner myself I am grateful for Wilson's zeal in this respect, but I fear that if he had read more Southern material—Calhoun's notion about Greek Democracy, for example, or some descriptions of secessionists such as Robert Barnwell Rhett, William Lowndes Yancey, Edmund Ruffin, and so forth—he would have been less charitable than he is about the South's role in the coming of war. Not that he whitewashes the South; he deals with George Fitzhugh, William Grayson, Olmstead's description of his Southern wanderings. But if there was a drive for domination, I am afraid that it was not confined to the citizens living north of the

Potomac and the Ohio. That side's drive merely proved more successful.

Economics, though, *was* much more of a factor than Wilson will admit. Except for a few remarks in the essay on Lincoln, Wilson largely ignores the subject. I wish he had read a little in *De Bow's Review*, Webster's correspondence with Amos Lawrence, Thaddeus Stevens' writings, or Broadus Mitchell's biography of William Gregg. The economic dimension would not have controverted Wilson's thesis, and might have reinforced it. His lack of interest in economic history comes out in his essay on Justice Holmes. Wilson doesn't like Holmes very much, and he depicts him as a Boston Brahmin hardened by war experience into a cold aloofness and detachment from society. When he scouts the misconception that Holmes was a "liberal" he is on firm (if often traveled) ground, but he fails to emphasize that the importance of Holmes to American constitutional law lies in the impact of Holmes's detachment upon the Supreme Court's attitude toward economic matters. Holmes dissented, that is, from the Court's practice of making its own economic prejudices into Higher Law; "the Fourteenth Amendment does not enact Herbert Spencer's Social Statics," he declared in a memorable opinion. This does not invalidate Wilson's theory about Holmes, but his failure to show the nature of Holmes's role in constitutional interpretation leaves us with an incomplete portrait of the man.

"The real causes of war still remain out of range of our rational thought," Wilson declares at one point. In his introduction, though, he is much more specific. Nations go to war, he seems to think, because of some behavioristic compulsion for power. "I think it is a serious deficiency on the part of historians and political writers that they so rarely interest themselves in biological and zoological phenomena" he writes. "In a recent Walt Disney film showing life at the bottom of the sea, a primitive organism called a sea slug is seen gobbling up a smaller organism through a larger orifice at one end of its body; confronted with another sea slug of an only slightly lesser size, it ingurgitates that, too. Now, the wars fought by human beings are stimulated as a rule primarily by the same instincts as the voracity of the sea slug."

This is an astounding analogy. It reminds one of nothing so much as the postscript that Theodore Dreiser attached to his novel entitled *The Titan*, describing the behavior of a fish known as *mycteroperca bonaci*, the "black grouper," which survives because of its instant ability to change color. Is the "black grouper" the creation of a beneficent, kind, idealistic universe, constructed on principles of honesty and truth? Dreiser asks gloomily. This is very close to Wilson's position; one recalls that Dreiser indeed used to enjoy the study of "biological and zoological phenomena." Life for Dreiser was, to his continuing horror and fascination, nothing more than an organic process, and thoughts and moral ideals merely the "mysterious chemisms" of the physical body. So too Edmund Wilson, one surmises. And surely a long engagement in the study of the conflicting moral claims of the protagonists in the American Civil War, in the examination of the incongruity between the "Battle Hymn of the Republic" and Sherman's performance in Georgia and the Carolinas, between Thomas Nelson Page's Old South and that described by Hinton Rowan Helper, is enough to make anyone highly skeptical of human ideals and human motives.

Yet can one leave it there? One can agree heartily that the holocaust of Civil War was an almost unmitigated evil, that the desire for power, the lust for political dominance, the greed for gain, all entered into the picture. Still, can one ultimately, finally, stop with that? The longer I think about the coming of the Civil War, the more it seems to me that Lincoln was essentially correct when he observed that "all knew that this interest [Negro slavery] was, somehow, the cause of the war." That is to say, the underlying cause was *moral*. A cruelly misunderstood and misguided morality to be sure, which took 600,000 lives, left a region devastated and a country corrupted, but still moral nonetheless. A nation of generally kind and God-fearing people failed wretchedly in identifying and solving its moral problem, chose, in fact, the worst possible solution to the problem. That is why, for me, the Civil War was not the action of a sea slug ingurgitating a smaller sea slug, but a human tragedy.

Despite Wilson's introductory remarks, the plausibility of his book seems to me not only dependent upon a nonmaterialistic, nonbehavioristic interpretation of the causes of the war, but indeed a refutation of his own contention. For the thirty or so men and women whom Wilson discusses seem to me to have acted and thought primarily on moral grounds. And no matter that their actions were in many instances terribly misguided, that moral considerations were not the only ones involved; if we search for the ultimate basis of their behavior we shall have to conclude, I think, that most of them were trying to do what was morally right. A fearful commentary on human wisdom indeed! Again the best summation seems to be Lincoln's: "Men are not flattered by being shown that there has been a difference of purpose between the Almighty and them. To deny it, however, is to deny that there is a God governing the world. It is a truth which I thought needed to be told; and as whatever of humiliation there is in it, falls most directly upon myself, I thought others might afford for me to tell it."

Whatever the pathetic failure of what has been termed a blundering generation, whatever the delusions, the psychological aberrations of the people whose writings Edmund Wilson so ably chronicles, the source of their collective motivation was distinctly not that of Walt Disney's sea slug. Wilson's rich, wonderfully interesting book, in the course of teaching us so much about nineteenth-century American literature, will surely attest to that.

PART II

Notes on a
Rear-Guard Action

It is said of General Robert Toombs that he never conceded, and that when the news of the great Chicago fire
reached the state of Georgia, the General went down to
the telegraph office to find out about it. Afterward he was
asked whether he had received any late reports, and he
replied that all possible protective measures were being
taken to prevent the spread of the flames, "but the wind is
in our favor."

Toombs's remark was widely and gleefully repeated by
his delighted fellow citizens, and we still rather enjoy it,
because of its invincible belligerency. The fact is, however, that much of its humor comes because even by 1871
it was so very quixotic, denying as it did that the war was
over. Barely six years after Appomattox Court House, the
South had all but unanimously conceded that the war was
both over and lost, that Chicago was not an enemy city any
more, and that the South was once more and forever part
of one nation indivisible. Except in the matter of race
relations, it has generally been acting on that premise ever
since. Even there it has been coming around recently;

the flare-up in Mississippi over the enrollment of James Meredith at the state university was an ugly and abortive protest, doomed to failure. South Carolina was much more sensible about the matter; loudly did its leaders vow resistance and loudly did its daily press trumpet defiance, but when the moment of truth came, law and order prevailed at Clemson College.

I wish I could attribute South Carolina's good manners entirely to idealistic motives, but I am of two minds about it. It was partly a matter of not wanting anything unpleasant to take place, because it would be bad publicity and might interfere with plans for industrial development. It is well known that industrial concerns do not set up new plants where there is widespread disorder and violence, and ever since Henry Grady's day the South has most of all been concerned with attracting industry. By and large it has been doing a pretty good job of it; the money has come South, the factories have sprung up everywhere, and no longer is the South a colony of the Northeast. With the money have come payrolls, and with payrolls have come schools, and with schools has come, however unequally, education. "Educate a nigger," I believe the motto used to be, "and you spoil a good farm hand." This is precisely what has happened. When you teach a colored man to read, you can't be sure that he will read only the instruction manual that comes with his employer's tractor. He might read the U.S. Constitution and, unless he has been properly warned off, he might even start believing it, and if that happens, there is no telling what will follow.

This is what went wrong in Mississippi, it seems to me. That Southern state tried to have it both ways. For many decades Mississippi paid very little attention to what was being said about the need for industry and payrolls, and went right on raising cotton. It was thus enabled, at least in part, to retain the kind of society that existed before the Industrial Revolution. But we know what happened to cotton after World War I; finally even Mississippi decided it had to industrialize. Two decades ago Mississippi embarked on what was known as the BAWI program: Balance Agriculture with Industry. I quote from an article by the director of agricultural and industrial development for the state in a 1953 publication entitled *Today's South*:

> Mississippi, steeped in the mellow tradition and romantic history of the colorful bygone era of the Old South, is today undergoing an industrial and agricultural revolution which is attracting national attention.
>
> A widely accepted program to "balance agriculture with industry" has passed after more than a decade from the experimental state into a time-tested formula for helping cure the state's economic ills.
>
> Today BAWI, as it is called, is paying off in employment and payrolls and in markets for the state's abundant natural resources.

Unfortunately for those who would have it otherwise, the state of Mississippi found what other Southern states had also discovered, that you can't do that sort of thing and expect the people who are affected by it not to change, colored people as well as white. Education is a very pernicious thing. The result was what happened at Oxford. By that time it was too late to go back and repeal the BAWI plan; the damage was done. The director of development's article, it seems to me, was quite prophetic; the industrial and agricultural revolution in Mississippi did indeed attract national attention, though not quite in the way that the state of Mississippi intended.

Oxford was in the news twice in that year of 1962. On two separate occasions, stories bearing its dateline were read throughout the world. One, of course, was the Meredith incident. The other, back in the summer, was the death of William Faulkner. The Meredith incident attracted the greater attention, perhaps, but I daresay that the death of the novelist will be remembered when the Meredith incident has been forgotten.

It will be so because the death of Faulkner is a great symbolic milestone in a momentous historical process that has been going on for a century, while the Meredith incident is only a momentary annoyance, which in the history books of the future will at most merit only a single sentence in a long chapter. The chapter will be entitled, "The End of the Old South." It will chronicle an American region's gradual absorption into the mainstream of American history. Most of the factual data is already in; the larger meaning is and has long since been apparent; the result is foregone. There is nothing that can change it now.

What do the death of William Faulkner and the admission of James Meredith into the student body of the University of Mississippi have in common? To the mobs of people who congregated about that campus, the thousands of United States Army troops who stood guard there, the newspaper and magazine reporters who came from all over the world to cover the story, there was no apparent connection. Relatively few of them had ever heard of William Faulkner. Those who had were doubtless too busy to think about him. Yet all the same, there was a relationship. For the novels of William Faulkner and the events that took place on the campus of the University of Mississippi were part and parcel of the same historical happenstance.

Faulkner was but one—the foremost, the greatest—of a number of talented novelists and poets who were born in the South about the turn of the century, and who came into prominence during the 1920's and 1930's. The noteworthy thing about these writers, so far as the South was concerned, was that they were the first group of distinguished writers to come from the South. The nineteenth-century South produced almost no writers of major stature, with the possible exception of Edgar Allan Poe. Compared with Melville, Hawthorne, Whitman, Thoreau, Emerson, Dickinson, James, what are Sidney Lanier, Joel

Chandler Harris, George Washington Cable, Henry Timrod, William Gilmore Simms, Thomas Nelson Page, Paul Hamilton Hayne? There is only Mark Twain, if we may claim him. H. L. Mencken, in the year 1920, wrote that so far as the fine arts were concerned, the South was a veritable Sahara of the Bozart. Who was to say him nay? Of course he exaggerated; Ellen Glasgow and James Branch Cabell were already publishing good work, but it was not until the decade after World War I that anyone took them very seriously. It was the twenties before there suddenly began to appear people in the South who could write books that people in the North and the West and in Europe might notice. And when they began to appear, they came almost at once, and in great number and brilliance. The novels, stories, and poems written by William Faulkner, Thomas Wolfe, Robert Penn Warren, Katherine Anne Porter, Eudora Welty, Erskine Caldwell, John Crowe Ransom, Allen Tate, Carson McCullers, Andrew Lytle, and others have attracted worldwide attention; it is impossible to judge the achievement of American literature during the decades after World War I without considering their work. They are in the mainstream. They dominate the scene.

What happened in the South that might cause this? This is a problem to which I have addressed myself on several occasions in the past. I shall not go into it now at any great length.* Suffice it to say that when a society undergoes great change, when its attitudes, its values, its patterns are violently disrupted, those of its citizens who have literary talents, which is to say the kind of imagination that seeks to give experience an order and meaning

---

* See "The South and the Faraway Country," *Virginia Quarterly Review*, Summer, 1962, pp. 444–59; and "Southern Literature: The Historical Image," in Louis D. Rubin, Jr., and Robert D. Jacobs (eds.), *South: Modern Southern Literature in Its Cultural Setting* (New York, 1961), pp. 29–47. Perhaps the best essay on this subject is Allen Tate's "The Profession of Letters in the South," in *On the Limits of Poetry* (New York, 1948), pp. 265–81.

through words and images, may well find it difficult or impossible to discover such order in their daily lives, and so may seek to create the order in stories and poems. Elizabethan England, moving from feudalism into mercantilism, was such a community; so was late nineteenth- and early twentieth-century Ireland; so was late nineteenth-century Russia; and so on. I do not insist that this is the only condition needed for a literary flowering, but it is certainly an important condition.

Now the Civil War, whatever its other effects on American life, served greatly to retard and postpone the impact of nineteenth-century industrialism on the Southern states; for one thing it all but destroyed the region's capital wealth, without which industrial development was impossible. When at last industrialism did come, however, it came swiftly and violently, with consequent great impact on what had been a rural, contained, agricultural society. To the generation of Southerners growing up in the early 1900's, the discrepancy between what they were taught to believe and what they saw all around them, between notions of truth, beauty, goodness, caste, class, conviction as enunciated by one's elders in home, church, and school, and the actual conditions of experience—the discrepancy between what should be and what actually was—must have been most puzzling.

No one knows exactly what it is that makes a man into a writer. I sometimes think it has something to do with a kind of masochism, together with an almost pathological desire for self-exposure. Allen Tate's description of Emily Dickinson I sometimes think is a word picture of all good novelists and poets: "Her poetry is a magnificent personal confession, blasphemous and, in its self-revelation, its honesty, almost obscene." In any event, the literary impulse, as I have suggested, surely has to do with a compulsion to give order and form to, or more accurately to discover them in, an experience that in real life seems not to possess sufficient pattern and logic. And of course a part of that experience is one's own self.

What I am suggesting is what many others have also suggested: that the so-called Southern Literary Renascence, that outburst of distinguished writing after World War I in a region hitherto bereft of literary achievement by its citizens, may be directly attributed to what the Mississippi director of development was talking about in his article on the BAWI plan—the fact that the Old South, steeped in tradition and historical loyalties, was undergoing a social revolution. What Southerners had considered to be eternal and unchanging truth was both changing and dubious. And its writers were quick to discover this, for indeed, it was abundantly present within their own minds and hearts.

Now all this is well and good, but it will not be worth saying unless it is clearly understood that it is *novelists* and *poets* we are talking about, and not social scientists. For these men and women are artists, and their response to the change within their society—a change, I repeat, existing within themselves—was that of art. They did not sit down and ask themselves, "How can I best illustrate the change in values going on in today's South?" They did not even think of such things at all, or if they did, it was not as writers, but as ordinary citizens did, as journalists, as pamphleteers, as businessmen, as politicians. Instead they thought of people, places, situations, which they made into characters, scenes, and plots. Any writer is primarily interested in people, usually himself. He writes a novel about people. His object is to show the way people are, which is to say, the way the world is. And if a novel is a good novel, it will do this with much perception, so that other people, reading the novel, recognize the truth of what the author is saying about people. The reader already knew it, but he didn't realize he knew it, and he didn't know it nearly so forcibly, until he was exposed to the novel.

Novelists, then, write about people, not political and social problems, and the humanness of their novels is what counts. But novelists are not just people; they are people of a particular time and place, and what they know is themselves in that time and place. The time and place known to the novelist I have been talking about was the twentieth-century South. They grew up in it, among Southerners, with Southern loyalties, Southern ties, Southern attitudes; they met the modern world. They observed the ways of modernity through Southern eyes, and at the same time they judged the institutions, customs, and habits of the South not through the tradition, but as moderns. It was, in other words, a time of midpassage.

Since they were Southerners, since the South and Southerners were what they knew, they wrote Southern books. I do not mean by this that they necessarily wrote "about" Southerners living in the South; rather, the kind of fictional world they created was one that took its lineaments from the Southern world they knew, and the concerns of the fictional characters they created were the concerns of Southerners. They tended to see life in the terms that their experience as Southerners presented itself. This was manifested in the way they used language, in the kinds of problems of human definition they thought important, in what they thought men were and what they thought men ought to be. These things being so, then, it ought to be possible for one to read their novels and poems, keeping in mind at all times that they are novels and poems and not social studies, in order to find out things about the South. And so I think it is.

I want to stress at this point, however, that it is one thing for a book to be "Southern," which is to say that it reflects and embodies Southern experience, and quite another for it to be "about" the South. Not all "Southern" books are about the South; for example, Katherine Anne Porter's *Ship of Fools* is not about the South, yet it is a "Southern" novel. By this I mean that the way that

Miss Porter looks at human beings, the things she thinks are important about them, the values by which she judges their conduct, are quite "Southern," even though none of the major characters are Southern, and indeed though most of them are not even American. Contrariwise, it is obvious that a play such as Jean-Paul Sartre's *La putain respecteuse* is "about" the South, but it is in no way Southern. We are not talking about subject matter when we say that a novel or a poem is Southern; we are talking about the way that the book is written and what it shows.

But it is not enough to stop here. We must make a further, perhaps more difficult, point: not only are books such as *Ship of Fools* not "about" the South, which is obvious, but, in a very important way, neither are books such as *Light in August* or *Look Homeward, Angel* "about" the South. This may seem strange; you might well ask, for example, how any book could be more nearly "about" the South than *Light in August.* Does not Faulkner set his novel in Mississippi? Does he not deal with the problem of whether a man is or is not a Negro, and what this means if he is so? Are not all the incidents those which are associated with the South? There is a lynching, the Civil War and Reconstruction are mentioned, there are Negroes and whites, tenant farming, sawmill operations, a country store, moonshining, and so on. What does it mean to say that such a novel as this is not "about" the South?

What I mean is simply this: there is no important attempt on the part of the author to make "real life" observations about the South. He was not interested in giving an account of typical life in Mississippi. His object was not to write a guidebook to that state, nor was it to make a political or sociological observation on the treatment of Negroes in Mississippi. He was not, that is, either historian or journalist, sociologist or psychiatrist. He was an artist, a novelist, and *Light in August* is not a treatise, but a tragedy. The laws which govern its characters' behavior, the meaning of the situations in which they find themselves, the outcome of those situations, are those of art, not those of journalism or social science.

It is precisely this matter that causes so much difficulty in the average person's comprehension of Faulkner, or for that matter of much additional Southern writing. Why, the question is so often asked, did Faulkner insist on portraying all Southerners as sadists, lynchers, nymphomaniacs, murderers, perverts, criminals, thieves, adulterers, miscegenists, racists, and so forth? Why didn't he show Southern life as it really is? Most Southerners aren't like that; not even most Mississippians are like that. Why did Faulkner malign his native region so consistently? Why did he continually write about all that violence and murder and filth?

We have all heard that question asked. And indeed, when one talks with people who do not know the South and is appalled to find that many of them do believe that Faulkner is describing typical Southern life, one has a certain sympathy for this objection. One can almost—though not quite—understand why, when Faulkner was awarded the Nobel Prize for literature, the editor of his native state's leading newspaper deplored the award and declared indignantly that Faulkner "is a propagandist of degradation and belongs in the privy school of literature." Admittedly it isn't very good advertising, though perhaps what took place at Oxford in the fall of 1962 makes the offense seem unimportant.

Yet however much we may sympathize with the objection, however much we may deplore the way in which so many people insist on reading not only Faulkner's novels but those of most other Southern authors as well, there is no real justification for blaming Faulkner for it. One cannot hold him responsible for the misuse of his novels. One can no more blame Faulkner for misrepresenting life in Mississippi than one can blame Shakespeare for misrepresenting life in England, or Sophocles for misrepresenting life in Thebes. Neither of the three was engaged in writing journalism; they were writing tragedies. Their object was not the representation of typical everyday human conduct; they were trying to show what certain men were like and thus what life is like, and to do this they were engaged in describing experience in its ultimate dimensions, those of life and death, heroism and suffering, bravery and cowardice, love and hatred.

So that if we want to discuss Faulkner and the South, or Wolfe, or Warren or any good Southern writer, we must remember that there is no intent on the author's part to give a journalistically authentic portrayal of Southern life. We must not read *Light in August* as if it were an explanation of why Negroes get lynched in Mississippi. In that respect it will prove very flimsy documentation. What *Light in August* has to tell us about the South is something else than that.

The central character of *Light in August* is a man named Joe Christmas who thinks he is part Negro though there is no real evidence that he is. Joe Christmas lives in a shed behind the house of a white woman, Joanna Burden, and at night he sleeps with her. At length she tries to kill him, but her pistol misfires, and he slays her instead. He flees, is hunted down, jailed, breaks free, and a posse corners him and shoots him to death. As he lies dying he is mutilated by one of the pursuers.

This is assuredly a very violent incident, not at all pleasant. Yet one cannot object to it as being in any way gratuitous violence. It is dramatically appropriate, the only kind of end which can properly come to Joe Christmas. It is almost as though it was what Joe Christmas wished to happen. What gives the novel meaning is *why* Joe wishes it to happen, which has to do with what kind of person Joe Christmas is. And what the novel has to tell us about the South depends upon our understanding of why Joe Christmas came to the end he did.

The key to Joe Chritsmas' death lies in his life. Born

illegitimately to a mother who died, he is taken to an orphanage where, perhaps because of his dark complexion —his father may not have been a Negro, but if not he was evidently a Mexican or a Spaniard with a dark skin—he is taunted by his playmates with accusations of "nigger!" and his sense of guilt and punishment is seriously shocked when he is bribed by a female hospital attendant when he thinks he has done wrong. This confusion of punishment is further intensified when he is adopted by foster parents who are fanatical Calvinists and who punish him brutally under the guise of inculcating justice and goodness in him. His doubt about his Negro ancestry continues to plague him so that, as the result of these and other incidents, he grows to manhood unable to accept love and tormented by his failure to know who he is, something he must know if he is ever to find his rightful place in society. The result is that he embarks on a long career of violence and brutality, culminating in his liaison with Joanna Burden. When this mutually destructive relationship ends, he goes almost willingly to his death.

This is but one, though the most important, of a number of closely interrelated sequences in the novel. What it depicts is the quest of a man to find out who he is. Joe Christmas does not know whether he is white or black, and he inhabits a society in which one must be either one or the other. The important point is that Joe *could*, so far as the society is concerned, pass as either. Indeed, he has at times lived in both guises. The problem then is one within himself. He needs certainty, he needs to be able to define himself as a man, and because of his upbringing he is unable to accept the limitations or the advantages of either choice. He rages against the need to assume an identity in society; his response to human limitation is violence. When even the ultimate violence he can commit, the ultimate blasphemy and rejection he can utter, fail to tell him who he is, fail to evoke an absolute standard by which he can measure himself, he chooses the only certainty still left to him: his own destruction.

Now what does this tell us about the South? It tells us, I think, that man needs to know who he is and what he is, and that a society in which men are fitted into roles which fail to allow them to define themselves fully as human beings must be a society of unrest, of violence, of suffering. But of course that is no revelation, is it? Don't the social scientists show us that, and in much more documentary fashion?

No, they do not. They don't show it to us; they tell it to us, by means of statistics, case histories, factual data. What Faulkner does in *Light in August* is to show us what it means to be a human being and not to know who one is and is not, to confront society and to try to live both without and within it, when one can do neither except at the expense of one's own identity. He shows us what it means, because he dramatizes it as a tragedy in which Joe Christmas, through not knowing how to be human and not being allowed to be himself, can find surcease only in self-destruction.

So that if we read this novel, and accept what it has to tell us, we will know, in a way that no nonfictional account, no sociological or journalistic analysis can tell us, the human meaning of racism—and not only that, but of all ways of treating human beings as less than human. With due reservation and skepticism as to the difficulty and even the absurdity of attempting to order one's life through works of art, I cannot conceive how anyone could read *Light in August* and ever feel quite the same about Negroes.

Of course I realize that in so saying, I may seem to have contradicted my original point, which was that a book such as *Light in August* is not "about" the South at all. And it is not: for the object of Faulkner in writing it was not to tell his readers about the South. Joe Christmas is not the "average" Southern Negro or even a portrait of a typical victim of a lynch mob. He is not, one is glad to say, a "typical" human being at all—for most human beings do not do the violent things that he did. He is an exaggeration, a tragic hero. Yet it is in his very exaggeration, his outlandish proportions, the intensity of his grief and fears and pains and desires, that he speaks most directly to us. By pursuing Joe Christmas' human dimensions to their ultimate proportions Faulkner is able to dramatize that humanness, to show it to us clean, unflawed by compromise or qualification. He shows us, that is, what it means to be a human being, and we recognize in this pervert, this murderer, this criminal, what is also present in ourselves. And since Joe Christmas is a Negro, or thinks he is, we can see that a Negro is a human being and what it must be like, again extended to the ultimate dimensions of tragedy, to try to be both human and Negro.

This is not something that can be measured. It cannot be transferred into the particulars of daily life, to serve as a guide to the improvement of race relations, to the sociology of rural Mississippi. It is not an attempt to describe the way things are in Mississippi. Thus it is not "about" Mississippi or the South. Yet the human insight it contains, the truth it has to tell us about compassion and cruelty and pride, speaks powerfully to the concerns of Mississippi and the South today.

For it is the nature of the Southern experience today that the large and elemental passions are in the news, at the surface of experience. We are assailed, in a most dramatic fashion, with human problems the most complex, the most urgent to solve. And it is impossible for us to look at these problems sideways. Caught up in the rending process of transition, we are brought face to face with events that possess instant and inescapable meaning. All our old loyalties, our historical attitudes, our instinctive responses, are up for examination. The compromises we have habitually relied upon to square conflicts between our ideas of the good and our knowledge of the imperfect ordering of our society are one after the other proving unsatisfactory.

I think we always knew, in the South, that we were not doing right by the Negro. But we also knew how very hard and how inconvenient it would be to do what was right. Both the right and the difficulty of doing right were very sharp realities, and we could not ignore their existence. So we worked out, as all human beings would naturally do, some very elaborate compromises with our integrity, and we persuaded ourselves that these would suffice. So they did, for a long time. But that time began running out on us many decades ago, and what we have been doing for the most part is trying to find new compromises and to beat a kind of grudging and dignified retreat. We have been waging a rear-guard action; we have been trying to keep the process of change from overwhelming us, while we were getting to where we had to go. I remember when I was a child, for example, that colored people, when mentioned in my hometown newspaper, were never called Mr. or Mrs. It was a little mark of indignity, part of a pattern of behavior. Nowadays this is no longer so; again, a small thing to be sure, but a sign that we are accommodating ourselves to the notion that Negroes are fully human beings after all. We have given up that line of defense and have retreated to new, prepared positions. Soon we shall give those up, and keep right on retreating. We shall keep retreating until, finally, one day, there will be no place else left to retreat, and to our amazement we will discover that the war is over. It will be over because there won't be anything left to fight about.

I do not want to minimize the ugliness and the unpleasantness of this rear-guard action. It is a discomforting business, and as events in Mississippi and more recently in Alabama showed, a very ugly one. Military historians would tell us, I believe, that rear-guard actions are among the most bitter of military operations. They are sullen, dogged, vicious affairs, with sporadic flares of violence and travail. Each battle, each engagement, is a repetition of the previous one. If one were to compile an anthology on historical principles of the defenses proposed by Southern spokesmen against justice for the Negro, beginning back in the 1830's and 1840's and continuing up to the present, what would be most appalling and most disconcerting to our pride would be the monotony, the sameness, of it all. We used the same arguments, with only minor adjustments for particular issues, against Daniel Webster and Abraham Lincoln that we have used against Earl Warren. (This is one reason, I suspect, why most of the professional historians that I know are opposed to segregation; they know how shopworn and unoriginal the arguments used in its favor are.) We go right on battling: against emancipation, against voting rights, against educational equality, against housing desegregation, against desegregated lunch counters, against integration of public transportation, against desegregation of theaters and libraries—I understand that they have reopened the library in Albany, Georgia, but have removed all the chairs—and so on. Think of it: a rear-guard action of more than a century's duration, fought as if each engagement were the only one that mattered!

This is what we have had to live with in the South for many decades, and I suppose it will go on for awhile yet. There is no use pretending that it has been very noble or very beautiful. It has been an ugly business, and it has marked all of us. It has consumed a great deal of time and energy that might better have gone into more productive activities. Furthermore, it has had the effect of diverting our attention from much more important things that have been taking place during much of that time. William Styron, who to my mind is the most distinguished Southern writer to have come on the scene since World War II, remarked in an interview recently, when asked whether he thought that the South was changing, that his home town of Hampton, Virginia, now looked like Bridgeport, Connecticut, and it had not looked like that when he was growing up there. If that meant change, he said, then the South had changed greatly. Of course it means change; of course the South has been changing. The whole pattern of Southern life has been transformed by the Industrial Revolution, and this is of crucial importance. Yet we have paid comparatively little attention to it; we have undertaken no coherent and extended critique of what we have been about these many decades.

Now you may say that this has been an inevitable change, and I would certainly agree. You may even say that it is, taken all in all, more desirable than not, and again I think I would agree. But the point is that we have let it take place haphazardly, willy-nilly; we have done little or nothing to control it, to see that it is done at the minimum cost to what we should like to retain in Southern life. I cannot but feel that we might have done a better job of industrializing and urbanizing than we have done. If you drive through downtown Richmond today you will find that all the historic dignity and beauty of that handsome city has been ripped out and destroyed. Was that necessary? Did Richmond have to pay that price for its industrialization?

It might have been prevented, had we thought about the problem. Likewise, had we spent the last quarter-century worrying, not about how to keep qualified Negroes out of our schools, but about what we could do to maintain and enhance the educational quality of our schools, how we could secure and keep first-class teachers; had we expended the same amount of emotional energy and intellect and money in improving our schools that we expended in our traditional rear-guard action; how changed our schools and our community might now be, and all for the better. As it is, we will still have the integrated schools, and neither the white nor the Negro stu-

dents will get a very good education in them. To paraphrase the Irish poet, behold this proof of Southern sense.

But of course that is a utopian dream. People do not
behave like that. They go on fighting their rear-guard
actions, dealing with immediate events, never worrying
about underlying causes, refusing to learn from the past
or to face the future. The historians look at the record of
what they said and did, trace out the causes and effects,
point to patterns, directions, motivations. How can there
be doubt as to what has taken place in the South, and what
will take place? Barring international calamity or collision
of planets, the outcome, the century-long direction, is as
certain and as predictable as any problem in applied science. Even those who lead the resistance to any such accommodation to the inevitable privately concede the futility of their opposition. Of course it's a lost cause, declares
a friend of mine in private. Yet he is a brilliant and promi-
nent newspaper editor who goes to work each morning and
composes vigorous editorials urging his fellow Southerners never to surrender, to stand fast. To persist in the face
of defeat, to remain defiant to the bitter end, we call this
bravery. And it is, of a sort. Yet sometimes I wonder
whether it would not require more bravery than that even
to act on the basis of one's reason and wisdom, though
one's emotions and one's sense of the state of public opinion urge the suppression of what one knows to be true.
It is hard to say. There is always that which is glamorous
and enticing about a rear-guard action. How much more
appealing is General Toombs's postwar attitude than that
of General Longstreet. All the same, it was Longstreet
who faced up to what had happened at Appomattox Court
House. The South admired Toombs's attitude, and it pronounced Longstreet a turncoat, even while assiduously
following the course of action Longstreet took. I fear that
it is not very respectable to be a prophet of the inevitable.

Yet, of course, reason does prevail. It has prevailed in
Texas. It prevailed more recently in South Carolina.

They might, at Clemson College, have chosen the path of Mississippi, but they did not. They were wise enough to see that a skirmish would serve no useful purpose. They had the example of Mississippi before them. I can read the sentence that will appear in tomorrow's history books. It will be something like this: "Similar bloodshed was avoided in South Carolina early the next year, however, when leaders of that state, realizing the harm that an outbreak of violence might do to civic peace and the state's efforts to attract large-scale industry within its borders, saw to it that the enrollment of a Negro architectural student at Clemson College was accomplished without incident."

Cooler heads prevailed. In Mississippi they did not. In Mississippi there was bluster, passion, violence. The mobs formed about the university; they fired shots into windows. People were killed; others were wounded. And while it was all taking place, over in the cemetery east of town there lay the body of a novelist who had died the summer before. I wondered, as I read the news stories, what he would have done during that crisis if he had been alive. I think perhaps he would have put on his coat and tie and hat and gone over to the campus, and stood quietly alongside of James Meredith.

Would it have made any difference? I doubt it. Most of the citizens who milled about the campus would not have known who he was, or if they had, they would not have cared. Who was William Faulkner to them?

He was, let us admit it, a utopian. His solution to the problem of the South was absurdly simple and entirely impractical. It is found in *Light in August* and every other one of his novels. It was, Love. That is the great theme of Faulkner: the failure of human love, the tragedy caused by its absence. He looked at the life he knew and saw its misery, its torment, its ugliness, and in every case the reason he found for the presence of misery, torment, and ugliness was the same: the failure of love. Joe Christmas is sadist, pervert, murderer; ultimately he is murdered by another sadist and pervert. Joe Christmas is these things, his murder is these things, because there was no love, because what love there was, was distorted, selfish.

Had there been love, had love been stronger than fear, then Joe Christmas would not have been sent forth inexorably on his path of violence. It is the same in all the other novels. In *The Sound and the Fury*, a dynasty collapses, a young man kills himself, a young woman destroys her integrity, an idiot is gelded, lives are ruined, warped, twisted, because there is no love. In *Absalom, Absalom!* a brother kills his brother, a woman goes childless, a man's plans for family and dynasty crumble, because what is sought is sought without love. And so on, in every one of Faulkner's tales.

He wanted the world to be a place where love is stronger than fear, compassion is stronger than hate. It was not such a world, and so he composed tragedies, showing what happened to people when love was absent. He showed the destructiveness of hate, the futility of selfishness, the viciousness of fear. He created human beings dominated by these passions, showed the ruin they wreaked.

His too was a rear-guard action. And in one sense I see all the great writers of the modern South as engaging in just such a rear-guard action. They wrote their novels and poems about human beings caught in a life of confusion, violence, change, people seeking to keep their integrity, to prevent themselves from being immersed in the chaos of time and transition. Examine the fictional worlds they created, the situations they made for their characters: in each instance it is love that mattered most, causing pain and destruction when not present, joy and triumph when realized. For that is mostly what literature is about.

If peace prevails in the South, and it will, if our region is ever to be a place where human beings strive to help other human beings instead of hurting them, then our novelists and our poets will be the prophets of such a time.

For in their novels and poems they have all been saying one thing, however utopian, however impractical: each man is a human being. Treat him that way. Nothing else will do. Whether he is black or white, rich or poor, there is no other way. Until that is done, neither the South nor the nation nor the world will ever know peace. Such is the language of Southern literature.

Two in Richmond:
Ellen Glasgow
and James Branch Cabell

Ellen Glasgow and I are the contemporaneous products of as nearly the same environment as was ever accorded to any two writers. From out of our impressions as to exactly the same Richmond-in-Virginia, she has builded her Queenborough, and I my Lichfield; yet no towns have civic regulations more widely various.

JAMES BRANCH CABELL

I

Richmond, Virginia, in the decades before the turn of the twentieth century, was a city with a past—the four years when it had been the besieged capital of the Confederate States of America. Lost Cause though it was, the Confederate tradition was of sustaining importance in Richmond. Most of the old and middle-aged men in the city had worn the gray; almost all, men and women alike, had shared in the ambitions of the new nation and had suffered in the common defeat. The hopeless bravery of the doomed Confederate cause had left memories that would shape Richmond life for decades afterward.

As the war years receded into the past, the heritage became a legend. All Confederate leaders became stainless and true, all engagements had been fought against overwhelming odds. Flesh-and-blood soldiery which had battled profanely and unwashed in the hot, savage summer campaigns became now, in retrospect, heroic, dauntless knights. Throughout the latter decades of the century the Confederate legend was industriously cultivated. Confederate memorial days, the numerous reunions of the old Army, the periodic dedication of statuary along Monument Avenue and elsewhere in Richmond, the storytelling of veterans who had fought through the war and of women who had waited at home—all combined to raise the halo of myth about the graying veterans who frequented the parlors of Richmond homes. "They spoke," James Branch Cabell remembered, "of womanhood, and of the brightness of hope's rainbow, and of the tomb, and of right upon the scaffold, and of the scroll of fame, and of stars, and of the verdict of posterity. But above all did they speak of a thin line of heroes who had warred for righteousness' sake in vain, and of four years' intrepid battling. . . ." General Lee, their leader, became "a god, or at any rate a demigod," and, "there was no flaw in it when, upon tall iron-gray Traveller, he had ridden among them, like King Arthur returned from out of Avalon, attended by the resplendent Launcelots and Tristrams and Gareths and Galahads, who, once upon a time, had been the other Confederate generals."

"To a child, who could not understand that for the health of human ideals every national myth needs to be edited and fostered with an unfailing purpose, the discrepancy was puzzling," Mr. Cabell wrote. For discrepancy there was; the Richmond that Mr. Cabell and Miss Glasgow knew as children was not a legendary city at all. Public and commercial life in Virginia during the 1870's 1880's, and 1890's was not conducted upon a noticeably mythological plane. Richmond was a busy commercial and industrial center, with a tremendous tobacco manufacturing trade, an extensive iron-and-metal industry (Miss Glasgow's father was manager of the Tredegar Iron Works), and distribution facilities that supplied goods to the entire Southeast. Within three decades after the war had ended, the city population and area had more than doubled; though never a boom town, Richmond recovered considerably more quickly and soundly than most Southern cities from the destruction of the war.

Nor were the former Confederates who dominated the city's business and political life mythological figures. They were men, with all the usual vices, habits, and compromises of men. Some did not hesitate to use the legend of the Lost Cause for political and financial profit, to talk of duty while seeking emolument. Richmonders were certainly no better, and no worse, than other Americans of the time.

The Richmond of the seventies, eighties, and nineties, then, was a contrasting mixture of the old and the new. The Confederate tradition was still very much alive; the days "before de Wah" were not forgotten, were indeed cloaked in an aura of romance more fabled and lovely than earth.

Even that witty old humorist George W. Bagby, known otherwise for his realistic portraits of Virginia life, dispensed with both irony and objectivity when he looked back on the good old days before the Union armies came. "Sorrows and cares were there—where do they not penetrate? but oh! dear God, one day in these sweet, tranquil homes outweighed a lifetime in the gayest cities of the globe."

And yet there was the everyday life of postwar Richmond, the mortal and gaslit city with the smoking factories, grain mills, warehouses, trolley cars, hotels, department stores, breweries, schools, and hospitals—no tranquil paradise, no Valhalla for martial heroes, but a busy American city.

As for the literature written by Virginians of the period, whatever its virtues and defects, it reflected little of the latter element of Virginia life. It was a romantic literature, set for the most part in the prewar period and the war years. By far the dominant author of the day was

Thomas Nelson Page, with his heartwarming tales of noble aristocrats, pristine belles, and faithful darkies. One of James Branch Cabell's characters pridefully extols a literature on the Page model: "I love to prattle of 'ole Marster' and 'ole Miss,' and throw in a sprinkling of 'mockin'buds' and 'hants' and 'horg-killing time,' and of sweeping animadversions as to all 'free niggers'; and to narrate how 'de quality use ter cum'—you spell it c-u-m because that looks so convincingly like dialect—'ter de gret hous.' Those are the main ingredients. . . ." To his last day Thomas Nelson Page never faltered in his appointed task of glorifying the old ways. He earned thereby an international reputation. When he died in 1923, after a distinguished career as novelist and diplomatist, the flag over the capitol in Richmond flew at half-mast, schools and colleges adjourned, and kings, premiers, and presidents telegraphed their messages of sympathy.

This was the time and place then, into which Ellen Glasgow and James Branch Cabell were born, and this was the literary milieu which they were soon to enter, and do so much to change.

II

Conventionally romantic though Ellen Glasgow's first two novels, *The Descendant* and *Phases of an Inferior Planet*, may seem to a modern audience, they were not considered so in their own day. For when Miss Glasgow published her first novel anonymously, in 1897, young Virginia ladies were not supposed to know about most of the considerations that motivated her protagonist as he strove to make his way in New York journalistic circles. The bleak pessimism that marked both that book and its successor drew hardly at all on Virginia literary models; as Rosewell Page declared several years later in a sketch of Miss Glasgow for the *Library of Southern Literature*, Miss Glasgow was nearer to Ibsen than to George Eliot. So she was, and nearer perhaps to Stephen Crane and Frank Norris than

to either of them. She had read much of the deterministic, naturalistic writing of the day; she was always vastly
interested in ideas and "kept up" with intellectual affairs
to the end of her life. Though properly loyal to his fellow
Virginian author, Rosewell Page tempered his encomium
with certain reservations: her second novel, he wrote, "is
in many respects real; but the keynote is one of pessimism." Pessimism, of course, was not an accepted literary
attitude in early twentieth-century Virginia.

It was not until her third novel, *The Voice of the People* (1900), that Ellen Glasgow turned to the Virginia
scene in her fiction. Once she did, she continued with it
until the end of her life. For the better part of forty years
she devoted her literary talents to an intensive scrutiny
of society in Virginia, exploring as many facets of it as she
knew existed. Though it is doubtful that she was consciously compiling a "social history" of Virginia from the
start, as she later claimed, there is no question that this
was what she was in effect accomplishing. She peopled her
novels with aging gentlemen and ladies of the "first
families," young blue bloods coming to grips with the
modern world, serene Episcopal communicants, gospel-
ridden Fundamentalists, freethinkers, heroines of high
birth and of low estate, good country folk, politicians,
bankers, lawyers, Confederate generals, clerks, factory
hands, industrial tycoons, ministers, farmers of tobacco,
peanuts, and wheat, dairymen, ladies of the old school and
women of the market place, emancipated modern girls and
tradition-bound ladies of high degree, Negroes and whites,
recent immigrants and old settlers, mountain and valley
folk and Tidewater aristocrats. "I intended to treat the
static customs of the country, as well as the changing provincial patterns of the small towns and cities," she wrote.
"Moreover, I planned to portray the different social
orders, and especially, for this would constitute the major
theme of my chronicle, the rise of the middle class as the
dominant force in Southern democracy."

The Voice of the People is the story of a poor farm boy's rise to political power, and is intended to typify the coming of the rural middle class into control of the state, a control it still retains today. Certainly in the year 1900 much of its contents must have appeared quite "realistic," even downright vulgar, to many readers. Not merely the lynching scene at the close, but such other matters as adultery, illegitimacy, a hint or two of loose sexual goings-on, conniving politicians—some of whom bore honored names —a no-holds-barred description of a state political convention, a less-than-idyllic description of the monotony and brutality of dirt farming, were unusual fare, especially in novels by young Southern ladies. In the 1920's Stuart P. Sherman declared that with *The Voice of the People*, "realism crossed the Potomac twenty-five years ago going North." Miss Glasgow herself thought it probably "the first work of genuine realism to appear in Southern fiction."

For all that, however, *The Voice of the People*, does not seem a very realistic novel today. The protagonist, Nick Burr, is nobody's realistic man of the world. As a boy he seems romantic and idealized; as a man, hollow and lifeless. The meaning of the novel depends on his being a martyr to truth, progress, and democratic ideals, and he is too unreal to be a martyr to anything. For the fact is that beyond the level of the pat abstraction, Miss Glasgow had no real knowledge of what the new democracy meant, and could give him no meaning. Once she had Nick elected governor and was forced to make good on his idealism, the only solution she could find for his career was to have him killed while attempting to save a Negro from being lynched.

It is with this novel that the modern reader first encounters an essential aspect of Miss Glasgow's "social history"—often enough the true social history lies not in what Miss Glasgow writes about it but in the fact that it is Miss Glasgow who is writing it. The rise of the common man to dominance in Virginia *ought* to be heroic and meaningful, she felt; but though she tried twice to achieve this meaning in her fiction, she never managed to succeed. In *One Man in His Time* (1922) her technique was more subtle, and by focusing, not directly upon the poor boy rising to power this time, but upon an aristocratic young Richmonder who comes to admire him, she managed several chapters of excellent social portraiture. Yet this novel too foundered on the same rock that had done in *The Voice of the People*. The most effective parts in the novel come when Stephen Culpeper, aristocratic young Queenborough resident, ceases to meditate about high political ideals and ponders instead the mores and manners of Queenborough society. In what is otherwise a poor novel we are treated to a little of what later became the focus of Miss Glasgow's best work: the aristocracy faced with defining its own shrinking function in the face of increasing middle-class infiltration. For that, as we shall see, was something Miss Glasgow *knew*, in a way that she could never know the ideological virtues of the new democracy.

In both these novels, what Miss Glasgow excelled in was the occasional moment in which a member of the first families of Virginia confronts someone of lower status in a situation that has social implications. At such times Miss Glasgow senses the problems of definition that are involved and presents them with real understanding. It is this theme that provides the best portions of all of Ellen Glasgow's novels. It is one part of the "social history" that is convincingly genuine.

Perhaps the most successful of all her early novels, *The Miller of Old Church* (1911), is based squarely upon this theme of the function of class. Jonathan Gay, highborn young dilettante, comes home to southside Virginia but cannot adapt himself to the nonaristocratic rural community. His closest attachment is to Molly Merryweather, a girl born out of wedlock to a mother from a country

family and a father with social status. But Abel Revercomb, the plain, virtuous miller of Old Church, loves
Molly, and Molly eventually comes to realize that the
good Abel is her true desire, thus electing a clean life of
honest toil with the humble miller rather than one of
aristocratic frivolity with her own class.

It is fascinating to watch Miss Glasgow at work, trying
to bring this off. By all Miss Glasgow's theories, and by
her intentions, the task should have been one of making
Molly worthy of Abel—he is the sturdy one, the man of the
people, the embodiment of the solid virtues of the new
man. But instead we find the author bending every effort
at making the plain, upright miller worthy of the tempes-
tuous, complex, aristocratic Molly.

It is a good thing that Jonathan Gay, Molly's far-from-
disinterested cousin, is shot to death before the novel ends,
as if to eliminate any possibility of Molly's backsliding.
We feel somewhat better, too, for knowing that, after all,
Molly is only *partly* aristocratic in birth, and she *was* born
out of wedlock. Even so, the final union is not quite convincing; for all of Miss Glasgow's valiant attempts at preparing for the result, one never quite feels that Molly is
ready permanently to wed and bed with Abel.

When a Glasgow heroine contemplates marriage, particularly in the earlier novels, the problem is usually one
of whether to marry beneath her social station or not to
wed at all. It is interesting to speculate upon this. For
Ellen Glasgow was a young woman of intellect, interested
in literature, in all the latest ideas. She declined the usual
coming-out party in Richmond society, concerned herself
instead with such matters as Henry George's *Progress and
Poverty* and Fabian socialism, joined the City Mission,
visited the inmates of charity hospitals. Yet as James
Branch Cabell has noted, Miss Glasgow was never remotely a social egalitarian. Certainly she seems never to have
found in Richmond society any eligible male with whom

she might be temperamentally and intellectually congenial.

The novel that followed *The Miller of Old Church* was *Virginia* (1913), which Miss Glasgow called "the first book of my maturity." One can agree wholeheartedly. The protagonist, Virginia Pendleton Treadwell, is a girl raised according to the old standards. "The chief object of her upbringing, which differed in no essential particular from that of every other well-bred and well-born Southern woman of her day, was to paralyze her reasoning faculties so completely that all danger of mental upsetting, or even movement, was eliminated from her future." Virginia falls in love with and marries a young playwright, who tries for a time to fit into the prevailing business life, then forsakes his earlier dramatic ideals, becomes a writer of comedies, and after becoming successful soon tires of his wife and deserts her for more sophisticated company.

Virginia is very much a creature of limitation, and Miss Glasgow's original intention was to satirize her inadequacies. But as Miss Glasgow tells us, during the writing of the book her irony grew fainter and "yielded at last to sympathetic compassion." Virginia does indeed grow in attractiveness and the reader's sympathy as the novel develops. At the last, one has the conviction that perhaps it is not Virginia's old-fashioned values that are at fault, but those of the crass new times.

Ellen Glasgow pictured Virginia Pendleton Treadwell as being everything that she, Ellen Glasgow, was not. She herself was not sentimental and old-fashioned; she was a realistic, intellectually alert modern. Yet when one reads the self-portrait of Miss Glasgow that constitutes her posthumously published autobiography, *The Woman Within*, one wonders. For the author of that memoir is more than a little sentimental, and despite her intellectual accomplishments very much an idealist of the old school. One feels that there is much more of Ellen Glasgow in Virginia

Pendleton Treadwell's make-up than her creator was willing to admit.

Because Miss Glasgow was able to conceive of Virginia as a limited, bounded person, she achieved a convincing and harmonious characterization. That part of Ellen Glasgow that was Virginia—the idealistic, old-fashioned, warmhearted Southern girl—she knew and understood very well, though she did not recognize it in herself. The other side of Miss Glasgow's character, the rebellious, intellectually alive, firm-minded modernist, she did not understand nearly so well, did not perceive the limitations involved therein. And when she put that kind of person into her novels, her troubles began.

Miss Glasgow's masterpiece, in her own estimation and in that of many readers, is *Barren Ground* (1925). "What I saw, as my novel unfolded," she wrote later, "was a complete reversal of a classic situation. For once in Southern fiction, the betrayed woman would become the victor instead of the victim." Dorinda Oakley, the central figure of the novel, is a farm girl who is betrayed in her love for Jason Greylock, a young man of high caste but weak will. Dorinda proceeds to rise above it. She flees to New York, earns a living there for a while, then comes back home and converts her father's rundown dirt farm into a prosperous commercial-dairy operation, achieving what is presented as a satisfying life. Her chief virtues, as we are frequently informed by the author, are her integrity and courage. Dorinda, says Miss Glasgow, was "universal. She exists wherever a human being has learned to live without joy, wherever the spirit of fortitude has triumphed over the sense of futility."

But where exactly does Dorinda's vaunted courage reside? Supposedly in her decision to turn her back on those things which as a girl she had most desired—love, affection, sexual fulfillment, a husband and family. She learns to "live without joy." She makes up her mind to become as hard, as unromantic, as business-minded as any man.

Her triumph is one of super-human self-sufficiency over human dependence and love.

It is a triumph, most of all, of sterility. For *Barren Ground* is an aptly named novel. Dorinda's life is a progressive espousal of barrenness. As a woman, she abhors, fears, sexual love. As a farmer, she converts the land from agriculture to pasture for commercial dairying. As a character, too, Dorinda is lifeless, impersonal, once the brief romance at the beginning of the novel is done. Her choice of the joyless existence is unconvincing: supposedly a passionate decision, it seems peculiarly coldblooded, inhuman. In writing *Barren Ground*, Miss Glasgow declared, she felt she had "found a code of living that was sufficient for life or for death." One agrees, ironically, for as a living, feeling, believable human being, Dorinda ceases to exist once her romantic moment is done.

Now there is no doubt that Miss Glasgow thought of herself in the same way she thought of Dorinda. She had "persevered in the face of an immense disadvantage," and no less than Dorinda had "faced the future without romantic glamour, but . . . faced it with integrity of vision." She had rejected the sentimental, the romantic, she felt, just as Dorinda did.

But the truth is that Ellen Glasgow only *thought* she was like Dorinda; in actuality she was much more. Persevere she did, and surely she possessed more than her fair share of "integrity of vision," of firm Presbyterian resolve to hold to her course in spite of all obstacles. But as a person—we have *The Woman Within* for witness, and the testimony of her friends, and the novels—she retained much of what she had Dorinda deny: the craving for affection, for acclaim, for admiration. There was no more gracious hostess in Richmond; she maintained many staunch friendships in the literary world. For fame, and acclaim, she was always most zealous. The lady who wrote *The Woman Within*, who wrote the *Selected Letters*, was no Spartan, like her Dorinda Oakley; she was much too human, much too warm a person for that.

If it was spiritual self-portrait, then, that Ellen Glasgow meditated in *Barren Ground*, as it so clearly seems, her effort was hardly complete. It leaves out too much; and I suggest that if we are to look for what is left out, the place to look is not in *Barren Ground* at all. It is in Virginia Pendleton Treadwell, the heroine of *Virginia*, feminine, eager for affection, in no way reconciled to a joyless, passionless, stoical life. Virginia Pendleton Treadwell, Miss Glasgow believed, was all that she herself was not; *she* was Dorinda, the firm-minded, the woman who would do without joy. She would deny the needs of Virginia; she would be strong, spurning the feminine weakness that required love, affection. She would be emancipated, "modern," unromantic, intellectual. She would be like Dorinda Oakley. But she was both of them. And, realizing this, we understand what Mr. Cabell meant when he remarked that the true theme of the "social history" was "the Tragedy of Everywoman, As It Was Lately Enacted in the Commonwealth of Virginia."

In *Barren Ground*, Miss Glasgow had written a novel about a woman who was defiantly superior to all need for joy. Now she proceeded joyfully to write three novels about people who were not so fortunate. In *The Romantic Comedians* (1926), *They Stooped to Folly* (1929), and *The Sheltered Life* (1932), she dealt directly and humorously with the ironies of love, marriage, procreation. Her heroes and heroines are all members of upper-level Richmond society, and the situations are drawn out of what is Miss Glasgow's most consistently successful medium—social satire, the aging aristocracy in a world turning steadily more bourgeois. Because she saw her people as limited creatures, she wrote stories with believable, reasonably complete characterizations. The dominant tone is ironical, accompanied by much compassion.

The central character of *The Romantic Comedians*,

Judge Gamaliel Bland Honeywell, has missed romance all his life and attempts at the age of sixty-five to capture it, only to realize dimly at the close that one cannot turn back the clock. Had he been a younger man, it would have mattered more, but as it is, the element of passion is so little in the picture that there is no feeling that the judge is being too cruelly punished for his sins. So deft is the characterization that we accept the judge for what he is.

They Stooped to Folly is also built around an aging male protagonist, Virginius Curle Littlepage. He is a middle-aged lawyer, fallible and human, and in proportion to these traits, we like him. He is married to a high-minded and virtuous lady, and he has a high-minded and virtuous daughter. He dreams of romantic passion and is attracted to a neighbor, Mrs. Dalrymple, a comely and not-so-high-minded woman. We wish he would gather up enough nerve to have the affair he desires, and once he almost does, but we understand it when he cannot finally do so, because Virginius is a contained, bounded creature, and Miss Glasgow intended him to be. The sensibilities of the protagonist are admirably fitted to the requirements of the story.

Miss Glasgow's next book was her triumph. *The Sheltered Life* (1932) is, more than any of her other books, a formal success, with characterization, plot development, and, above all, the tone of the prose working in near-flawless harmony to produce a little masterpiece of sensibility. The theme is that of a young girl's progression from innocence to human involvement. Jenny Blair Archbald's sensibilities are effectively shaped to the requirements of the adolescent characterization. Her drive toward passionate engagement in human desire represents something of a fated, explosive action in which she seems almost helpless in the bonds of her mortal sensuality. Similarly, her grandfather, old General Archbald, is sympathetically and beautifully done and provides an effective thematic and dramatic counterpoint for Jenny Blair. She is too young to know what she is doing; he is too old to be able to act.

Surely this is one of the most significant perceptions of the "social history"; for what Jenny Blair Archbald basically represents is a well-born young woman, raised "traditionally" and with all the old romantic illusions carefully nurtured in her, suddenly come face to face with reality. Nothing she has been told or taught is of any real use to her in coping with it. The general's wisdom, that of the past, cannot serve as guide or model. She will have to discover her own way. Miss Glasgow manages this insight without being either sentimental or smug.

With *The Sheltered Life* Miss Glasgow ended her period of social satire. She turned back to her earlier high seriousness, and while in certain matters of technique her last two novels are superior to the earlier novels of this kind, they are distinctly less successful fiction than the satirical novels immediately preceding them. When Miss Glasgow abandoned comedy, I think, she abandoned her true forte. Only in satire could she maintain the kind of objectivity about her people that made them believable and credible in their own right.

In *Vein of Iron* (1935) she returned for good to those who suffer and live without joy. She returned, too, to the plain folk, seeking to show, as the title of the novel indicates, the human will to endure. Ada Fincastle, the heroine, lives a blighted existence, as does everyone else in *Vein of Iron*. As in *Barren Ground* what is striking is the passivity of the characters. They merely endure. The next impact is not sympathy and admiration for Ada's rockbound qualities, but something more akin to weariness. Ada never seems a thinking, hoping, acting person, with whom the reader can feel any real rapport.

As nearly always in Miss Glasgow's novels, sex is portrayed as something ugly and ruinous for all concerned. Ada goes off into the woods with Ralph, and the result is an illegitimate child. In *Barren Ground*, Dorinda's liai-

son was equally blighted. In *The Sheltered Life* there is
suffering aplenty because of the promiscuity of George
Birdsong. When Abel Revercomb embraces Molly Merryweather early in *The Miller of Old Church*, Molly is re-
pelled. "I suppose most girls like that sort of thing, but
I don't, and I shan't, if I live to be a hundred." Virginius
Littlepage almost misbehaves with Mrs. Dalrymple in
They Stooped to Folly, then returns home to find, almost
as cause and effect, that his wife has died. Milly Burden
of that novel conceives an illegitimate child. Annabel
feels physical revulsion for the old judge in *The Romantic
Comedians*. As early as *Phases of an Inferior Planet*,
marriage for the hero and heroine is quickly followed by
desperate poverty and the death of their child, whereupon
their union disintegrates.

Miss Glasgow describes, in *The Woman Within*, a visit
she made early in her career to a professional literary ad-
visor, who made improper advances. " 'If you kiss me I
will let you go,' he said presently; but at last I struggled
free without kissing. His mouth, beneath his grey mous-
tache, was red and juicy, and it gave me forever afterwards
a loathing for red and juicy lips." The tremendous physical revulsion and fear explicit in that description is surely
paralleled in her fiction.

In Miss Glasgow's last novel, *In This Our Life* (1941),
there is no true happiness or pleasure to be found for anyone. Written while its author was ill and often unable
for months at a time to continue work, it is the story of
impoverished townsfolk, vaguely members of the old aristocracy, but for whom such identification has ceased to
have any real meaning. Once again everything is a tired,
bloodless novel. The "social history" of Virginia ends on
a note of exhaustion.

When we examine the "social history" to see the accomplishment of Miss Glasgow's panorama of novels about
Virginia life, from the pre-Civil War (*The Battle-Ground*,
1902) to the 1930's, we are impressed with the unevenness

of her chronicle. The more successful novels—*Virginia, The Romantic Comedians, They Stooped to Folly, The Sheltered Life*—stand out brightly. What is notable is that, in each of these, Miss Glasgow is dealing primarily with protagonists of the upper classes, the old families. In each one we see the breakdown of the old aristocratic tradition before the onslaught of modern life. They are all novels of *loss*—and what is lost in them all is the aristocratic possibility. The Southern woman of the old school in *Virginia* loses because her old-fashioned virtues, those of Southern Womanhood, cannot cope with the demands of the twentieth century. The old judge in *The Romantic Comedians* feels that his life has been loveless and futile, but when he attempts to recapture his youth, he becomes not only further saddened but is made ridiculous as well. Virginius Curle Littlepage in *They Stooped to Folly* is rather futile from the start, and what he discovers is the impossibility of doing anything positive for himself or his friends and family. In *The Sheltered Life* Jenny Blair Archbald, nurtured on old-fashioned romance, runs right into disaster in the real world, while old General Archbald, his day long since done, cannot do anything to prevent it. Each time there is failure. And each time, too, the reader's sympathies are actively engaged, and the characterizations shine forth convincingly. Miss Glasgow understood these people; they were her own kind. What she knew, what she could portray perceptively and fully, was the collapse of the old order. Given that theme, she seldom faltered.

But when that was not her theme, her novels failed. *The Miller of Old Church* failed because the thematic intention ran counter to the characterization. Molly Merryweather should, by the dictates of all that is modern and democratic, find strength and happiness in the plain but good miller—yet Miss Glasgow wound up straining to make the miller temperamentally worthy of Molly, instead of the other way around. Both *The Voice of the People*

and *One Man in His Time* failed because the man of the
people who was supposed to bring honesty and progress to
Virginia life could not be imbued with a dramatic characterization to fit the thematic meaning. In *The Battle-
Ground*, her Civil War romance, she attempted to show
the planter aristocracy in full heroism and glory; what
she produced was a thinly sentimental pastiche, without
firmness or conviction. In *Barren Ground* and *Vein of
Iron* she turned to the common folk for her protagonists,
but the heroines of both novels could only suffer lifelessly,
and the rockbound fortitude with which she sought to
endow them is not strength of will so much as stolid
passivity. They are not interesting people; they are tire-
somely heavy. Oddly enough, she attempted in each of
these novels to provide, at the close, a hopeful ending; in
every case it seems unreal, forced.

What the social history in fiction succeeds in recording
vividly is the breakdown of the old families, their failure
to find meaning and function in the new middle-class
democracy. When the attempt is to portray the virtues of
the way of life that displaced them, and of the people who
succeeded them in command, the novels are unconvincing. The true social history, then, is observable not only
in what Miss Glasgow succeeded in doing, but in what she
could not do. She could not give a meaning to twentieth-
century democracy in Virginia. As a novelist, all she knew
—and she knew that so well—was the failure of the old
order. Her best work is rooted in its collapse.

III

Ellen Glasgow thought of herself as a realist. "What the
South needs is blood and irony," her pronouncement
went—and she felt that as a novelist she was chiefly engaged in providing both these elements. By contrast,
James Branch Cabell insisted that he was a romantic. For
realism in literature he had considerable scorn. "Veracity," he remarked, "is the one unpardonable sin, not mere-

ly against art, but against human welfare." And again: "If 'realism' be a form of art, the morning newspaper is a permanent contribution to literature." He composed most of his fiction about an imaginary, faraway land he called Poictesme, and the time he most often selected for his work was not the twentieth century but the hazy medieval. He was in no way concerned with what a social historian would seize upon. Politics, class conflicts, economic transition, the impact of modernity upon the Virginia aristocracy—what have these to do with Mr. Cabell's fiction, whether set in Poictesme or, as sometimes happened, in Lichfield, his own version of Richmond? His people find satisfaction only in dreams; his protagonists are preoccupied with escape.

It is not surprising, then, that the term "escapist" has been applied to his work. Poictesme, the critics declared in the socially conscious decade that followed Mr. Cabell's heyday of the 1920's, was a cloud-cuckoo land, having no purpose other than to divert and to amuse. His swift decline in popularity during the 1930's has been ascribed directly to his failure to come to grips with the problems of his time. "Cabell and Hitler," declared Alfred Kazin, "did not inhabit the same universe."

Similarly, his relationship to the South, and to Southern literature, has been put down as one of flight. A thorough aristocrat, he is supposed to have looked out on twentieth-century Richmond-in-Virginia, frowned upon what he saw, and conjured up instead a better never-never world of imaginary heroes, noble deeds, and grand passions, all of which were notably lacking in the modern South. "Because he disliked the world he saw outside his Virginia home," Marshall Fishwick has written, "James Branch Cabell invented one inside his Virginia mind."

Perhaps. Yet before accepting so simple a solution, it might be wise to examine a few of those novels and see just what sort of satisfyingly heroic and aristocratic life Mr. Cabell purportedly sets up in protest against the mundane present. Let us take a closer look at those romantic novels of escape which were so popular during the twenties and are so little read today. For if the Cabell canon is so everlastingly far removed from reality, we might wonder why it is that so engaged, so serious-minded a critic as Edmund Wilson learned to become such a vigorous champion of Mr. Cabell's work, to the extent of declaring that the Cabell cult of the twenties was unfortunate because its effect "was eventually to leave the impression that its object was second-rate, and this is unjust to Mr. Cabell, whose distinction is real and of an uncommon kind." Surely Mr. Wilson is not noted for his advocacy of escapism.

Let us look, then, at a few of the novels. *Figures of Earth* (1921), the seminal work in the multivolumed *Biography of Manuel* that probably constitutes Mr. Cabell's major achievement, has to do with a swineherd who likes to sculpt figures out of clay. Manuel soon postpones sculpting, however, and departs to seek adventure. He wins in turn the love of the queenly Alianora and the divine Freydis, but leaves them both, more than mortal though they are, to win back from death one Naifer, an ordinarily attractive woman of no special charm. With her he subsequently lives and rears children in the Duchy of Poictesme, whose sovereignty he gains after considerable maneuvering and adventuring. His life at home with Naifer is not especially blissful or romantic, but he prefers it, even so. At the end, as he departs for Valhalla, he sees one of his earthen statues. "What is that thing?" he is asked. "It is the figure of a man," he replies, "which I have modeled and remodeled, and cannot get exactly to my liking. So it is necessary that I keep laboring at it, until the figure is to my liking and my desire."

It would be hard to say just how Manuel's life represents an escape from the crass present and into satisfying romance. His heroic deeds have produced a dukedom, true; but what is it ultimately worth to him? He has not given life to the statue he sought to sculpt. There is still the third window of the palace, through which he cannot bear to look, and which represents all the things he had hoped to be, all he had meant to achieve and did not because he was mortal and had grown old without getting around to them.

It is most clear that Manuel's life was *not* one of satisfyingly heroic achievement. His own inescapably mortal nature, his preference for comfort and compromise, for the familiar, left him at the last not a whit more "successful," in his own eyes, than might have been the case had he lived in mundane Richmond-in-Virginia in the twentieth century, instead of in medieval Poictesme, where the heroic possibility was supposedly abundant. The net effect is a denial of all possibility for mortal achievement in deeds—not because of crass times, not because of the absence of the aristocratic possibility, but because of the nature of man. Only the earthen figures, unsatisfactory, unfinished, remain after Manuel has gone.

So in transferring his fictional world from the present to the faraway past, Mr. Cabell has not exactly "escaped." Quite the contrary: the past has turned out to be very much like the present, and that seems to have been Mr. Cabell's point. Not only in *Figures*, but in others of his Poictesme novels, the same discovery is made: the romantic, glorious past is found by its inhabitants to contain no more satisfaction than the present.

Gerald Musgrave, in *Something about Eve*, continually searches after beautiful women who will not cloy, as his mortal mistress cloys; but each new daughter of Eve turns out to be but a replica of Evelyn Townsend. The protagonist of *Jurgen*, visiting eternity, turns away from fair Helen's bed, because he knows at last that only by so doing will he be able to preserve the illusion that she, unlike all other women, is something special. Florian de Puysange, not so wise, seeks out the lovely Melior of his dreams in *The High Place*, and she soon proves to be no different from his earthly wives and mistresses. Again and again the Cabellian hero manages to controvert the laws of chronology and to escape into a never-never land, but his findings are always the same. He is still human; he is still subject to the usual limitations of mortality.

Mr. Cabell, H. L. Mencken has written, is "really the most acidulous of all the anti-romantics." His "gaudy heroes," he notes, "in the last analysis, chase dragons precisely as stockbrokers play golf. . . . Art, argues Cabell, is an escape from life: a doctrine quite beyond challenge. The artist seeks surcease from reality by creating an ideal world. *Soit!* But once he has moved into it he finds to his dismay that it is made of the same silicon, carbon, aluminum, oxygen, hydrogen and calcium that make the real one."

What the Cabell hero always finds beyond time and space is still more mortality.

It should be obvious, then, that there is something of the social history of Virginia in the Cabell novels too. Like Miss Glasgow's they too were composed by a modern descendant of the old aristocracy, a member of one of the first families of Virginia. They too were written in a time of progress, of great material advancement, of developing political democracy, when the old aristocracy lost the remnants of what control over state destinies remained to it after the Civil War had ended its hegemony. Yet what we have in the Cabell novels is hardly a hymn to progress and democracy; it is a skepticism that goes far beyond the usual lament for the "Good Old Days before de Wah" and into a wryly comic denial of the efficacy of works, a scouting of the possibilities of lasting, satisfying, heroic existence at any time.

It is odd that Mr. Cabell's novel *The Silver Stallion* (1926) has not been more thoroughly investigated for the commentary it embodies on the author's own times, in particular the last decades of the nineteenth century in the South, when the old Confederates were being so assid-

uously mythologized and the Lost Cause was being transformed into a legendary struggle of heroes. This novel,
which seems to me one of the best of Mr. Cabell's many
works of fiction, chronicles the growth of the legend of
Manuel the Redeemer after his death. We follow each of
Manuel's former cronies as they attempt unsuccessfully to
reconcile the growing deification of Manuel and the fic-
tionalizing of their joint exploits with their actual memories of the leader and the times they once knew. Each
must come to terms with the legend. One after another
they struggle against it, protest against its unreality, then
make their adjustments. Some accept it, bow to the counterfeit legend, falsify their own roles. Others retire from
the scene, pursuing their private realities and forbearing
to challenge the public mythmaking. Finally even Don-
ander, the Christian God that Manuel believed in, winds
up in a pagan heaven by mistake and passes his days by
making his little creations of worlds, obeying the customary rituals.

At the last Jurgen the pawnbroker, son of one of Manuel's old warriors, talks with Dame Naifer, Manuel's
widow, and decides that the growth of the legend may be
all for the best. Everything has fitted into the myth, which
is palpably false and humbug—and *he* knows, for he helped
to invent a story that set the mythmaking off. Yet the
legend has become more real than the truth.

Is this not precisely what happened with the myth of
the Confederacy in Mr. Cabell's own day? In Richmond,
too, certain first-class fighting men were made into stainless heroes, often in spite of themselves. In Richmond,
too, the legend of the Lost Cause was made to replace the
actual events themselves. As a child, Mr. Cabell had seen
it happen, and the discrepancy had been puzzling: "It was
confusing, the way in which your elders talked about
things which no great while before you were born had
happened in Richmond. . . . Richmond was not at all
like Camelot or Caerlon upon Usk; and so you found it

kind of curious that the way in which your elders talked, upon platforms, reminded you of your *Stories of the Days of King Arthur,* by Charles Henry Hanson, with illustrations by Gustave Doré."

This process of mythmaking, set forth so quaintly by Mr. Cabell in *Let Me Lie,* is precisely the subject of *The Silver Stallion.* The deceased Manuel's wife, Naifer, and her spiritual adviser, Holmendis, were, with the help of the population of Poictesme, busily creating a national saint out of a mortal and unsaintly man and turning his deeds and those of his followers into a legend that was only in few respects similar to the truth. In the end the myth, the legend of Manuel the Redeemer, triumphed. When Jurgen the pawnbroker ascends the statue of Manuel that his widow has caused to be erected, he finds that the jewels that adorned it were "one and all, and had been from the first, bright bits of variously colored glass." Naifer had sent Jurgen up the statue to assay the value of the jewels, for she, who had herself built the statue, had so forgotten what the reality was, as to come to believe, too, that the glasswork was jewelry!

Yet as Jurgen ponders the matter, he decides that the statue of Manuel the Redeemer was no mere fraud. Made though it was of counterfeit jewelry, nevertheless, "you knew the shining thing to have been, also, the begetter of so much charity, and of forbearance, and of bravery, and of self-denial—and of its devotees' so strange, so troublingly incomprehensible, contentment. . . ." Clearly the effect of the Manuel legend upon the succeeding generations of Poictesme had been entirely beneficent. It had civilized, ennobled, made more virtuous those who believed in it.

Of what importance, Mr. Cabell has asked, is the myth, whether for Poictesme or Richmond-in-Virginia? He answers by declaring that mythmaking is the single most important fact of all human activity. He includes in this category not only Manuel the Redeemer, or the Confederate legend, but all mortal beliefs, including religion itself. "Men have, out of so many thousand years of speculation," he has written, "contrived no surer creed than . . . that 'in matters of faith it is necessary to believe blindly.' Men have discovered no firmer hope than that, in defiance of all logic and of all human experience, something very pleasant may still be impending, in—need I say?—bright lands which are in nothing familiar."

For Cabell, the dream was the myth, and the only important literary activity. He could discover nothing else sufficiently real and deserving of attention. The conviction he held about the everyday activities of humans, whether in Richmond or Poictesme, had to do with the briefness and evanescence of men and what they did in time. To be alive was to be doomed in time: "We live *in Articulo Mortis*; our doings here, when unaffectedly regarded, are but the restlessness of a prolonged demise; and the birth-cry of every infant announces the beginning of the death-agony."

In creating and articulating myth, therefore, he was far from trying to avoid reality; rather, it was on precisely such terms that reality presented itself to him. So-called realism in art, he felt, was merely the art of paying attention to the mileposts along the way, instead of to the journey itself. "To spin romances is, indeed, man's proper and peculiar function in a world wherein he only of created beings can make no profitable use of the truth about himself. For man alone of animals plays the ape to his dreams."

Whether or not Mr. Cabell's deductions are sound is one thing; what is important is that he held the conviction, and based his art upon it. And that, it seems to me, is a telling observation about his time and place, and his relationship to them. This was what modern-day reality in Richmond meant for one discerning artist. His faraway Poictesme became for him the stage upon which all that mattered most about men was the direct and unsheltered subject of scrutiny. The meditations to which the statue of Manuel the Redeemer inspired Jurgen are no less serious because they were occasioned by events in legendary Poictesme, rather than by a contemplation of the statue of George Washington in Capitol Park in Richmond.

I have, I fear, made Mr. Cabell out to be a rather serious and somber writer. This is a mistake; the Cabell novels are ordinarily anything but grim. He is essentially a comic writer, and those who have placed him in the lineage of Boccaccio, Rabelais, Petronius Arbiter, Laurence Sterne are generally correct. Mr. Cabell is amused by the world; his novels are constructed upon that amusement. If the laughter seems sardonic sometimes, when the absurdities of his people seem only too recognizable to us, then we must remember that Mr. Cabell considers that amusing too.

The Cream of the Jest (1917), for example, contains some hilarious situations. A novelist named Felix Bulmer Kennaston gets hold of the Sigil of Scoteia, which, if he will clutch it as he goes to bed, will transport him into a dream world of timeless adventure. He becomes Horvendile, the master storyteller, and roams through time in space with a lovely and immortal maid named Ettare, while during his waking hours he writes a novel that has a career very much like Mr. Cabell's *Jurgen* of several years later. Finally Felix Kennaston finds the other half of the Sigil of Scoteia in his wife's boudoir. She was Ettare all along, he decided, and neither could tell the other, for neither was aware of the other's role. But his wife, puzzled by the significance Kennaston attaches to the Sigil, suggests he discuss it with his friend Harrowby, a student of the occult. Harrowby may be able to interpret the strange hieroglyphics on the Sigil.

His wife's suggestion, however, as we learn from Harrowby, is not prompted by any belief in the occult. It is simply that the Sigil is nothing more than the lid of a cosmetics jar, manufactured by a company of which Harrowby is an owner. Harrowby does not tell Kennaston, of course; he does not wish to shatter the poor fellow's illusions.

The scene in which Harrowby "deciphers" the mystery of the Sigil is absurdly comic. All of Kennaston's fanciful theorizing is built on something as mundane and insubstantial as the seal from a jar of cold cream! The description of the deadly serious Kennaston puzzling vainly over the secret message imprinted by the cosmetics manufacturer, finding in the tin disk the inscription for wild and sublimely soaring flights into unreality, is almost wickedly ironic. Kennaston seems in the direct line of "my father" in *Tristram Shandy*, of Don Quixote.

But, as with all great comic artists, there is pathos behind the absurdity. At the last, is Felix Kennaston actually the absurd, impractical, ludicrous dreamer that Harrowby and his other Lichfield neighbors think him? Has he really wasted his days, as even his wife Kathleen believes? After all, Kennaston's pursuit of the radiant Ettare produced, in his waking hours, some very Cabellian novels, and brought him impressively close—much closer than his down-to-earth neighbors will ever come—to what any man hopes to achieve: beauty, immortality, art. Does it matter ultimately that the Sigil is only a cosmetic tin? For that matter, *was* that all it was? After all, Kennaston's valuation of the Sigil made possible so imposing a superstructure of dreams. Eventually what will remain of Kennaston will be the novels that grew out of the dreaming, and which in their imperfect way manage to retain a little of the wondrous vision. This alone is far more than his neighbors will leave behind. Which interpretation of the Sigil is real, then—the mundane world's, or Kennaston's? Who was at last the "practical" man—Kennaston the dreamer or Harrowby the responsible citizen? Mr. Cabell asks us this riddle, and the answer would seem to be a rather formidable commentary on the efficacy and value of that everyday life from which he was supposedly escaping so capriciously.

The famous *Jurgen* (1919) is likewise a comic book, including some episodes of rather low comedy at that. Tired of his wife, Jurgen the pawnbroker is granted the Faustian privilege of journeying through time and space. He regains his youth, by which is meant above all his aptitude for romantic love. In succession, he visits and tarries for a while with Guenever, who is all chivalrous and highborn beauty (and also a little slut); Anaïtis, the incarnation of pagan, carnal delight; the Hamadryad Chloris, innocence, rustic bliss incomparable; and Florimel the vampire, all that a *femme fatale* can hope to be. There is, furthermore, the chance for Jurgen to make love to Helen herself, who is also his childhood sweetheart Dorothy la Desirée, all perfect, imagined, personally desired loveliness, the dream of one's youth, the embodiment of idealized romantic passion.

In cavorting with these various maids and matrons, Jurgen proves "a monstrous clever fellow," and Mr. Cabell's sense of pornographic symbolism is hard at work. Yet once again the final impression is one of considerable irony. Jurgen decides, having had his choice, to go back to his unglamorous, middle-aged wife, Dame Lisa, who is what he had learned to become accustomed to. For all her faults, all her shrewishness and her failure to "understand" Jurgen, she is the known quantity, the compromise men make with ideals. Jurgen might indeed attain immortality, the stars, the heights of romance and art; being man, he prefers marriage instead. Here again the legendary trappings of Poictesme do not produce an escapist romance; they only heighten the irony. The incorrigible humanness of the characters triumphs.

But if the quest for unattainable beauty, for perfect art, never succeeds, it is nonetheless a continual quest. The Cabell hero is a prisoner in time; he is mortal and must die, and as a mortal he cannot know fulfillment. For the artist, as a man, life represents a continual diminution of his urge to create, a hopeless and failing quest for the impossible act of pure creativity. Still, of all man's activities, only art can offer any hope of survival. It alone endures beyond death—capriciously and erratically, to be sure, but it endures.

One conviction runs through Mr. Cabell's work: The indomitable nature of man. Man knows neither why nor how he exists, but he *is*. Limited, fallible, he is a creature of courage and endurance, the central image of creation. For man has his dreams, and though he cannot for one moment prove or demonstrate their truth, they afford him his only and supreme hope: "We are being made into something quite unpredictable, I imagine: and we are sustained, through the purging and the smelting, by an instinctive knowledge that we are being made into something better. For this we know, quite incommunicably, and yet as surely as we know that we will to have it thus."

At bottom, all Mr. Cabell's cynicism, and his fond and fastidious mockery of human pretense and conceit, is based upon a kind of visceral and rock-bound humanism, a conviction that in the very absurdity of his dreams and his playing man is demonstrating that he can and will survive. The mythmaker is supreme, because it is he who, by dreaming, confutes the very nature of mortality: "And it is this will that stirs in us to have the creatures of earth and the affairs of earth, not as they are, but 'as they ought to be,' which we call romance. But when we note how visibly it sways all life we perceive that we are talking about God."

Thus did his meditations lead one Richmond novelist to decide, in the early decades of this century. His books were written in the years when the kingdom of works seemed more important than ever to his fellow citizens, whether in Richmond or elsewhere, and it is difficult to see them as anything less than a critique, wry, comic, penetrating of his times. Art did not, for Mr. Cabell, finally lead nearly so far away from the social scene as has been generally thought. And remembering Felix Bulmer Kennaston and the Sigil of Scoteia, one wonders just how unrealistic Mr. Cabell's viewpoint will finally turn out to be.

IV

They were the first of the modern Southern writers. Decades before the Fugitives began assembling at Vanderbilt, before William Faulkner in New Orleans started work on a novel, before Thomas Wolfe decided to leave North Carolina for Harvard and a career as playwright, these two residents of Richmond were writing fiction. When Ellen Glasgow published *The Descendant* in 1897, James Joyce had not yet enrolled at the University in Dublin. Marcel Proust had published only one slight volume of occasional pieces. T. S. Eliot was a child in St. Louis. John Crowe Ransom was nine years old.

During their early years, the South was still mostly a conquered province; the predominantly agricultural economy of a relatively static, threadbare region had not yet been seriously changed by the industrial and commercial expansion that was transforming the Northeast and the Midwest. Only in a few Southern communities were the factories more important than the market places.

But one of these was Richmond. For Richmond was closer to the industrial cities of the North. The manufacturing interests that the Civil War had created to provide for the armies fighting just beyond the suburbs, the railroad network that had kept the city provisioned and supplied with commodities from the lower South, hung on after the war and made Richmond one of the cities in which the industrial ethic of the New South first took hold. Earlier than Tennessee, earlier than the whole lower South, Richmond espoused the new ways. And if, as seems likely, much of the impetus behind the Southern literary outburst of the twentieth century arose from the tensions resulting from the clash of the old ways and the new, then it is not surprising that Richmond should be the place where the first major authors of the Southern Literary Renascence arose.

Miss Glasgow died in 1945, Mr. Cabell in 1958. What their eventual places in the literature will be, it is difficult to say. So much of Ellen Glasgow's work seems dated now; only a few of her novels stand up in their own right, rather than as specimens in the transition from romanticism to realism in Southern literature. In any event, her place in Southern literary history would seem to be secure; it was she who led the way into the twentieth century, and the writers who came afterward, many of whom now seem more important than she, followed in her footsteps and explored the new country that she had first visited. If from Thomas Nelson Page to William Faulkner there has been a tremendous transformation, then it is hardly too much to say that it was Ellen Glasgow who made the transformation possible.

Mr. Cabell is another matter. His novels are almost all out of print. As a writer he was always something of an exotic; he has had few disciples, Southern or Northern. By contrast with Miss Glasgow, his role in the twentieth-century development of Southern literature was not crucial. As far as American writing as a whole goes, it is true that *Jurgen* played a part in the modern emancipation from puritanism in literature, but that aspect of his work seems least important now. Today he has only a few readers. Yet for those few he is unique, inimitable, providing something that no other modern writer offers. His work does not "date," does not seem limited to a period; it is perennially fresh, wise, and witty. There are other writers like him in the English language—writers who will never be widely popular, but will never be forgotten, who will continue to amuse and delight some few readers possessed of the taste and sophistication for the proper appreciation. That is the way Mr. Cabell would have liked it; in literature as in life, he was an aristocrat all the way.

Literary fashions come and go; nothing is more transient, more precarious than popular acclaim. But for Ellen Glasgow and James Branch Cabell at their best, some lines from a poem by Mr. Cabell in *Chivalry* will suffice for an epitaph:

> For I have got such recompense
> Of that high-hearted excellence
> Which the contented craftsman knows,
> Alone, that to loved labor goes,
> And daily does the work he chose,
> And counts all else impertinence!

The Image of an Army

At the close of the War between the States, Father Abram Ryan, the poet laureate of the Confederacy, penned some verses which were set to music. The song was called "The Conquered Banner," and it has remained one of the best known of Confederate hymns. One of its stanzas ran as follows:

> Furl that banner! True, 'tis gory,
> Yet 'tis wreathed around with glory,
> And 'twill live in song and story,
>   Though its folds are in the dust;
> For its fame on brightest pages,
> Penned by poets and by sages,
> Shall go sounding down the ages . . .
>   Furl its folds though now we must.

Father Ryan's was a fairly common expectation: that future generations of Southerners would be able to draw the inspiration and the material for great literature from the tales of their warring forefathers. An army such as the Confederacy's, and a chieftain such as Robert E. Lee, could scarcely fail to provide the image by which poets and novelists could create a heroic literature, commensurate with the loftiness of the subject matter. A young Virginian, John Hampden Chamberlayne, expressed the idea quite well in a letter to his sister, written in the autumn of 1862 when he was an artilleryman in the Army of Northern Virginia:

When by accident I at any time see Gen. Lee or when I think of him whether I will or no, there looms up to me some king-of-men, superior by the head, a Gigantic figure, on whom rests the world,

> With Atlantean shoulder, fit to bear
> The weight of empire.

Was it a King Henry whose son was lost at sea, whereafter he never smiled? In the weight he carried to suppress all joy forever, he was but a fool to this Lee. When you and I are white haired and tell huge stories about these times to awe struck youngsters white haired around us then the shadow of Lee lengthening through the years behind him will mark a continent with a giant form.

In the hundred years that have elapsed since the Civil War, there has been no dearth of attempts to tell the story of the Confederate army in fiction and verse. More than a thousand novels have been written about the war by Southerners alone, and the poems must surely number in the tens of thousands. In a study entitled *Fiction Fights the Civil War,* Dr. Robert A. Lively waded through some five hundred novels of the war in order to show how the changing attitudes of Northern and Southern writers provided an important index to American social and political history. Each season produces a new crop. Some few Civil War novels—Margaret Mitchell's *Gone with the Wind,* Allen Tate's *The Fathers,* Andrew Nelson Lytle's *The Long Night,* Stark Young's *So Red the Rose,* William Faulkner's *The Unvanquished,* Caroline Gordon's *None Shall Look Back,* Evelyn Scott's *The Wave,* Ellen Glasgow's *The Battle-Ground,* Thomas Nelson Page's

Meh Lady, Mary Johnston's *The Long Roll,* Clifford Dowdey's *Bugles Blow No More,* George Washington Cable's *The Cavalier* and *Kincaid's Battery,* to name a baker's dozen—are interesting work, often of high literary excellence, and well worth reading.

Most of the South's Civil War fiction, however, is wretched stuff. Only the fiercest chauvinism can make *Surry of Eagle's Nest, Macaria, Tiger-Lilies, The Little Shepherd of Kingdom Come, The Clansman,* and shelfload after shelfload of novels of similar caliber into palatable literature. Professor Lively assures us, after reading five hundred novels, that "my own experience with a mass of second rate novels suggests that the effort would be more than an adventure among the Philistines. The rapid achievement of technical proficiency by historical novelists has guaranteed a certain quality to their efforts which is fairly impressive." A kind judgment, surely, and perhaps it comes because Professor Lively is a historian rather than a literary scholar (though his critical analysis of various novels would seem to belie it), and he may be a bit timid about making final critical judgments in a field of scholarship foreign to his own training. Either that, or Mr. Lively's earlier researches in economic history made even second-rate fiction seem interesting by comparison.

What with the fascination that the Civil War has exerted on the South's writers ever since the 1860's, it seems strange that so little really good fiction has been produced about the Confederate army. There has surely been no shortage of good writers, especially in recent decades when Southern novelists have been producing work of the first importance. Yet the fact is that from a region that has produced Faulkner, Wolfe, Warren, Welty, Cable, Lytle, Glasgow, and others, and which possesses so vivid a historical symbol as the Civil War, there has not been really outstanding work of fiction written about the Confederate soldier and his times.

There have been good novels, competent novels. Yet in

their best books, most of the South's outstanding writers
have not been primarily concerned with the Confederacy.
Soldiers and statesmen and battles have figured in their
work, but no single Confederate war novel exists which
we can read and then say with satisfaction and admiration,
That was the *Lost Cause; that* was Lee's army.

William Faulkner, perhaps the contemporary South's
finest novelist, illustrates this point. He has written one
novel, *The Unvanquished*, primarily about the war as
such. It is an interesting, well-written narrative. But it is
not comparable in scope or artistry to the same writer's
Absalom, Absalom! Indeed, in *Absalom, Absalom!* there
are a few scattered war sequences which despite their
brevity and secondary role in the novel present far more
of what a Confederate military historian has called "the
inspiration of personalities, humble and exalted, who met
a supreme test and did not falter," than the entire narrative of *The Unvanquished*. Likewise, Ellen Glasgow's
The Battle-Ground is a poor thing compared with *The
Sheltered Life* or others of her best novels. Robert Penn
Warren's only Civil War novel has to do with Yankee
soldiers. George Washington Cable's Civil War romances
are neither so amusing as *The Grandissimes* nor so socially
perceptive as his fine Reconstruction novel, *John March,
Southerner*. Caroline Gordon's *None Shall Look Back* has
not the strength or scope of several of her novels about the
modern South. And so on.

"Where the plowshare of war cut deepest," Chancellor
Kirkland of Vanderbilt wrote several decades after Appomattox, "the first fruits of tradition and of story ought to
grow. The burden of Southern sorrow and suffering ought
to elicit a burst of Southern song." But his prediction has
not come true. The effect of the South's history on its
literature has been profound, but the war itself awaits its
fictional chronicler. There is no *War and Peace* about the
South and its army. There is not even an *A Farewell to
Arms*. All we have is *Gone with the Wind*, a novel com-

parable only in physical size. We have no Prince Andrew; only Ashley Wilkes. Instead of Natasha, we have only Scarlett O'Hara. Above all, we have no Bezukhov, no fictional protagonist for whom, as Andrew Lytle has said of him, "his own ordeal and his country's can become one."

Discussing the fiction of the South, Herbert Marshall McLuhan remarks that "the impersonal social code which permits a formal expression of inward emotion makes it quite pointless for people to interpret one another constantly, as they do in most 'realistic' novels. There is thus in the Southern novel a vacuum where we might expect introspection. . . . The stress falls entirely on slight human gestures, external events which are obliquely slanted to flash light or shade on character." Though Mr. McLuhan's diagnosis fits some Southern novelists better than it does others (surely Quentin Compson, Jack Burden, and Eugene Gant are introspective characters of a most extraordinary kind), it is certainly true of a writer such as Caroline Gordon. Here for example is Rives Allard, the chief male character of *None Shall Look Back*, looking on at a crucial moment in Southern destiny, when General Nathan Bedford Forrest pleads in vain with Braxton Bragg to let him seal the Confederate success at Chickamauga by cutting off the Union army from Chattanooga. Rives listens to them arguing, and then follows as the irate Forrest rides off with an aide:

Riding behind the two dark figures he raised his clenched hand in impotent fury. When he had first heard the conversation between the two generals he had been excited to think that he, a private, was receiving information about important maneuvers. That emotion seemed trivial now. The incidents of the morning seemed trivial, too, and vain. He thought of George Rowan, dead and buried on the field. He had felt pity for the dead man as he laid him in his grave but now he knew envy. If the Confederate cause failed . . . and for the first time he felt fear for its outcome . . . there could be no happiness for him except in the grave.

That is all. The chapter ends there. There is no introspection, no meditation upon what Rives Allard has seen,
and what he thinks of it. There is no opportunity for us
to explore, whether through Rives's eyes or Miss Gordon's,
the impact of a Confederate soldier's first realization that
the war might be lost. All we get is a clenched fist and a
half-dozen terse sentences. Nor would an intense reverie
on Rives's part be appropriate in Miss Gordon's novel. In
her fiction, it would seem forced, didactic. The meaning
of that moment, and of the entire war, must be resolved
entirely in terms of symbol, in what Mr. McLuhan describes as "slight human gestures, external events." There
is no room for self-revelation at all.

What might seem an opposite extreme to Miss Gordon's
almost complete externality is the technique of a novel
such as Stark Young's *So Red the Rose*. Here is Sallie
Bedford of that novel as she thinks about her husband
and the war:

She saw that the suspense of the Vicksburg siege was always at
the back of Malcolm's mind. She herself had been busy with
the children and with the managing of the place. Somebody
had to do that, for children must eat . . . and now, talking
with her husband in the solitude of the bedroom sometime
past midnight, she understood more profoundly what it meant
if Vicksburg fell. Vicksburg was the last Confederate strong-
hold on the Mississippi. Its fall meant that the North would
possess the river from St. Louis to New Orleans; that the
Confederate territory would be cut in half, the eastern and
western; that the Northern men now in this country would
be freed to be used elsewhere in the war against the South.
If the Southern leaders were not mad, Malcolm Bedford said
over and over, they would know that the fall of Vicksburg
would mean defeat and the end of the war. "No use trying
to speak of the ruins that would follow," he said to his wife.
"Oh, no use speaking of it."

"Darlin,' don't put your hands up to your head like that,"
she said, and turned away to find something she could do
about the room.

And there follows a lengthy exposition of the progress of the Federal campaign against Vicksburg.

Where Miss Gordon's characters were mostly silent about the events of the war, Stark Young's people spend a great deal of time discoursing on it and thinking about it. They do so almost exclusively in historical terms, however. There is almost no interpolation of the historical events into the more subjective consciousness of individual characters. Mr. Young's people deal with the events of the Civil War with complete objectivity, as if they were spectators who, from a distant vantage point, watch the coming and going of foreign armies on a battle map. His approach to characterization and dialogue is reminiscent of that of a wartime novelist, August Jane Evans Wilson, in *Macaria*, who has two female characters discuss the progress of events as follows:

"A long, dark vista stretches before the Confederacy. I can not, like many persons, feel sanguine on a speedy termination of the war."

"Yes . . . a vista lined with the bloody graves of her best sons; but beyond glimmers Freedom. . . . Independence. In that light we shall walk without stumbling. Deprived of liberty we cannot exist, and its price was fixed when the foundations of time were laid. I believe the terminations of the war to be contingent only on the method of its prosecution. Agathocles, with thirteen thousand men, established a brilliant precedent, which Scipio followed successfully in the Second Punic War; and when our own able generals are permitted to emulate those illustrious leaders of antiquity, then, and I fear not until then, shall we be able to dictate terms of peace."

Seventy years of literary history and aeons of literary judgment saved Mr. Young's dialogue from that, but actually the notion of what fictional characters ought to say and think is similar in both novels. It was Mr. Young's taste and intelligence, not his method, that made the difference. The characters of both novels speak, and think, with mannered formality and propriety. They react to events in quite conventional, literal fashion, exemplifying the official point of view, so to speak, of the South, and they thus serve as their author's commentary on the events of the war. So while at first glance their loquaciousness may seem to contrast with Caroline Gordon's externalized male protagonist of *None Shall Look Back*, actually they are the other side of the same literary coin. They are designed for defense of the Southern Way. The picture of the war is not predicated on individual terms. The characters serve as spokesmen for the region's attitudes, as the authors conceive of them. Despite Rives Allard's failure to enlarge on his thoughts on the subject of the Confederate cause, he is nevertheless intended by the author to exemplify a social system, a school of character, the region. At bottom the author's intention is patriotic; Rives Allard is the prototype of a society. His death is intended to symbolize the failure of his cause. Primarily he exists to embody the cause. We see Rives from the outside, and we see the Bedfords and the McGehees of *So Red the Rose* from the outside. The limits of their characterization are defined by their role as symbols of what for their author is an essentially noble and praiseworthy society.

It is this attitude toward the Civil War on the part of many Southern novelists, I think, that determines the form that numerous Southern war novels have taken. It is admirably summed up in a statement by Mr. Walter Sullivan in an essay on Southern war fiction. In the Old South, he says,

the honor and the pride were there, not as individual virtues in isolated men, but as part of the public consciousness, the moral basis on which the culture was constructed. This is the reason that the War has been used so often by so many Southern writers. It is the grand image for the novelist, the period when the "ultimate truths," with which Mr. Faulkner says the writer must deal, existed as commonly recognized values within a social framework. It is the only moment in American history when a completely developed national ethic was brought to a dramatic crisis.

Mr. Sullivan thus ascribes to Civil War fiction an essential basis in social commentary. It is written in order to pay homage to a society, and to demonstrate the moral values which characterize that society.

Similarly, Donald Davidson notes of *So Red the Rose* that "the Bedfords and McGehees, in their histories, dwellings, and personal peculiarities, represent different and complementary aspects of Southern life," and he remarks that in the characterization of Hugh McGehee "Southern society has produced an example of the unified personality, in tune with its environment while also commanding it," so that therefore we may assume "that Southern Society at the outbreak of the war was tending toward such an ideal."

In conceiving of the Civil War as the testing ground for the virtues of antebellum society, as well as the occasion of its destruction by materialism, the novelists heretofore mentioned are in effect striving to fulfill a charge given to young Southern writers by Thomas Nelson Page. Addressing an audience of college students in the late 1880's, Page took for his topic the Old South. "What nobler task," he asked, "can [the young Southern writer] set himself than this . . . to preserve from oblivion, or worse, from misrepresentation, a civilization which produced as its natural fruit Washington and Lee!" That was precisely what Page himself sought to do . . . in *Meh Lady*, in *Red Rock*, in *Two Little Confederates*, and in every other story he wrote about the Civil War in Virginia.

For better or for worse, Page has spoken for the vast majority of Southern writers who have taken the war for their subject matter. For while individual writers may differ greatly on how best to preserve and honor the image of antebellum Southern society, behind their novels rests the same attitude toward the war as the climax of a social system which, for all its faults, was far preferable to that which followed it. From *Macaria* to *None Shall Look Back*, the Southern war novel has usually been concerned with portraying the social structure of Southern society, with the individual characters intended primarily for that purpose.

So important has that social ideal been that in many Southern war novels little attention has been paid to the actual war itself. Ellen Glasgow, for example, saw the war almost exclusively as an event in a social history. She has written that "in *The Battle-Ground* I have tried to portray the last stand in Virginia of the aristocratic tradition," and, again, "What I tried to do in *The Battle-Ground* was to write, not literally a novel of war, but a chronicle of two neighboring families, the Amblers and the Lightfoots, who had lived through a disastrous period in history. If I used the Civil War as a background, it was merely as one of several circumstances which had moulded the character of the individual Virginian, as well as the social order in which he made a vital, if obscure, figure." The war as such constitutes only a small portion of the text; Miss Glasgow's emphasis is on prewar life. This existence she portrays in almost idyllic hues. In its time *The Battle-Ground* was shocking in its harsh realism; times have long since changed, and now the book seems merely a conventional love story. Miss Glasgow was impressed by her boldness in daring to make a Southern mountaineer, who did not own slaves or landed estates, one of her Confederate soldiers. Actually, however, Pine Top, her "common man," is treated with much condescension by Miss Glasgow, who sees him entirely through aristocratic eyes. Today one finds little impressive realism in *The Battle-Ground,* and the devastating social irony Miss Glasgow thought she was composing now seems mild and inoffensive. Her prewar society is properly romantic, her plantation belles glamorous, her Confederate soldiers cavaliers all. She seems much closer to Thomas Nelson

Page than to Thomas Wolfe or William Faulkner. Her picture of the life "before de Wah" is in roseate colors, and the war is important only as it destroys the old society.

The Civil War scenes of George Washington Cable are actually much more realistic than Miss Glasgow's, for all their light touch and for all Cable's unwillingness to take life very tragically in his fiction. As seen in *Kincaid's Battery* and *The Cavalier*, Cable's war is a time of adventure and romance. But despite his melodramatic love stories, there is a certain realistic honesty to his characters, a flesh-and-blood quality that makes them into believable people in their own right instead of exemplars of Southern social patterns. Occasionally there is a flash of real emotion and pathos, as in *The Cavalier* when Cable depicts a Confederate troop riding back after an engagement:

And yet a lovely ten miles it was, withal. You would hardly have known this tousled crowd for the same dandy crew that had smiled so flippantly upon me at sunrise, though they smiled as flippantly now with faces powder-blackened, hair and eyelashes matted and gummed with sweat and dust, and shoulders and thighs caked with grime. Yet to Ned Ferry as well as to me . . . I saw it in his eye every time he looked at them . . . these grimy fellows did more to beautify those ten miles than did June woods beflowered and perfumed with magnolia, bay and muscadine, or than slant sunlight in the glade or grove.

The fine understatement and tangible quality of that passage, however, with its touching image of the Confederate soldiers, is one of the few serious looks that Cable casts at the Confederate army-as-army in his novel. The social muse has pervaded his aesthetic, too . . . not in an idealized presentation of prewar society, to be sure, but in his inability to take the Confederates seriously for very long at a time. The creoles are missing in *The Cavalier*, though present in *Kincaid's Battery*, but this is still the world of *Old Creole Days*, in which highborn Southerners play idly at life, in this case the war. Earlier in Cable's life, as Jay B. Hubbell has said, he had "felt a certain scorn for luxury-loving creoles and easygoing Southern planters." *Kincaid's Battery* and *The Cavalier* date from the later period, and Cable is no longer scornful. Nevertheless, he still considers the South's aristocracy essentially frivolous creatures, and this attitude usually prevents him from viewing the war with sufficient seriousness to make possible anything beyond the limits of comedy.

The social approach to the war, of course, is completely dominant in Stark Young's *So Red the Rose*, which takes the war quite seriously. There are no scenes of Confederate armies in full combat, however; the book is a story of the war on the home front and its effect on Southern plantation life. Donald Davidson rightly sees the novel as drawing into focus "the battle between tradition and anti-tradition that has been waged with increasing bitterness since the Renaissance." *So Red the Rose*, he says, "is a large-scale narrative in which events of national importance exert catastrophic force upon the life of the Bedfords, the McGehees, and their kin, friends, visitors, slaves . . . the whole complex of plantation life and, by implication, of Southern life in general." The novel is a story of the downfall of traditional Southern society before the onslaught of anti-traditional Northern materialism, and the war is merely the device by which this social tragedy is effected.

Caroline Gordon's *None Shall Look Back* is more of the same, done by a different kind of artist but one who shares the same essential purpose. "At the end of the book," Walter Sullivan points out, "every single character who has remained constant to the Southern ethic has either been killed or sadly broken. Of all the immediate Allard kin, only Jim, who represents the spirit of commerce, is seen to thrive in the end." A staunch advocate of the well-planned novel, Miss Gordon has carefully constructed her characters and her plot to accomplish that result. The dissolution of antebellum Southern plantation society provides *None Shall Look Back* with its form, and its limitations as well. The whole purpose is to show the downfall of a society before superior force and internal weaknesses, and her characters are not permitted to develop in any direction not contributing to that end. This rules out such themes as the personal impact of war on an individual sensibility, the hammering out of the individual soul on the anvil of conflict, the growth of compassion and understanding amid the cataclysm of suffering . . . the themes, that is to say, that make up the chief concern of *War and Peace.*

Allen Tate's *The Fathers* is another case in point. An extremely well-written, incisive novel, it is concerned with the defects in antebellum Southern society that brought its ruin when war came. It is not really a war novel, nor was it intended to be. Mr. Tate depicts the advent of George Posey, a "morally neutral" person, as Walter Sullivan has it, into the traditional society of northern Virginia. With the coming of the war, the society's ethical code is no longer sufficient to act as a guide for behavior, and the prewar Virginia world collapses. In Lacy Buchan, the narrator of *The Fathers,* Mr. Tate created a well-drawn sensitive character, but he was not interested in taking Lacy beyond the onset of the war. We leave him after the battle of First Manassas, when the fighting in Virginia is only beginning. Lacy does not himself serve as a major protagonist; he is a relatively uncritical narrator, through whose eyes we witness the events of the novel. Nor is there any attempt to show the Army of Northern Virginia itself.

DuBose Heyward's *Peter Ashley* is even less concerned with the embattled Confederacy and its soldiers than Mr. Tate's *The Fathers.* He desires to show the South preparing for secession, not fighting for independence. His theme is the transformation of a doubting Unionist into a loyal Confederate soldier. Southern society becomes so caught up in the fervor for secession that at the onset of hostilities even the most reluctant of secessionists ceases to oppose separation. Peter Ashley is above all a Charlestonian, and once the issue is drawn, his loyalty to his society is such that there could be no question of his not "going with my native state." Mr. Heyward's frame of reference is almost exclusively political; there is none of the curiosity about the underlying social and ethical structure that produced the political attitudes which mark Mr. Tate's *The Fathers* or Miss Gordon's *None Shall Look Back.*

Though William Faulkner's *The Unvanquished* takes place for the most part during the war and involves considerable fighting, it too is not really a novel about Confederate armies. It is a behind-the-lines story, about an elderly Southern lady and two small children, one white, the other Negro, who became embroiled in the fighting when their area is overrun by Yankees. A very exciting narrative indeed, it chronicles the breakdown of peaceful ethics and the increasing hold that violence takes on community life, until after the war young Bayard Sartoris dramatically rejects further recourse to killing. The focus is on young Bayard, and we watch him as he experiences the war as a child and finally grows to manhood during the war's aftermath. But the episodic quality of the story —it is not a continuous narrative but a series of stories, originally published separately—prevents Bayard's personality from being developed in depth. Only in the final, Reconstruction episode are we really allowed to look within Bayard's consciousness.

Thus far, *Absalom, Absalom!* is really Faulkner's best novel that deals importantly with the Civil War. A far more profound book than *The Unvanquished*, there are several brief but memorable war scenes in it. But the Civil War is but one among many developments in the rise and fall of Thomas Sutpen and his grand design over the course of a half century. The war serves mainly to postpone for four years the wrecking of the self-made Mis-

sissippi baron's hopes for a plantation dynasty. Yet even
in passing, Faulkner masterfully illuminates the Confederate cause and the men who made up its armies. The
picture of Charles Bon writing a letter to Judith Sutpen
by campfire as Joseph E. Johnston's depleted army trails
after Sherman's hosts in North Carolina will be remembered long after most of the lieutenants and colonels of
the fictional Confederacy have been forgotten.

The war is also only a phase, albeit the climactic one, of
Andrew Lytle's *The Long Night*. Pleasant McIvor is a
man seeking revenge against a clan of men who murdered
his father. Only after his personal war causes the death of
a Confederate comrade does Pleasant renounce his purpose, and then it is in order to leave the army and flee to
the hills, where he must live with himself and the knowledge of what he has done. Some of Mr. Lytle's battle
moments, notably Shiloh, are skillfully done. In the total
purpose of the novel, however, the war and the soldiers
are but the culminating incident of a story not essentially
concerned with the Confederacy.

There are, of course, many Southern novels primarily
focused on the fighting itself. Perhaps the best known is
Mary Johnston's *The Long Roll* and its sequel *Cease Firing*. Miss Johnston's novels have been justly praised for
their fidelity to detail, their intimate presentation of Confederate operations both from command and rear rank.
But in truth it must be said that this is about all her
novels have to commend them to a modern audience; they
are fictionalized history, with characters designed primarily to furnish individual plot suspense and thus give body
to the historical events of the war. Miss Johnston is desirous of one thing above all: to show how well Southerners fought. As Mr. Lively points out, here is "the true
historical novel . . . the gospel according to Sir Walter
Scott, in which actual historical personages are always close
by on the wings of the fictional stage, and in which recorded fact is used to shape the developing story to the

pattern of actual circumstances." The external, historical events completely dominate the fictional elements, and the subplots and characterization are always subordinate to Miss Johnston's central purpose: the telling of "the Southern side of the war."

Fictional characterization and plot suspense are even less important to Evelyn Scott's *The Wave*, even though, paradoxically enough, most of the events described therein are fictional. *The Wave* is a panoramic view of the war, North and South, as it changes the lives of hundreds of persons. It contains numerous episodes, with the characters of each one different. Miss Scott's intent was to take the external, history-book story of the war and translate it into the lives of numerous Americans, of various social castes and positions. The end result is still the historical war, however, and the fictional characters are not of any structural importance. Miss Scott's intention is primarily expository: to present typical Americans caught up in a social revolution, in order to describe the revolution.

We have noted a few of the better Civil War novels written by Southerners. As we have seen, some are chiefly concerned with the impact of the war on the social pattern. The war is not seen in them as an ordeal in itself so much as the catastrophe that destroyed antebellum life. The characters in these novels tend for the most part to be representative of certain Southern traits and attitudes, and in their reaction to the events of war the society's own characteristics and values are illustrated.

Other novels view the war only as an episode in a larger story, so that the image of the Confederate soldier and armies is not developed in detail. Still other novels, though concerned primarily with the war, seek primarily to give historical events some human relevance, and the fiction is subordinated to the battle reports.

What is lacking in all these novels, from Mary Johnston to William Faulkner, from August Evans Wilson to Caroline Gordon, is the quality that makes a novel such as *War and Peace* more than just an artistic representation of Russian society during the Napoleonic wars, or more than a mere justification of Russian strategy and tactics during the 1812 campaign. And that is, a protagonist, or protagonists, for whom the war becomes the great personal experience of his life, transforming the individual, so that the novelist shows a great character developing in a time of stress . . . a man in whom, as Andrew Lytle has said of Bezukhov, a personal crisis and his country's crisis are so joined and fused that they become one. There is, in short, no Southern counterpart of Pierre Bezukhov, no character who can exemplify and embody the South at war, in whose actions and through whose eyes and mind the Southern cause can be understood. And without such a character, the image of the Confederate soldier and the wartime South is fragmented and incomplete.

To find a Southern character with the qualifications of a Pierre Bezukhov, we must look elsewhere than in novels. We must look to nonfiction. For there is no fictional Confederate soldier one-half so convincing, and so memorable, as some of the real-life Confederates as seen through their diaries, letters, and memoirs. In particular I think of John Hampden Chamberlayne as seen through the letters that comprise the volume entitled *Ham Chamberlayne, Virginian*, from which I quoted earlier. Nor is there a novel about a Southern family undergoing the ordeal of war, deprivation, death, and defeat nearly as vivid or as exciting as the story that unfolds in the letters of a Charleston, South Carolina, family, as published in a volume of their correspondence, *The Mason Smith Family Letters*. Much the same might be said of that moving journal of wartime life in the trans-Mississippi, *Brokenburn: The Diary of Kate Stone*. Such real-life narratives as these drawf the fictional accounts of the embattled South.

Ham Chamberlayne, for example, was a young Richmond lawyer and a promising literary man. He was thus quite articulate, and—in a way that no fictional Southern soldier has yet been allowed to be—extremely reflective and thoughtful. In the paragraph previously quoted from his letters, he speaks of the gigantic stature of General Lee, and the shadow that Lee's personality is likely to cast in future years, which "lengthening through the years behind him will mark a continent with a giant form." It is high Confederate rhetoric, of a sort not unfamiliar to readers of Confederate narratives. But what is quite unfamiliar in Confederate writing is the passage by Ham Chamberlayne that immediately follows:

> Big thing! ! !
> Why is it that I can never let myself loose and write on without feeling somehow ashamed? There must be some taste of the ludicrous in high degree of emotion of whatever kind the instant we cease to sympathize with it.

Here Ham Chamberlayne is being completely frank and analytical. He is looking right at himself, thinking out loud, so to speak. We are *inside* his consciousness, and because his mind is a very keen and observant one, we are given a picture of a Confederate soldier unmatched in its depth and sincerity. There is self-perception, awareness of subjective, personal reaction. The young Confederate expresses his awe and admiration for his commanding general, and then shyly balances his rhetorical outburst with another observation that reveals his awareness and honesty in a way that lets us believe instantly in him and trust him entirely. We know, as we somehow never know for sure in fictional Confederates, that he is not merely orating for the effect his words will have, that he is not striking a pose consciously designed to illustrate the characteristics of a society. The result is a remarkable picture of a man. Observe, too, the very next paragraph of that same letter to his sister:

> How great a teacher is this abominable "civil combustion," as Gordon Tacitus has it. "Heaven and earth come together to

overwhelm me," said the Spider when the turks head swept away his dirty web. India saw hundreds of women and children murdered, Lucknow suffered siege, Cawnpore massacre; in Balaklavan trench and Scutari hospital, fever, frost, wound and want slew each his thousands; Italian crops were trampled by Gaul & Hun amidst smoke and death; but we were very comfortable. 'Twas so far off. Now the turks head sweeps some of us. Whereby we will learn how to read history, while we make it for ourselves.

This is the kind of detachment, of lofty vision, that we get in *War and Peace* when Prince Andrew lies wounded under the blue sky or when the captured Bezukhov observes his captors and his fellow Russian prisoners. It is a philosophical passage of unusual depth and perception. We see a sensitive, devoted soldier—and Ham Chamberlayne was a completely sincere Confederate and a brave and skilled artillerist—looking at himself, his region, the war with a disenthralled wisdom, marveling at what is happening to moral Virginia men. I do not know any other depiction of the Army of Northern Virginia, its soldiers, and the society from which they came that can come close to it for vividness, integrity, and a high-minded realism. Nor in any Confederate war novel I have read is there a moment such as that in *Ham Chamberlayne, Virginian* when, writing to his mother from the trenches of Petersburg in the gloomy December of 1864, he suddenly interpolates this comment: "But the whirligig of time ever brings round its revenge as Goethe says . . . that man of peace whom to quote now is to bring echoes from a dead past already almost inconceivable." Coming in the middle of a long letter full of news of friends, restrained expressions of grief for the dead, an account of a narrow escape in a raid, and a description of a girl of whom he has become enamored, the understatement of the passage adds to its poignancy. Its effect on the reader is similar to the passage about the returning Confederates previously noted in Cable's *The Cavalier,* but it is all the more moving and pathetic because of what goes before and after it.

Likewise the account of the Mason Smith family's wartime years, as seen in the letter from a mother and her children and friends, is a behind-the-lines portrait of almost tragic dimensions. The letters that the mother wrote from Richmond in 1864 at the bedside of her dying son, wounded at Cold Harbor, have a genuine quality of grief and loftiness about them that gives dignity and stature to an episode that in most Civil War fiction would have been stylized and sentimental. As we read the *Mason Smith Family Letters* we get a picture of what the war meant to the South such as no single Confederate novel provides.

Both *Ham Chamberlayne, Virginian* and the *Mason Smith Family Letters,* it must be remembered, are correspondence. They are not private meditations. They are written, to be sure, to close friends and intimates with whom relatively few constraints are expected, but they are nevertheless necessarily external and objective. Particularly with Ham Chamberlayne's letters this makes the accomplishment all the more remarkable. For even as frank and as honest as he was, he must necessarily have marshaled his thoughts to formalize them for others. What might a good novelist do with such a character, in similar circumstances? For like Tolstoy with Prince Andrew, he could show us what his fictional character was thinking and feeling, directly, subjectively. The formal constraint required of Ham Chamberlayne even when writing to one as close to him as his sister would not be involved. And Aristotle's dictum about history and poetry holds good for the Civil War, too; the probable impossible more nearly approches the universal experience. If Ham Chamberlayne could give us what he does, think what would be possible in fiction.

But so far there has been no Ham Chamberlayne in Southern war fiction. There is no character of intelligence and sensibility such as he, who could go through a war, fight well enough to win battlefield promotion and high commendation, maintain his intellectual interests as best possible, compose book reviews from the Petersburg trenches, and all the while see what was happening to him and his fellow soldiers and friends back home as from the outside, with the perception that comes at moments of absolute detachment. He was not a "typical" Confederate, to be sure, but there must have been many others like him. Nor was Prince Andrew a "typical" Russian. It is in the image of men like Ham Chamberlayne that a novelist might fashion a Confederate soldier capable of the insight and intelligence needed to inform a protagonist of a great novel. Anyone of lesser stature and intelligence would not do, just as the story that Tolstoy tells in *War and Peace* would have been impossible without Prince Andrew and Pierre Bezukhov.

It must be emphasized that, among other things, *War and Peace* is a great social novel. It describes a country, a people, and a culture. Its portrait of a Russian society during the Napoleonic wars is masterfully done. But the social portraiture was achieved not by a concentration on social types at the expense of the personal insight and individuality of its chief characters so much as through such insights. If we compare *War and Peace* with Thackeray's *Vanity Fair* we see its superiority at social portrayal. Looking at English society of the early 1800's from outside his characters, Thackeray achieved a superb satire. But Tolstoy showed Russian society through the eyes of a protagonist of complete honesty and perception, and the result is more than just satire. Rather there is a quality of profound understanding and compassion accompanying the critical objectivity.

The moral for Southern writers, I think, is obvious. If they would write of the Civil War with the breadth and penetration of great literature, they must be willing to bring to the Confederacy not merely loyalty but also understanding. They must write not in defense but in analysis. The defense will then take care of itself. Tolstoy did not seek to "defend" Napoleonic Russian life, but that was what he achieved. Similarly Southern writers must be willing to see the Civil War South, its soldiers, its noncombatants, for what they were, as individuals, and not as they represent certain preconceived social virtues. They must be willing to open up their regions and its armies to the insights of a Ham Chamberlayne. They must face up to the creation of a protagonist of intellectual depth and vision, through whose eyes the war and the society that fought it can be seen without the condescension that would be needed to force the story into the limited perceptions of a too literal, too restricted intelligence. Anything less will fall short of complete portrayal.

It is precisely here that *Gone with the Wind* fails. It has the requisite qualities of sweep and range, but where Miss Mitchell did not succeed was in her perception of character. Scarlett O'Hara is an interesting lady, and Rhett Butler a fine figure of a man, but neither sees deeply enough into what is happening to provide the perspectives that make *War and Peace* a great work of literature. Only Ashley Wilkes might have furnished the subtlety and depth to be to the embattled South what Bezukhov was for Napoleonic Russia. But Miss Mitchell never dared to venture into Ashley's mind. From first to last, *Gone with the Wind* is Scarlett's story, and therein the limitations of author and story are contained. To unfold a story of the range of *War and Peace*, Miss Mitchell could only provide the moral perceptions of a Becky Sharp, and even there she was the inferior of Thackeray in social discernment and satirical acuteness. She was never able to make Rhett Butler into an individual; he is a type at all times. Ashley Wilkes, whom she intended to be a type, is her only believable male character of any importance. The scenes of besieged and burning Atlanta, Scarlett's struggle for existence back at Tara after the evacuation, the mobilization of the Klan during the Reconstruction, are exceptionally fine action sequences, but they stand by themselves in an otherwise shallow story. Where underlying the events of *War and Peace* there is a profound philosophical and moral foundation, behind the events of *Gone with the Wind* there is nothing. The surface is often rich and glittering, but deeper than that Miss Mitchell could not go.

In his study of Civil War fiction, Robert A. Lively notes that "stories of Northern life are focused on the abilities and the characters of single heroes or heroines, individuals whose society is depicted as the hostile setting for their lonely struggles and ambitions. With a Southern writer, on the other hand, families or whole communities tend to divide the author's attention and stretch his canvas to cover a social rather than a personal scene." The concentration on individuals possible to Northern novelists brought about a book like Stephen Crane's *The Red Badge of Courage,* in which the individual in battle, his subjective reactions, his fears and hopes, are everything. Crane produced an unforgettable picture of youth at war.

But that is all. The story exists in a vacuum; only the informed student can recognize it for a Civil War battle story, probably set in Chancellorsville. *The Red Badge of Courage* is the ultimate achievement in a completely subjective, completely isolated war narrative, with the protagonist existing without benefit of society, history, reflective thought, abstract idea, or accumulated knowledge.

I doubt that a Southerner could have written a book such as Crane's. Southern novelists, whether writing of the war or of other subjects, have never been able to view man alone, by himself, outside of any society, existing with no sense of past or future, thinking only of the immediate instant. In any Southern war novel the Confederate soldier would have to be a Confederate as well as a soldier, and the war cannot be separated from the region that fought the war. It is not the way of writers like Faulkner, Wolfe, Warren, and others to isolate a man from all that surrounds him and gives perspective to his life and thoughts. For Southern novelists man exists in a society, and they must fit him into it.

What the Southern novelist who would create a great Civil war novel can do is not to forsake his sense of society and history, but add to it the ability of a Crane to see the lonely individual soul as well. He must not let the society obscure the individual; rather he can look at the war and the society through the individual and create an individual capable of realizing the full psychological, social, and above all ethical dimensions of the subject. He can show the Civil War as a tremendous social cataclysm, but one that happened not to waxen images but to men, in a region peopled by individuals who are not stereotyped as social exemplars but released by a social code into their full stature as men. Through the perceptions of such a protagonist, the full tragedy of the Civil War might be captured in fiction.

The Southern
Muse:
Two Poetry Societies

"Down there," wrote H. L. Mencken, "A poet is almost as rare as an oboe-player, a dry-point etcher, or a metaphysician." If by poet he meant anyone who composed verses, he was wrong, of course. There were countless Southern ladies who filled the newspaper poetry columns with their lyrics and kept the little book presses busy turning out slim volumes of perishable sentiment. But if by poet he meant one who wrote good poetry, Mencken did not in the year 1920 exaggerate. Since Sidney Lanier the Southern states of the American Union had produced no poet of more than local and seasonal interest. In Chicago there was a Renaissance in poetry going on, and in England T. S. Eliot had published *Prufrock* and was working on other poems. But in the South all was still.

Or so it appeared; actually the poets were gathering there too. In Nashville a group of young men were meeting once a week at James M. Frank's house to read and discuss each other's work. In Charleston DuBose Heyward and Hervey Allen came together on Wednesday nights at John Bennett's home and talked over their verse.

In New Orleans Julius Weis Friend and John McClure were planning a magazine. In Oxford, Mississippi, the student newspaper, *The Mississippian*, was publishing verse by an undergraduate at the University of Mississippi named William Faulkner. By the very next year the results began to be evident. In 1921 three new magazines and a poetry year book appeared in the South. The magazines were *The Fugitive*, of Nashville; *The Double-Dealer*, of New Orleans; and *The Reviewer*, of Richmond; and the year book was that of the Poetry Society of South Carolina. A year later Harriet Monroe could fill an issue of *Poetry* magazine with a Southern selection.

Of these publications, the two most important, so far as Southern poetry was concerned, were *The Fugitive* and the *Year Book of the Poetry Society of South Carolina*. Though *The Double-Dealer* published the first stories of William Faulkner and Ernest Hemingway, it was an eclectic little magazine with no strong Southern roots which presented poetry from all over, including much from Nashville. *The Reviewer*, edited by Emily Clark and others, contained work of many of the most illustrious writers of the 1920's, but it did not represent the center of a Southern poetry movement.

The Fugitive, on the other hand, constituted a veritable literary revolution; it was the organ of an energetic and highly articulate group of young Southerners with common literary aims and interests. In Charleston the Poetry Society was founded by Heyward and Allen in a conscious attempt to instigate a revival in Southern poetry, and its most active members thought of themselves as kindred workers. During the years that followed, when people mentioned Southern poetry, it was to these two groups that they referred.

To the observer in the early 1920's there seemed to be strong similarities in the poetry groups of Nashville and Charleston. Both were made up of young Southerners who wanted to write, and who thought the creation of poetry a respectable goal in life. The leaders of both groups were in conscious revolt against the accustomed notions of what poetry and poets should be in the South. *"The Fugitive* flees from nothing faster than from the high-caste Brahmins of the Old South," that magazine announced in its first issue.* "We believe that culture in the South is not merely an ante-bellum tradition, but an instant, vital force, awaiting only opportunity and recognition to burst into artistic expression," began DuBose Heyward's foreword to the first number of the *Year Book of the Poetry Society of South Carolina.* Both groups rejected the Daughters of the Confederacy ideal for Southern poetry; both wanted poems to be something more than rhymed platitudes. And both groups began producing poems that were much more than that.

They thought of each other as fellow workers for a common cause. The Poetry Society *Year Books* noted with approval the activities of their Nashville brethren, and several times announced the award of prizes to them in the Society's annual competitions. In 1924, when the finances of *The Fugitive* were at low ebb, one of the Nashville poets suggested the possibility of merging their magazine with that of the Charleston group.

Yet, despite the apparent similarity, these two Southern poetry groups were essentially dissimilar—in their aims, their functions, their attitudes toward the South and toward the writing of poetry. Only by geographical and historical proximity could the Nashville Fugitives and the Poetry Society of South Carolina be considered kindred groups. In the distinction between them lay a commentary on what modern poetry was and would become.

Today almost no one reads the poems of the South Carolinians for reasons of other than historical interest. Those members of the group whose work came to warrant

* Quoted by Louise Cowan in her authoritative study, *The Fugitive Group: A Literary History* (Baton Rouge, La., 1959). Throughout this essay I have drawn liberally on Miss Cowan's fine book.

any attention are remembered today as novelists and play-wrights—Heyward for *Porgy,* Allen for *Anthony Adverse,* Josephine Pinckney for *Three O'Clock Dinner,* Henry Bellamann for *King's Row,* John Bennett for the children's book he wrote many years before the Society came into existence, *Master Skylark.* Of all these only *Porgy* importantly survives today, and as an opera by Heyward and George Gershwin.

The Fugitives of Nashville, on the other hand, included poets now numbered among the most important American writers of our century—John Crowe Ransom, Allen Tate, Donald Davidson, Robert Penn Warren. It would be impossible to compose a history of modern American poetry without paying close attention to their work.

Because these two Southern poetry groups, which seemed for a time to be so similar in origins and aims, made such disparate contributions to American literary life, it is interesting to explore the ways in which they were different. To begin with, their very nature was dissimilar. The Nashville Fugitives were a closely-knit group of young poets existing in order to write poetry and to criticize each other's work. Fugitive meetings were not social occasions. The members came together each week with carboned copies of their latest poems, which they passed around and commented on. The meetings were no-holds-barred affairs, with each Fugitive engaging without protocol in strenuous give-and-take discussion, defending and attacking. By contrast, the meetings of the Poetry Society of South Carolina were formal, public events, in which members of the society gathered on announced occasions to hear poets read from their work and lecturers speak on literary topics. At a typical Fugitive meeting there were seldom as many as a dozen participants present; the Poetry Society of South Carolina consisted of several hundred members of whom only a very few were practicing poets. The Fugitives existed to write poetry, and for no other reason; their magazine was a vehicle for their work. The Poetry Society of South Carolina's announced role was that of fostering poetry within the community. Membership in the Fugitives was on the basis of interest and a shared desire to write; the Poetry Society of South Carolina's membership list, as Frank Durham records in his excellent biography of DuBose Heyward, was first recruited by Heyward and Hervey Allen by running through the Charleston telephone directory for a list of hundreds of names.

The Fugitives at no point in their existence enjoyed much community cultural status, even though the magazine was subsidized for a while by the Nashville Associated Retailers. Allen Tate has written of how, while the Fugitive poets were being "read in the editorial offices of the *Nouvelle Revue Française* in Paris, they were gently ridiculed in the suburbs of Nashville." The very first issue of *The Fugitive* was chided in the editorial columns of the *Nashville Banner* for a "loss of spontaneity" in its poetry, and the second number was written off in that newspaper as being academic, doomed never to be "either popular or influential until it adopts a more intelligent brand of subjects for its poetical effusions and a more humanely understandable manner of dealing with them."

By contrast, during the first decade of the Poetry Society of South Carolina's existence the editors of both local newspapers served as presidents of the organization. The Poetry Society thought of itself as a communitywide cultural organization. Summing up the Society's contributions in 1928, John Bennett saw the group as having "contributed to the enjoyment of thoughtful life in the community, . . . maintained a wholesome relationship between the social life of the city and the intellectual life of the time, . . . assisted to make this community a center of interest to intelligent travel, . . . attracted to it as a winter haven many persons of distinction, [and] helped to place it in the guide-book as a notable center of creative and critical art"—as well as having fostered poetry and in-spired writers.

An amusing and telling insight into the difference be-tween the two groups is given in an incident that occurred in 1923, described by Frank Durham in his biography of Heyward. In that year the Poetry Society's Southern Prize of $100 was awarded to John Crowe Ransom of the Fugi-tives for his poem "Armageddon." The poem described, with considerable irony and detachment, a meeting be-tween Christ and Antichrist. The customary practice was to print the contest-winning poem in the annual *Year Book*. But members of the Poetry Society's leadership grew worried that publication of so atheistic (!) a poem might cause good Charlestonians to resign in droves. So with Heyward's acquiescence the matter was resolved by bringing out Ransom's poem not in the *Year Book* but in a little brochure distributed "to such members of the so-ciety as express a desire to have it"! One can hardly imagine the members of the Nashville group permitting similar considerations to operate in the editing of *The Fugitive*. The Nashville magazine was a private affair of poets; the *Year Book* of the Poetry Society was a com-munity activity; and there the difference lay.

We see the distinction between the two groups clearly from another perspective when we consider the attitude each took to the South. The Poetry Society of South Caro-lina was avowedly and proudly Southern in its interests. Its first *Year Book* contained a rebuttal to Mencken's "The Sahara of the Bozart," in which it extolled the South as a place for literature. (By contrast, Allen Tate is said to have carried a copy of Mencken "around under his arm" during his early Nashville years!) The first book of poems by Heyward and Hervey Allen was entitled *Caro-lina Chansons* and bore the subtitle of "Legends of the Low Country" (1922). In their preface the two young men pointedly proclaimed that their intention was "to call attention to the literary and artistic values inherent in the South, and to the essentially unique and yet nationally interesting qualities of the Carolina Low County, its landscapes and legends. . . ." Repeatedly the Poetry Society's *Year Books* stressed the importance of using Southern material as subject matter for poetry. "Where is the Southern poet who has adequately done the Carolina coast country?" Henry Bellamann asked in 1930. "One waits for a poet saturated with its past to lift it to a large expression, to give it its vast dignity, its grieving and mournful reality, its pathos and its peculiar solace."

The Fugitives, on the other hand, resented the concept of "Southern" poetry. Its members were, especially during the early 1920's, not so much opposed to the use of the South as self-conscious subject matter for poetry, as simply uninterested in it. Even so, when Harriet Monroe devoted a review to praise of Heyward's and Allen's *Carolina Chansons* for its picturesque use of Southern material, several of the Fugitives felt impelled to protest the notion that Southern poets ought to write poetry about the South. Donald Davidson wrote in *The Fugitive* that many Southern poets "will guffaw at the fiction that the Southern writer of today must embalm and serve up as an ancient dish. They will create from what is nearest and deepest in experience—whether it be old or new, North, South, East, or West—and what business is that of Aunt Harriet's?" As Tate wrote to the acting editor of *Poetry*, the Fugitives "fear very much to have the slightest stress laid upon Southern traditions in literature; we who are Southerners know the fatality of such an attitude—the old atavism and sentimentality are always imminent."

It was not until much later in the decade of the 1920's that several of the Fugitives grew consciously interested in the Old South, and their concern culminated in 1930 with the Agrarian symposium entitled *I'll Take My Stand*. Even so there was an essential difference between this book and the writings of the South Carolinians. The Charleston poets strove primarily to *use* Southern themes and Southern subjects in verse. Tate, Ransom, Davidson, and Robert Penn Warren grew concerned with what they considered to be the growing abandonment by the South of its manner of life in favor of the industrial and commercial civilization of general America and particularly the Northeast. "What shall we do who have knowledge / Carried to the heart?" Tate's protagonist asked in his "Ode to the Confederate Dead," identifying the plight of the modern Southerner with that of the intellectual man searching for values in an increasingly fragmented and divided world. For the four Fugitive poets who became Agrarians—and Louise Cowan has noted that these were the Fugitives whose dedication to literature was the most uncompromising and complete—Southernness was an underlying attitude of mind and heart; for Heyward, Allen, and their associates it was considered primarily as subject matter for poetry.

Actually, of course, the South provided both groups of poets with subject matter, but more importantly it made itself felt in the writer's attitude toward language, the way in which he envisioned men and their relationship to nature and to society. It would be difficult to find lines more markedly "Southern" in attitude and spirit, for example, than those that conclude Ransom's poem "Conrad in Twilight," published long before any of the Fugitives began thinking very much about the South's Agrarian heritage:

> Autumn days in our section
> Are the most used-up thing on earth
> (Or in the waters under the earth)
> Having no more color nor predilection
> Than cornstalks too wet for the fire,
> A ribbon rotting on the byre,
> A man's face as weathered as straw
> By the summer's flare and winter's flaw.

One might compare these lines with the closing stanza of DuBose Heyward's poem "Buzzard Island" as published in the *Year Book* of the Poetry Society for 1922:

> Beyond these rice-fields and their crawling streams,
> Young voices ring; white cities lift and spread.
> This is the rookery of still-born dreams;
> Here, old faiths gather after they are dead,
> Out-lived despairs slant by on evil wing,
> And bitter memories that time has starved
> Home down the closing dusk for comforting.

Both poems describe a Southern landscape; Heyward's even has a footnote identifying the spot. Both attempt to establish the melancholy aspect of evening in the open fields. The difference is that Heyward's stanza is filled with abstractions, while Ransom's lines are concerned with the concrete evocation of the actual scene itself. Heyward asks us to imagine dreams, faiths, despairs, and memories as wild birds; Ransom shows us a place and a man's visage. Ransom's diction, too, is strikingly colloquial and Southern; there are no lines in the Heyward poem comparable to "Autumn days in our section / Are the most used-up thing on earth."

This difference in diction points up perhaps the most crucial distinction between Fugitive poetry and that of the South Carolina Poetry Society. The best poetry of the Nashville writers displays a highly literate, intellectual attitude toward language. It is no accident that all the Fugitive poets were university men, closely associated with Vanderbilt University in Nashville. From the very beginning they were concerned with language, with poetry as a rigorously disciplined craft. Even in the 1920's the leading Fugitives were producing incisive essays in criticism, and the successive issues of their magazine showed a steadily increasing concern for the formal problems involved in the writing of poetry. They were highly interested in the work of Eliot, I. A. Richards, Pound, and other leaders of the new poetry. As noted, Fugitive verse was from the beginning criticized for its "loss of spontaneity," its intellectual qualities. Writing to Tate, one of the Fugitives quoted Ransom as having remarked at a meeting that "it is the Fugitive habit never to name the Thing, to paint all the picture except the central figure"; Fugitive poetry must not be sentimental or obvious, it must be intellectual as well as emotional. Around Ransom, Tate, Warren, and a Vanderbilt student of a few years later, Cleanth Brooks, there developed in the 1930's a critical approach to poetry in terms of its formal properties of language and paradox that Ransom was to term the New Criticism. In the Fugitive days the interest in diction that led to this was already shaping up. The schism between those Fugitives who held to the "traditional" attitude toward the language of poetry and those who advocated the more intellectual, "modernist" approach (actually, as Tate said, just as "traditional" as the other) developed early in the history of the group; it centered around the concept, championed in particular by Tate, of the "packed line," crowded with dynamic, highly charged imagery.

No such preoccupation with problems of form and technique is recorded in the writings by members of the Poetry Society of South Carolina; of all the little essays and manifestos published in the *Year Books* during the 1920's, not one exhibited any vital concern for what to the Nashville poets was a compelling problem, that of the language of poetry. The South Carolinians wrote little criticism, whether in the *Year Books* or elsewhere. Only occasionally did they discuss in public the matter of poetic diction, and then the occasion was usually one for defending the "traditional" approach. In the *Year Book* for 1926 Josephine Pinckney praised her group's emphasis on local color as having imposed "a concreteness and a gay hue that have crowded out the poetry of abstract ideas, unsuitable to the finest poetry, and alien to the Southern temperament." The next year the *Year Book* linked Ransom and Davidson (not Tate!) with the poetry of Eliot and Pound, and approved John Gould Fletcher's strictures on the intellectual character of such work.

Curiously enough, when viewed with the perspective of more than thirty years of modern poetry it is the work of the South Carolinians, not the Fugitives, that seems most addicted to the poetry of "abstract ideas." What could be more abstract in diction, for example, and less concrete, than the final stanza of Miss Pinckney's poem "Dead Poet" in the 1924 *Year Book*?

> Till in the presence of his shielded eyes
> Death's dignity had shamed our common sense,
> And we confessed his right to being wise
> Who now held knowledge of our going hence.

Her poem, to be sure, deals with a dead poet, rather than "poetry," but it is not a particular dead poet so much as a representative of what poets should be. Throughout the poem she is dealing with abstract concepts, ideas. What Miss Pinckney was doing in her strictures on the Fugitive use of abstract ideas in poetry was confusing subject matter with texture and diction. Though the South Carolina poets wrote about concrete subjects such as marshes, houses, people, gardens, islands, waterways, milk boats, and the like, the language they used was filled with abstraction. Of all the Charleston poets, it seems to the present writer, only one gave evidence of any compelling interest in the concrete properties of words, and then only spordically. This was Beatrice Ravenel, who in a poem such as "Humming-Bird" was capable of lines such as these:

> The air is of melted glass,
> Solid, filling interstices
> Of leaves that are spaced on the spine
> Like a pattern ground into glass . . . .

Miss Ravenel's work is all but forgotten, but she alone of all the better poets of the Poetry Society could sometimes exhibit in her work an occasional concern with the language medium. A poem such as "The Yemassee Lands" represents the South Carolina poetry at its most verbally interesting level; while for Heyward, Allen, Miss Pinckney, Archibald Rutledge, John Bennett the language of poetry must be simple, obvious, immediately intelligible. Their poetry offered no challenge to its readers, no insistence that, as Allen Tate wrote somewhat later, modern poetry be difficult, since, like sixteenth-century Metaphysical poetry, it "requires of the reader the fullest cooperation of all his intellectual resources, all his knowledge of the world, and all the persistence and alertness that he now thinks only of giving to scientific studies." For Tate, poetry in the twentieth century "must have the direct and *active* participation of a reader who today, because he has been pampered by bad education, expects to lie down and be *passive* when he is reading poetry."

It is not surprising that many of the Charleston poets turned increasingly to popular fiction in the later 1920's and afterward. They were from the start *popular* writers, who directed their work at a wide audience. It should be noted again that not one of the leading South Carolina poets was a university teacher, while all four of the major Fugitive poets turned to the university, where they *taught* literature. If it is true that in our society the university has become almost the only place, except for the very wealthy, that it is possible to make literary activity one's chief professional interest without turning to *popular* literature, then the difference between the Fugitives and the South Carolinians becomes clear. The only one of the Nashville group who ever achieved a large popular audience has been Robert Penn Warren, much later in his career, and his fiction has always enjoyed a strong intellectual, "highbrow" vogue even while being fairly widely read.

Yet intellectual and "highbrow" though the poetry of the Fugitives has often seemed, it too is gradually becoming "popular." A generation of readers has been trained in the techniques of language that Eliot, Pound, and the leading Fugitive poets introduced into literature; for this generation the disciplined diction of "modernist" poetry presents no such barriers as once seemed so formidable to those who criticized The Fugitives' poetry for its "loss of spontaneity." As with all revolutions in sensibility, it was necessary for modern poetry to create an audience. Now that audience exists, and the poems of Ransom, Tate, and the other Fugitives, once considered so difficult, are read with delight and appreciation.

But that audience, let it be remarked, is not the Southern community to which the poems of the South Carolina Poetry Society were addressed. It is much more of an intellectual, specialized audience than that, and whether affiliated with a university or not, it exists—in Southern cities as well as Northern and Western ones—as a kind of cultural elite, set apart, so far as important aesthetic interests go, from the general, television-watching community. The "dissociation of sensibility" against which some of the Fugitives used to warn in their Agrarian and post-Agrarian phases has to that extent taken place; indeed, the early reception of Fugitive poetry shows that it already existed by the year 1920.

Agrarianism as practiced in Nashville was an attempt to head off the trend toward the fragmented modern community, to protest the abandonment of a social ideal in which, as Ransom wrote, man and nature "seem to live on terms of mutual respect and amity, and his loving arts, religions and philosophies come spontaneously into being." The Agrarians depicted the Old South at its best as a symbol of such a society. Presumably in this kind of community the high arts would not be limited to a cultivated intellectual minority group but available to all. Ransom has long since abandoned the idea of Agrarianism as a possible way of stemming the tide, and now sees the best hope for the future in "pockets" of culture which, presumably, would eventually broaden their boundaries and encompass the full citizenry. Tate and Warren too, while not adopting Ransom's notion of cultural "pockets" as such, tend in their later writing to regard any hope for renewed cultural "wholeness" as residing within the individual living *in* the industrialized, fragmented society, and working to restore order from within. Tate has envisioned the problem as a religious, humane mastery of power. Thus Davidson alone of the four leading Fugitives who became Agrarians has continued to write and think in terms of the South as corrective to contemporary cultural fragmentation.*

One might look at the contrasting fates of Fugitive and South Carolina poetry and find in it some corroboration for Ransom's diagnosis of cultural "pockets." For in the 1920's the writers of the Poetry Society of South Carolina attempted to deny the growing schism between the high arts and the average citizen of the community, and the result was only impermanent "popular" poetry. By contrast, despite their later protest as Agrarians, the Fugitives never sought to compose their poetry in language that would make it easily available to the Southern community, and as poetry it has lasted very well.

In 1927, surveying the Poetry Society of South Carolina's first seven years of existence, Josephine Pinckney noted the growing controversy over modernism in verse

---

* See Ransom's essay, "The Idea of a Literary Anthropologist and What He Might Say of the *Paradise Lost* of Milton," *Kenyon Review*, XXI, No. 1 (Winter, 1959), 121–40, for a statement of his most recent position on the matter. Tate's essays in the volume entitled *The Forlorn Demon* (Chicago, 1953) set forth his views. In *Fugitives' Reunion*, Rob Roy Purdy, ed. (Nashville, Tenn., 1959) there is an interesting statement by Warren on *I'll Take My Stand* as it concerned him (pp. 208-10). Davidson has continued to write extensively on the subject of the South and American society. See *Southern Writers in the Modern World* (Athens, Ga., 1958), and several of the essays in *Still Rebels, Still Yankees* (Baton Rouge: Louisiana State University Press, 1957).

and predicted that "perhaps during the next seven years this society will witness and take part in a greater conflict than it has yet experienced." So it did; and in the battle, the forces represented by the Nashville Fugitives and the Poetry Society of South Carolina were arranged on opposite sides so far as the issue of the language of poetry was concerned. Four decades later it was "these new intellectuals" of Nashville, as Miss Pinckney termed them, who had won.

All the King's Meanings

The late Huey Pierce Long, governor of and United States Senator from Louisiana until his assassination in 1935, has been credited with inspiring four novels since his death. Two of them, Robert Penn Warren's *All the King's Men* and Adria Locke Langley's *A Lion Is in the Streets*, have been best sellers. The other two, John Dos Passos' *Number One* and Hamilton Basso's *Sun in Capricorn*, have not done so well financially.

Of the four, *All the King's Men* seems to be the one that has the best chance for an extended literary life; it is one of those rare books that makes its appeal both to the intellectual and to the popular reader. It has even gone into the Modern Library reprint series, the proprietors of which select their titles with a view toward the long haul. In his preface to this edition, Mr. Warren ascribed the book's general popularity to its journalistic relevance, and he declared emphatically that *All the King's Men* is not about Huey Long at all. "Certainly it was the career of Long and the atmosphere of Louisiana that suggested the play that was to become the novel," he admitted. "But suggestion does not mean identity, and even if I had wanted to make Stark a projection of Long, I should not have known how to go about it." Mr. Warren went on to say that Long was but one of the figures implicit in the character of Willie Stark, and that another was "the scholarly and benign figure of William James."

Mr. Warren ought to know what the tie-in is between Huey Long and Willie Stark if anyone knows; and yet an annoying paradox exists here: because the fact is that of the four novels "about" Huey Long, it is most certainly *All the King's Men* that best captures the picture of the historical King Fish, and of Louisiana during the 1920's and 1930's when the King Fish governed. No one, I believe, who can read these four novels with reasonable dispassion will dispute that. To be sure, Hamilton Basso did, in a rather long essay on the Huey Long legend in *Life* magazine some years ago. But Mr. Basso was prominently identified with the anti-Long faction in Louisiana during the 1930's, and I suspect that his complaint that Mr. Warren has eulogized the King Fish is at least partly explained by that quite understandable partisanship. Mr. Basso even objected to *A Lion Is in the Streets* on the same score, and I doubt that any halfway objective reader would conclude after perusing Mrs. Langley's novel that Long came out very well. Whatever the artistic faults of *A Lion Is in the Streets*, no one could reasonably claim that Mrs. Langley advocates or is even willing to tolerate men like Long in politics.

Mr. Basso's objections to the contrary, I think that most readers familiar with the South of the 1930's will testify that *All the King's Men* is a remarkably accurate reporting on those times. And this is not only in the more intangible "atmosphere" of those times, but even in the events themselves; Mr. Warren's account of the death of Willie Stark, and the causes, is factually closer to the death of Long, for instance, than are the death scenes in any of the other three novels.

Yet Mr. Warren denies the identification, which certainly seems paradoxical; and so that I may attempt to resolve the apparent paradox, I am going to propose what may be another paradox. This is, that Mr. Warren was able to write the best book "about" Huey Long *because* he was furthest from his subject. His very lack of motivation and dedication to "tell the truth" about Huey was what made it possible for him to do just that. What is meant by this can best be seen through a look at the four "Long" novels.

Mr. Basso's *Sun in Capricorn* is rather easily disposed of; it is a slight affair, with no great pretension about it. The central character of the book becomes the victim of a slander plot engineered by one of the lieutenants of "Gilgo Slade," the Long-like governor of the state. The attack is directed against the central character because his uncle is Gilgo Slade's opponent in the gubernatorial race, and it takes the form of an accusation that the central character's girl friend has violated the state moral code by going to bed with him. The last several chapters are built around a race to get the young lady on a train for New York before the police come. A political rally for Gilgo Slade causes the highways to be blocked off and almost results in the girl's being caught, but finally she gets away, and Gilgo Slade is shot to death by the central character's brother—though for political reasons only.

The novel is neither high drama nor a commentary on the state of man on Louisiana earth during the 1930's. It is simply a thriller. It attempts no development of the character of Gilgo Slade, who remains a sinister but shadowy background presence. The novel fulfills Mr. Basso's own criterion for novels "about" Huey Long: there is no doubt that Gilgo Slade is a fascist, a menace, a scoundrel, and a despot. But he is not much of a fictional character; and since Mr. Basso was attempting a novel and not a treatise on unconstitutional government, he failed to achieve his purpose entirely. No matter what one might think of its political attitude, *Sun in Capricorn* is indifferent art.

A Lion Is in the Streets, by Adria Locke Langley, is a book of considerable more pretension than *Sun in Capricorn.* It is about four times as lengthy, and of all the "Long" novels it had the best initial sale, topping even Mr. Warren's book and far outdistancing both Mr. Basso and Mr. Dos Passos.

Mr. Basso singled out *A Lion Is in the Streets,* along with *All the King's Men,* for castigation because it presented Huey Long in partially favorable terms. How he arrived at this evaluation is somewhat puzzling. On the political plane, Mrs. Langley's novel is faithfully anti-Long. Using flashbacks to review the career of "Hank Martin," the Lion, Mrs. Langley tells a tale about a poor boy burning with zeal to improve his lot and the lot of those around him. He rises to political power, but immediately he is corrupted by it. In the end he is assassinated by one of the "little people," who thus preserves democracy and popular government. The whole point of the book is that power corrupts and absolute power corrupts absolutely, and Mrs. Langley eschews both subtlety and symbolism to make it crystal clear that that is what she means. Thus Hank Martin's wife Verity, the "conscience" of the novel, is actually glad that her husband has been done to death:

The glow of the western sky pinked the leaves of oak and magnolia, and in the distance was the sheen of the silvered river. A great love of this country swelled and pushed within her. Spreading her arms toward the world she pleaded silently, Don't—oh, don't turn on your bed as a door on its hinges. You're my kinsmen— you're the people! Only the people can blow the trumpet—the incorruptible trumpet of faith and justice, of equality and truth. And blow certain, she pleaded. Oh, trumpet, blow certain!

The only possible objection that Mr. Basso could have to Mrs. Langley's politics would be that she made her

Huey Long-like protagonist honest and public-spirited at first, and then let him grow corrupt as he gained power, instead of making him thoroughly hypocritical and corrupt from the very outset. Surely, even granted Mr. Basso's objectives, that seems rather too partisan and unfair. A much more legitimate complaint is that *A Lion Is in the Streets* is a badly written book. The characterization, from Hank Martin on down, is stereotyped; the transformation in Hank Martin's character is simply not credible in terms of the novel's structure. We are told that Hank is becoming corrupt and is losing his principles; the author leaves it up to us to make it believable. Hank is overdrawn all the way through, too; the dialogue that Mrs. Langley invents for him approaches the burlesque.

". . . There's a clear, bright somethin' liken to a fast-runnin' brook in you, 'n I come to that brook 'n I spill the blackness in me, 'n I feel all clean agin." Taking her hand he placed it over his heart and sealed it there with one of his own. " 'N I get all filled up 'n go as plain as if it was the handwritin' for me on the wall. My beginnin's is allus with you. Liken to that brook y' got in y'. Its beginnin's is in some high place."

Mrs. Langley is laying it on rather thickly there, and it is a fairly representative passage. The whole of *A Lion Is in the Streets* is flashy and gaudy; in particular there is an outlandish scene in which a big city underworld king is eaten alive by thousands of brightly plumaged birds, with Hank Martin and a vixen named Flamingo officiating. It might really have happened, for all I know; but in the novel it is comically bizarre. The vixen Flamingo is not one of Mrs. Langley's happier creations. We first meet her when she attempts to feed Hank Martin's wife Verity to an alligator, and thereafter she keeps turning up time after time, jarring our tolerance of fictional coincidence on each occasion. A chapter on the art of fiction could be written by comparing Mrs. Langley's use of coincidence with that of Mr. Warren in *All the King's Men*. The

apparent coincidences become the structure of Mr. Warren's novel, and are not really chance meetings at all.
They are brought off by the inevitability of fate and the
plot, and are no more haphazard, at the last, than the
events of the Oedipus plays that they so resemble. Whereas Mrs. Langley's coincidences occur because of the apparent luck of the draw, to make the plot work out
smoothly.

A more exciting comparison for *All the King's Men* is
with Mr. Dos Passos' *Number One,* the second volume of
his Spotswood trilogy and since published along with the
other two novels under the general title of *District of
Columbia.* For in John Dos Passos we have a worthy comparison with Mr. Warren, and the measure of Mr. Warren's achievement in *All the King's Men* is more fully
understood when the book is considered alongside of
Number One.

Both novels have several technical and structural similarities. Mr. Warren and Mr. Dos Passos both chose to
focus their attention not on the Huey Long-like politician, but on one of his aides. In neither novel does the
aide serve simply as a chorus; neither *All the King's Men*
nor *Number One* achieves its final meaning in the rise
and fall of the Boss, but rather in the effect of the Boss's
fortunes upon the aide. Indeed, in *Number One* the Boss
doesn't suffer either assassination or disaster; when threat-
ened, he merely offers up the aide, Tyler Spotswood, as a
convenient scapegoat.

The figure of Homer Crawford is less easily likened to
Huey Long than is Mr. Warren's Willie Stark. Crawford
is the backwoods messiah type, with some of the mannerisms and traits we recognize as Long's, but there is not the
strong similarity in setting and historical events that we
find between Willie Stark and Long in *All the King's
Men.* And the main reason for this is that Mr. Dos Passos
never goes in much either for setting or for historical
events. His Chuck Crawford is simply a demagogue, ob-

viously inspired by Long, and Crawford's role in *Number One* is to show by example that strong men endanger democratic government. The lesson is meant for Tyler Spotswood, and us. Much of Homer Crawford's success is due to Tyler Spotswood's help, and when Homer then ditches Tyler as soon as it becomes expedient, we have the final irony to make Tyler—and us—aware of Crawford's ruthlessness and lack of principle. Tyler Spotswood finally learns what it means to play with fire, and is at last able to realize that as an American citizen it is his responsibility to fight power, not abet it. Through Tyler's misfortunes we are taught a lesson in political attitude.

Robert B. Heilman has said of *All the King's Men* that "the author begins with history and politics, but the real subject is the nature of man; Warren is no more discussing American politics than *Hamlet* is discussing Danish politics." This I think is just about as valid for *Number One* as it is for Mr. Warren's novel; the vast difference between the two novels lies in their authors' tremendously disparate conceptions of what is involved in "the nature of man." I think this difference is apparent in almost every phase of the two novels, and we can get at it from the very beginning.

All the King's Men opens as Jack Burden and his companions are driving along a white concrete highway in Louisiana:

MASON CITY.

To get there you follow Highway 58, going northeast out of the city, and it is a good highway and new. Or was new, that day we went up it. You look up the highway and it is straight for miles, coming at you, with the black line down the center coming at and at you, black and slick and tarry-shining against the white of the slab, and the heat dazzles up from the white slab so that only the black line is clear, coming at you with the whine of the tires, and if you don't quit staring at that line and don't take a few deep breaths and slap yourself hard on the back of the neck you'll hypnotize yourself and you'll come to just at the moment when the right front wheel hooks over into the black dirt shoulder off the slab, and you'll try to jerk her back on but you can't because the slab is high like a curb, and maybe you'll try to reach to turn off the ignition just as she starts the dive . . . .

From the highway Mr. Warren proceeds to the countryside, and the rednecks who inhabit it, and then begins on the people who share the car with Jack Burden, showing how they are reacting to the trip. We see Sugar Boy, the bodyguard-driver; then Tom Stark, son of the Boss; then Lucy Stark, Tom's mother and the Boss's wife; until finally the car pulls up to a stop at a drugstore. Before that car has stopped and Willie Stark has gone into action, Mr. Warren has given us perhaps two thousand words to get us into the situation. In the long third sentence of the opening passage he evokes several varieties of sensory experience, and in the sentences that will follow he continues this process. Even the rhythm of the prose contributes to the mood, constructed as it is with a multitude of short coordinate clauses coming one after the other, and joined by the same conjunction each time, with none of the variety possible through subordinate construction. The whole passage is designed to get across the sense of a drive through Louisiana on a hot day, with one image after another looming up and then receding behind the speeding car, to touch off the casual and rather monotonous thought patterns. There is a quietly desperate feeling about the whole thing, and Mr. Warren shows us how this feeling is in various degrees shared by the participants of the scene that is to follow. Were this not done, then the electric effect of Willie Stark orating at the drugstore would not be properly grasped. The riders in the automobile are not content to sit back and enjoy the trip; they are bored and nervous, and they are anxious to get where they are going even though they have no particular desire to go there. What they are waiting for is the emotional stimulus of Willie Stark's personality, which they know will necessarily be available when they arrive and he goes to work.

By contrast, Mr. Dos Passos gets *Number One* under way with a prelude, in italics:

When you try to find the people, always in the end it comes down to somebody,
somebody working, maybe:
a man alone on an old disk harrow yelling his lungs out at a team of mean mules (it's the off mule that gives the trouble, breaking and skittish, pulling black lips back off yellow teeth to nip at the near mule's dusty neck); it's March and the wind sears the chapped knuckles of the hand that clamps the reins; levers rattle; there's a bolt loose under the seat somewhere. . . .

and so on for about six hundred words. The passage is filled with details, and yet paradoxically it is a completely abstract piece of writing. It is not a particular place or individual being described, but merely a farmer—any farmer: "the people." Something of the same effect might have been achieved had Mr. Dos Passos chosen to include a painting as a prelude, instead of the prose passage. Its link with the story that follows is completely on an ideological plane, by intention of the author; and this is true as well of several other such italicized passages inserted between chapters of *Number One.* In them the author shows us "the people" in specimen form—a mechanic, a radio ham, a businessman, and finally a catalogue of occupations, which ends with the injunction that

weak as the weakest, strong as the strongest,
the people are the republic,
the people are you.

To repeat, these passages have no structural or textural relationship to the story proper; when the plot opens, the scene is a hotel room, and we get Tyler Spotswood thinking for perhaps a hundred and fifty words before the dialogue between him and a cohort begins and the plot proceeds to advance. The italicized preludes serve by their very contrast to remind us of what the "real people" are. But the only real people in *Number One* are the politicians. The "real people" remain out of it entirely, so that when Tyler Spotswood is reminded at the finish to keep his faith with them, the credibility of that final resolution depends entirely upon the reader's willingness to accept that evaluation of their democratic worthiness. And while I am quite able to do this, I do not like being told to do so by a novelist. I prefer him to prove his case on its own artistic merits.

Tyler Spotswood "discovers" democracy in the process of political betrayal. Mr. Dos Passos' novel makes its appeal to the reader as political animal, and this is true from the first pages onward. On any other plane save the political, there would be no need and no reason for the reminder about the "real people."

By contrast, the opening pages of *All the King's Men* begin unfolding for us no merely political animals. Right away we sense that it is not simply a political reason that has those people driving toward Mason City with Willie Stark. What we get is several people going somewhere in Louisiana on a hot day; immediately Mr. Warren gets about his appointed task of giving us these people in their time and place *on many planes of activity*. The devotion to the sensory texture of the scene, rather than to the political affiliations alone, begins the job. Whereas Chuck Crawford of *Number One* possesses life and importance only insofar as he symbolizes a political strong man, Willie Stark of *All the King's Men* becomes a compelling person in his own right, and the political implications are only part of the total story. This is apparent from the first chapter on. Nor is the figure of Willie Stark made the ultimate object of the novel's meaning; instead it becomes the cause of the action, upon which all the various planes of the characters' individual existences are focused, thus giving a unity and a progression to the multitudinous scene about it.

Like *Number One,* Mr. Warren's book is a political novel, in that the question of civic attitude toward government is prominently aired. But unlike *Number One,* it is also a social novel, a moral novel, a philosophical novel—a novel of the meaning of history and society and of man in a time and place. At the end of it Jack Burden, the central character, has come through to a knowledge possible only through tragic experience, and I think it possible to say that *All the King's Men* possesses the proportions of tragedy.

Jack Burden's tragic experience lies in the knowledge of time. It is symbolized by the Cass Mastern journal. Jack has not been able to make sense of it. He cannot understand why Cass Mastern acted as he did. Not until the events transpire that cause Anne Stanton to become Willie Stark's mistress, that cause the death of Willie, Adam Stanton, and Judge Irwin, and that paralyze Tom Stark, does Jack comprehend the meaning of the journal. And the meaning is that man must take care to move and act in the convulsion of the world, accepting full responsibility for his acts both as they draw on the past and create the future. Because Jack was a divided man, he could not fathom the motives that impelled Cass Mastern to act as he did. Cass Mastern had accepted the full implications of his responsibility, and Jack could not understand why.

Therefore, Jack Burden put aside the journal of his ancestor, which he had proposed to edit as his doctoral dissertation, and he went to work for Willie Stark. He believed in Willie's good faith, and he found in Willie's realism and strength a kind of absolute. Yet it was not satisfactory, and when Jack did reprehensible things because he thought Willie Stark's ends justified them, he was attempting to live a role as a divided man. He tried to ignore his responsibility to both himself and society, to separate artificially his personal loyalties and beliefs from his work with Willie Stark—and the world tumbled down on him.

It is the split sensibility of Jack Burden that causes the death of Judge Irwin, his true father—and causes Jack to discover that the Judge is his father. The Judge has brought Jack up as a child, and has been his friend, but Jack works for Willie Stark, and he turns up evidence for Willie to show that the Judge once accepted a bribe. It is "true," and so Jack will use it without regard for personal loyalty, old friendships, or the knowledge that the Judge has done full atonement and has lived an upright life ever since. For Jack Burden can compartmentalize his life into separate experiences, or thinks he can, and thus refuse to consider one action as having any bearing on another. But unfortunately for his peace of mind, that was not so. As Jack says, "It was the 'Case of the Upright Judge' and I had every reason to congratulate myself on a job well done. It was a perfect research job, marred in its technical perfection by only one thing: it meant something."

Split sensibility, evasions of responsibility: these things bring death to Willie Stark, cause the death of Jack Burden's father, and make the whole world of *All the King's Men* possible—and impossible.

Yet Mr. Warren's counsel in his novel is not for one moment that of the subjective idealist. He is not declaring that Jack Burden's actions, or Willie Stark's, either, violated some sort of abstract ethical principle and that therefore the disasters came. Indeed, one of Jack Burden's sins is a bit of subjective idealism in his make-up, Mr. Warren intimates: he rationalizes away personal responsibility for his own misdeeds by considering only what he believed was the ideal end of his action. Jack refuses to consider "the truth" in the light of the whole situational context, and of his knowledge of human fallibility; instead he separates his "research" into the Judge's past from all other considerations. And his father dies. Similarly— Adam Stanton's downfall comes about because, as Robert B. Heilman says, he "takes insufficient account of the facts" when they fail to conform to abstract ideals.

The lesson of the Cass Mastern story is that wholeness embodies the acceptance of evil and guilt, and it is wholeness that Jack Burden finally learns to seek. As Norman Girault has written, Burden learns at last "that it is only through an acceptance of the evil in his nature that man can achieve good." He learns, too, that the knowledge given to men is never quite certain. And finally, Jack Burden realizes that men must strive "for that state *least* wasteful of human good."

And here is the answer to those who, like Hamilton Basso, contend that *All the King's Men* is a deification of men like Huey Long. If Mr. Warren has any political message in his novel, it is that in any realm, including the political, a supposedly desirable end does not justify vicious means. Willie Stark dipped too deeply in evil to achieve his purposes. In Girault's words, "the Boss's integration has been doomed to fall because it has rested on an unsound base." We recall Willie's advice to Jack Burden: "Man is conceived in sin and born in corruption and he passeth from the stink of the didie to the stench of the shroud. There is always something."

Jack Burden finds "something." He finds out that Judge Irwin, whom Willie Stark wants to ruin, had in his youth accepted a bribe. When he confronts the Judge with this knowledge, the Judge commits suicide. And then Jack's mother tells him that the Judge was his father.

Judge Irwin could have made Jack Burden withhold the evidence of the long-ago dishonesty had he wished, merely by telling Jack that he was his father. But the Judge didn't. He preferred to go to his death rather than make that claim.

It is Judge Irwin's example, more than anything else, that makes Jack Burden realize that honor has its place, along with the stink and stench, in the life of man. And the full realization of this comes later, after Willie Stark and Adam Stanton are dead, and Jack knows, now, that his mother, whom he had thought selfish and cold and loveless, has been in love herself. She questions him about the night of the interview with Judge Irwin which resulted in the Judge's death:

"—did he—was there—" she was looking away from me.

"You mean," I said, "had he got into a jam and had to shoot himself? Is that it?"

She nodded, then looked straight at me and waited for what was coming.

I looked into her face and studied it. The light wasn't any too kind to it. Light would never be kind to it again. But she held it up and looked straight at me and waited.

"No," I said, "he wasn't in any jam. We had a little argument about politics. Nothing serious. But he talked about his health. About feeling bad. That was it. He said good-bye to me. I can see now he meant it as the real thing. That was all."

She sagged a little. She didn't have to brace up so stiff any longer.

"Is that the truth?" she demanded.

"Yes," I said. "I swear to God it is."

"Oh," she said softly and let her breath escape in an almost soundless sigh.

The interview has taken place at the railroad station, and afterward Jack's mother boards the train and it pulls away for the West:

I looked after the dwindling train that was carrying my mother away until it was nothing but the smudge of smoke to the west, and thought how I had lied to her. Well, I had given that lie to her as a going-away present. Or a kind of wedding present, I thought.

Then I thought how maybe I had lied just to cover up myself.

"Damn it," I said out loud, savagely, "it wasn't for me, it wasn't."

And it was true. It was really true.

If Burden were Warren, or merely speaking for Warren much as a Greek chorus represented the commentary on the action, the import of this scene would only be that Warren wished to inform his readers that Burden had done an act of selflessness rather than selfishness when he lied to his mother. But that is not the impact of that last line at all. What it means to the reader, and must mean in the context of the novel, is that Jack Burden as protagonist has faced up to his responsibility at last, and realizes that he has done so.

Nor is it any vacant, burned-out finish that Jack Burden and Anne Stanton have achieved. The conclusion of *All the King's Men* does not leave them in a Snug Harbor such as the characters of O'Neill's *Strange Interlude* find, in which they will "pick flowers together in the ageing afternoons of spring and summer." Jack Burden disavows any such idea as that when he remarks that "it looks as though Hugh [Miller] will get back into politics, and when he does I'll be along to hold his coat. I've had some valuable experience in that line." Burden has by no means abandoned the world to seek his salvation in the hermitic fashion that the scholarly attorney did. This is not at all the solution of *All the King's Men*. On the contrary, Mr. Warren has Burden declare at the last that he and Anne must "go into the convulsion of the world, out of history into history and the awful responsibility of time."

So that now we may return to the question of whether *All the King's Men* is "about" Huey Pierce Long of Louisiana. I think the answer is, yes, it is "about" Long, but not "about" him in the way that *A Lion Is in the Streets* is "about" him. Rather, it is the very detachment with which Robert Penn Warren as artist could observe the Louisiana scene that makes the novel both an independent work of art which does not require a predetermined set of political attitudes for its effect, and at the same time a breath-taking depiction of the time and place of Long in Louisiana. Where other, lesser novelists were constricted and hampered in their art by their engagement in the political milieu from which they were attempting to draw the raw material for their art, Mr. Warren was able to see Huey Long in relation to the world in which he existed, and through his superior insight and artistry present the total picture—not just the political side of it, not just one man's role in it, but something of the total length and depth.

It is the failure to recognize what Mr. Warren was doing that resulted in all the complaints about *All the King's Men* being a glorification of Huey Long, and Mr. Warren as apologist for fascism, and so forth. The usually astute Mr. Robert G. Davis, for example, interpreted, in the New York *Times*, Mr. Warren's novel as the author's guilty rationalization for having edited the *Southern Review* with Long money,* and he concluded his review with the complaint that "Warren does not ask—the question apparently has no imaginative appeal for him—whether American tradition does not demand that we fight men like Long with all the democratic means at our disposal in order to preserve in this country and in the world free, open, pluralistic societies in which individual rights are protected by law and in which ultimate control is vested below in the people and not above in Willie Stark." Had Mr. Warren set himself to work along the lines of the problem as seen by Mr. Davis, *All the King's Men* would have been not a novel, but a political tract. Mr. Davis asks, purely and simply, that when Mr. Warren writes a novel involving a political figure, he drop everything else and dedicate all his efforts to attacking the political figure. Unless *All the King's Men* presents a political sermon designed to produce results on election day, it has failed; that in effect is what Mr. Davis's approach would maintain.

Even on ideological grounds, Mr. Davis's contention,

* Mr. Warren felt so guilty about his editorship of the *Southern Review* that he and Cleanth Brooks have since edited a volume of short stories from that magazine.

and the way he phrased it, are invalid. American tradition does not "demand" that a novelist fight anybody or anything; rather it is the land of novelists like Ilya Ehrenburg that makes that particular demand. Mr. Davis would surely not maintain that because Hamilton Basso's *Sun in Capricorn* fulfilled the ideological requirement he set up, it is a better work of art than *All the King's Men*; and yet that is what his theory would imply.

There is a pholosophical moral implicit in all this, but it is in the literary moral that I am interested. Mr. Warren achieved both the tragedy and the social commentary, and transcended the regional and political limitations, by heeding that counsel of wholeness—sound and shape, smell and feel, ethics and politics, sociology and dramatics—in the telling of his tale. If one may borrow Mr. Warren's own summation of William Faulkner's achievements and apply it to *All the King's Men*, "he has taken our [Southern] world, with its powerful sense of history, its tangled loyalties, its pains and tensions of transition, its pieties and violence, and elevated it to the level of a great moral drama on the tragic scale." In the last analysis it was the story that mattered to Robert Penn Warren: all the magnificant social, political, and philosophical portraiture was incidental to his artistic purposes. Mr. Warren's story gave the counsel of wholeness, but it was because *All the King's Men* itself embodied the wholeness that it succeeded where other novels fell short.

Flannery O'Connor
and the Bible Belt

If I join a community where a tongue other than my own is the medium of intercourse, I simply must learn the language of the place to the best of my ability.

GUSTAVE WEIGEL, S.J.

There is much to be said for the theory that what makes a writer is a built-in conflict of vision, together with the desire to resolve it. Let him be born into one set of values, and let him be instructed in another and opposed set of values in the life he confronts each day, and the result will be either schizophrenia or else a new perception whereby his experience will be thrown into the sharp illumination that comes of seeing things in stereoscopic distance.

This thesis has frequently been applied to the Southern writers of our time, who were moderns reared in a traditional kind of society that during their youth was in the process of breaking up. They saw the new through the eyes of the old, and vice versa, and their stories and poems gave form and order to the human image in changing times.

Whatever else may be said of this notion, it does seem to be borne out in the instance of Flannery O'Connor. For this young woman of genius, who in an all-too-brief literary career established herself as one of the finest writers of her time, was surely exposed to several of the most revealing and dramatic contrasts of viewpoint and value possible to her time and place. She was a Southerner, born in a city but reared in the rural South, from which she journeyed forth for long stays in the Midwest and Northeast. As if that were not enough, however, she was also by birth and by faith a Roman Catholic, which in the rural, Protestant South is an alien sect. Beyond the Southern cities the religious sentiment is evangelical all the way—some low-Church Episcopalians and some Presbyterians, who generally constitute the cultural and financial elite, but especially Methodists and Baptists, the last-named ranging from the solid middle-class respectability of the large churches to all manner of Hard-Shell, Fundamentalist, Revivalist, Pentecostal, and other primitive offshoots of evangelical Protestantism. In the little wooden churches of the backcountry South and in the unpainted tabernacles of the Southern urban slums, the Pope of Rome is a minion of Satan, and a Catholic priest a mysterious and dangerous man.

The ways of the fundamentalist South, especially in its more primitive levels of religious experience, are not those of the Roman Catholic Church. Primitive Protestantism in the South is puritanical, much more so than the Presbyterian church itself is nowadays; the struggle against Satan is individual, continuous, and desperate, and salvation is a personal problem, which comes not through ritual and sacrament, but in the gripping fervor of immediate confrontation with eternity. The rural South is not so much Christ-centered as Christ-haunted. PREPARE TO MEET THY GOD, the signs along the highway counsel the motorist, and WHERE WILL YOU SPEND ETERNITY? "The people believe strongly in an anthropomorphic Satan," an Episcopal bishop has written. "One gets the impression that they believe more in the reality of Satan than in the reality of God."

Miss O'Connor, one critic remarks, "has imposed her

Catholic theology on the local image, and the marriage of Rome and South Georgia is odd to say the least." It is that, and it is also highly revealing. The Catholic novelist in the South, as Miss O'Connor herself tells us, "is forced to follow the spirit into strange places and to recognize it in many forms not totally congenial to him. But the fact that the South is the Bible Belt increases rather than decreases his sympathy for what he sees. His interest will in all likelihood go immediately to those aspects of Southern life where the religious feeling is most intense and where its outward forms are farthest from the Catholic." Both her novels and most of her short stories are directly concerned with religion. In the commentary that follows, I want to discuss this strange union of evangelical Protestantism and Roman Catholicism as it manifests itself in Flannery O'Connor's novels. I shall neglect the short stories both because I have on several previous occasions written about them, and because it is especially in the two novels that she conducts an exploration of backwoods Southern primitive Protestantism. It is only fair, however, for me to point out that I think Miss O'Connor was primarily a short story writer, one of the very best of her century, rather than a novelist. I mean this in much the same sense that Malcolm Cowley means it when he declares that William Faulkner was likewise a short story writer rather than a novelist: "his stories do not occur to him in book-length units of 70,000 to 150,000 words" and "almost all of his novels have some weakness in structure." But if in these novels we sense some structural flaws, if especially some of the secondary characters seem insufficiently developed to fit the longer form of the novel, nevertheless, the two novels that Flannery O'Connor has left us are remarkable works of fiction and not likely to be forgotten any time soon.

The behavior of Southern rural Christians of the primitivistic persuasion has of course long been a stock in trade of the Southern writer. For a novelist such as Erskine Cald-

well, who exploited the Georgia countryside in books that
have achieved record-breaking sales, the Southern preacher is a humorous figure, and a backwoods revival an exploration into sexual comedy. Miss O'Connor's depiction
of Southern rural Protestantism, however, never stops at
the comic surfaces. Underlying the often pathetically
crude and naïve exteriors of Southern fundamentalism she
recognizes the presence of an intense spiritual life, which
however grotesque its forms is authentic and very much
worthy of respect.

Like Caldwell, and also another Georgia writer, Carson
McCullers, Miss O'Connor has throughout her career
showed an affinity for the strange, the grotesque, the deformed. In abnormality she has perceived the exaggeration, the outsized proportions whereby a commentary is
made on the normal and conventional. Her characters are
for the most part not "normal" or "sane"; neither, for that
matter, are William Faulkner's, and for the very good
reason that in the exaggeration, the grotesque proportions
of their people, a telling critique is thereby possible of
the "normal and sane." Yet there is a considerable difference between the grotesque as handled by Miss O'Connor
and Faulkner on the one hand, and by Caldwell and Miss
McCullers on the other. Caldwell dotes on the physically
grotesque; he gives us a Georgia freak show. Sister Bessie
of *Tobacco Road*, with her nose so turned up that she is
imperiled when it rains, serves the purposes of low comedy
and little more. Miss McCullers likewise goes in for the
physically deformed and maimed in her work; for her,
however, grotesqueness is designed not to provoke amusement but to convey the sense of loneliness and isolation
that comes with abnormality. Pain is the motif of her
fiction; her characters move about in a haze of *Angst* and
misery. In her best work, the strange novella entitled *The
Ballad of the Sad Café*, a tall, sexless, masculine woman
and a hunchback dwarf convey through their very odd-
ness and deformity the loneliness, the pain of thwarted

and unfulfilled love that is Miss McCullers' picture of our experience.

Like Faulkner, however, Miss O'Connor's version of Southern Gothic emphasizes not so much physical as mental and spiritual deformity. She has, it is true, some physical grotesques among her characters, but even with these she makes no attempt to capitalize on the reader's curiosity about the morbid and unnatural. Rather, her true grotesques are those who are spiritually maimed and twisted, who cannot view the everyday life around them with the equanimity and complacency that ordinary, "well-adjusted" people manage. Asked once why it was that Southern writers tend to dwell so often on freaks and grotesques, she replied that the South was the only American region where a freak could still be recognized when seen. The roster of Miss O'Connor's freaks is brilliant and frightening. From Hazel Motes in *Wise Blood,* who preached the Church Without Christ and who ultimately blinded himself to shut out the vision of sin, to Francis Marion Tarwater of *The Violent Bear It Away*, struggling vainly to escape from the terrible burden of baptism and prophecy laid upon him by his fanatical old great-uncle, Miss O'Connor's people are afflicted with a savage inability and unwillingness to accept the normal conditions of everyday life and are driven into violent deeds of protest and retribution.

It is in this light that Miss O'Connor views Southern fundamentalist Protestantism. The fanaticism and torment that characterize the emotion-torn, apocalyptic primitive Protestantism of the backcountry South, with its revivals, evangelists, testimonies, visions, prophets, and hallucinations, become in her fiction the unlettered, naïve search for spiritual existence in a world grown complacent and materialistic. Her sympathies lie not with the prosperous, well-adjusted, comfortable middle-class churches, but with those who stand outside the respectable community, refuse to accept its accommodations and compromises, and preach the fire and the plague. They alone, she implies, are willing to confront evil; they alone believe in redemption; only for them is the Devil a real and tangible presence. "I see a damned soul before my eyes!" the child evangelist declares. "I see a dead man Jesus hasn't raised. His head is in the window but his ear is deaf to the Holy Word!" And she points her finger at the educated, rationalistic schoolteacher who has been watching her and telling himself how wretched is the kind of religion that would exploit a little child in this manner. The schoolteacher drops to the ground in terror and dismay and fumbles for the switch that will turn off his artificial hearing apparatus and restore him to the blessed condition of silence. The easy tolerance, the complacent rationalism of the schoolteacher are for the moment quite helpless against the onslaught of religious fervor of the child.

I do not want to imply that Miss O'Connor, though a Roman Catholic, feels that the wild, hallucinatory emotionalism, the primitive and unlettered evangelicism of the Bible Belt is the true apprehension of God. It is rather that as a Roman Catholic in the modern South she considers fundamentalist Protestantism a manifestation, however grotesque and distorted, of a belief in the supremacy of the spirit over the materialistic ethics and bland rationalism of modern "respectable" theology, and an assertion of true religious identity in a society rapidly losing its sense of dependence on God. That Miss O'Connor's attitude is not an uncommon one for a Roman Catholic may be illustrated by a quotation from a recent work by a Catholic theologian, the late Father Gustave Weigel, S.J.:

Even though the fundamentalist is traditionally opposed to the Scarlet Woman of Rome and her ways, yet he clings to certain positions which are as fundamental for him as for Catholics. He believes in the divinity of Jesus of Nazareth, the Virgin birth, the objectively atoning death of Jesus and

His physical resurrection. The liberals vacillate ambiguously in their adherence to these dogmas. In consequence, the Catholic feels sympathy for the Fundamentalist in spite of the latent antipathy felt by that group toward Catholicism. The liberals are far more friendly and cordial but the Catholic is appalled by their radical reconstructions of Christianity.

Yet despite this agreement on certain theological essentials, the way of the primitive fundamentalists is not the way of the Catholic, and it is a mistake, I feel, to read Miss O'Connor's novels without remembering this—for reasons that I shall discuss later in this essay. In the primitive fervor, and also the error, of fundamentalism she perceives the waste and the horror of that spiritual integrity. We must keep in mind that in their blind and confused zeal, the protagonists of both her novels commit crimes. Their warped but powerful consciousness of human sinfulness gives them purpose and integrity in a materialistic society, but it also leads them to do grievous harm. In part, of course, this is the fault of society: in a world in which God is ignored, those who cannot acquiesce to godlessness are forced to travel along strange paths, and in their ignorance to do evil deeds. A society which fails to instruct its members in righteousness drives them to hate. Such is Miss O'Connor's South, as depicted in her novels.

Hazel Motes, the protagonist of Miss O'Connor's first novel, *Wise Blood*, is just such a person. Imbued as a child with a fanatical sense of guilt for his sinfulness, he comes out of the army to find the hamlet where he had lived deserted. Naïve, ignorant, confused, he sets out for the city of Taulkinham, obsessed with the need to deny the existence of Christ. He buys an old Essex automobile to serve as his temple, and he moves about the city preaching the Church Without Christ. He sins, blasphemes, degrades himself. Jesus did not die for you, he tells the townsfolk; there is no sin, no redemption of sin, no salvation. But the citizens of Taulkinham respond only with utter unconcern. He visits a prostitute, not out of desire but out of the compulsion to sin by fornication. "What I mean to have you know is: I'm no goddam preacher," he tells her. "That's okay, son," the woman responds. "Momma don't mind if you ain't a preacher." He finds a blind revivalist and his daughter; the man has supposedly blinded himself to justify his belief in Christ's redemption. But the blind man proves to be not blind at all, and his daughter is a hard-bitten slut. A clever evangelist sees Haze preaching his Church Without Christ, breaks into the gathering, calls Haze the Prophet, and seeks to ally himself with him in order to extract money from the crowd. Haze refuses, whereupon the evangelist finds another man to serve as prophet for such a church. Haze runs over this false prophet with his automobile; as the man lies dying in the road, Haze denounces him for pretending not to believe in Christ when actually he does. Haze hears the false prophet's dying words, "Jesus hep me," and from then on he is without rest. Ultimately he blinds himself, sleeps with barbed wire wrapped around his chest. His landlady asks him why he does these things. "It's natural," he tells her. "Well, it's not normal," she declares. "It's like one of them gory stories, it's something that people have quit doing—like boiling in oil or being a saint or walling up cats. . . . There's no reason for it. People have quit doing it." To which Haze replies, "They ain't quit doing it as long as I'm doing it." Eventually he is found dying in the winter streets of the city, and the police, after hitting him over the head to keep him quiet, bring him back to the landlady, but he dies on the way.

There is also Enoch Emery, a loveless, unattractive youth who like Hazel Motes has come to the city from the backwoods, and who wants friendship. Haze will have none of him, but Enoch continues to tag along; Haze is his Prophet, and Enoch is overcome with the sense of having a mission, which consists finally of stealing the mummified body of a man from a museum and giving it to Motes. After that he steals a gorilla suit and we last see him as, wearing the suit, he frightens away a man and a woman who are out in the country watching the view.

The theological ramifications of *Wise Blood* have been widely noted. As Jonathan Baumbach points out in an excellent essay on the novel, both Hazel Motes and Enoch Emory come to the city of Taulkinham in search of help. Hazel blasphemes, sins, preaches the denial of Christ's redemptive power, seeking to provoke a response, to be struck down for his sinfulness, to come up against something greater than himself if only in negation. But the city merely ignores him. The citizenry of Taulkinham—modernity, civilized urban society—is so "well adjusted" to its comfortable complacency that a prophet stalking its streets to preach that there is no God is considered a freak, a harmless religious fanatic who is simply unnoticed. For the city dwellers the denial of Christ and His redemption is not important; they are not troubled by such matters. If at the end Haze, a blasphemer and a murderer, is saved, it is because alone of them all he has the integrity to know guilt, to feel that he is "not clean."

As for Enoch Emery, he comes to Taulkinham looking for love, for human affection, but nobody wishes remotely to know him or love him. When he steals the mummy from the museum and presents it to Haze, he is giving him the ultimate proof of what men are if there is no God and no redemption—shrunken figures of dust. And it is only when Enoch steals the gorilla costume and comes out to frighten the spooning couple that he is able to evoke any sort of human response to his existence.

Miss O'Connor's intentions in *Wise Blood* are stated squarely in the little prefatory note she wrote for the second edition of the novel when it was published in 1962:

That belief in Christ is to some a matter of life and death has been a stumbling block for readers who would prefer to think it a matter of no great consequence. For them Hazel Motes' integrity lies in his trying with such vigor to get rid of the ragged figure who moves from tree to tree in the back of his mind. For the author Hazel's integrity lies in his not being able to.

Haze is indeed a freak, a grotesque figure, but is he not thereby "natural"? Rather, as Haze replies to his landlady when she tells him that civilized people no longer mortify their flesh to punish themselves for sinfulness, it is the complacent, secular society of the city that is "unnatural" if man is the religious creature that both Catholic and Protestant theologies believe he is. And it is just such an "unnatural" society that forces the Hazel Moteses and Enoch Emerys to find meaning only in violence. The violence of Hazel Motes is the warped and inarticulate protest of one for whom salvation is of crucial importance, against a society for whom God is dead. That Enoch Emory becomes in effect a wild animal is likewise to be expected in a society which will not offer him elementary love and compassion.

The same theme is present in Miss O'Connor's other and much later novel, *The Violent Bear It Away*, but the protagonist of that novel is both less bizarre and more sympathetic a character than Hazel Motes. Discussing the task of the Catholic novelist as she sees it, Miss O'Connor has written that "when I write a novel in which the central action is baptism, I know that for the larger percentage of my readers, baptism is a meaningless rite; therefore I have to imbue this action with an awe and terror which will suggest its awful mystery. I have to distort the look of the thing in order to represent as I see them both the mystery and the fact." The reference is obviously to *The Violent Bear It Away*. In this novel a youth, Francis Marion Tarwater, has been charged by the fanatical old great-uncle who has reared him with the task of baptizing an idiot cousin and then taking on his burden of prophecy. With his great-uncle the youth had lived on a farm remote from the city. On one occasion an uncle, a school-teacher named Rayber, had come out from town with a welfare worker to try to take the youth from the old man, but the great-uncle had driven Rayber away, wounding him twice with a rifle in the process. When the old man dies, young Tarwater, instead of burying the great-uncle as he had been enjoined to do, decides to burn down the farmhouse with the old man's body inside, and afterwards heads for town, where he joins Rayber and the school-teacher's mentally defective son Bishop. There ensues a contest in which Rayber, who though he once exposed himself to the great-uncle's fanaticism has secured an education and become an expert in educational psychology, seeks to rid the youth of his compulsive attachment to the old man's fanaticism.

Tarwater does not want to baptize the idiot child Bishop, as his great-uncle had commanded, but so strong is the hold that the old man's memory has on him that the injunction is constantly in his thoughts. To save Tarwater from fanaticism, Rayber takes him on tours of the city, trying to win his confidence and to acquaint him with what the schoolteacher considers the attractions of the modern world. Tarwater, however, is not impressed. One night the youth steals out of Rayber's house and, with the barefooted and half-dressed schoolteacher in pursuit, goes to a revivalist meeting in which a little girl delivers a highly rhapsodic address on God's love. The schoolteach-er, who is watching through the window, is at first disgusted with the way in which the girl's innocence is being exploited; then he begins to feel a growing emotional yearning for her, and imagines, when the child keeps glancing toward his face in the window, that some "miraculous communication" is taking place between them—only to have the girl point to him and denounce him for his unbelief. When Tarwater comes out of the meeting and joins the disconcerted Rayber, the youth seems finally on the verge of breaking through his distrust and suspicion and wanting to talk with his uncle. But the distraught, confused Rayber refuses to respond. The next day the opportunity is gone, and the youth is as hostile and closemouthed as ever.

By now Tarwater has come to feel that the only way he can throw off the yoke of his dead great-uncle's will is to drown the little boy Bishop, in whose features he sees the old man's. Rayber takes Tarwater and Bishop to a lake resort not too far from the site of the great-uncle's one-time farm, and after a time he lets Tarwater take Bishop out in a rowboat. When much later he hears a cry across the water, he knows what has happened.

Tarwater has drowned Bishop, but in so doing the youth realizes that he has not repudiated the old great-uncle's command but instead has obeyed it, since the drowning also constituted the act of baptism. Despairing and desperate, the youth makes his way back to the site of the farm; on the way he is picked up by a sex pervert, drugged, and attacked. Finally he gets to the farmhouse; he had left it after setting it afire, thinking that in so doing he had cremated the dead great-uncle's body. Now he finds that the old man's body had not been in the house at the time; a Negro neighbor had removed it, dug a grave, and buried it. The will of the old man has been fulfilled; he has been buried and Bishop has been baptized. So Tarwater, after setting fire to the woods, sets out for the city, confirmed now in the mission of prophecy bequeathed him by the dead old man, going forth to warn the children of God of the terrible speed of mercy.

When *The Violent Bear It Away* appeared, it was savagely attacked by several Roman Catholic critics, including the novelist Robert O. Bowen, who wrote that "beyond not being Catholic, the novel is distinctly anti-Catholic in being a thorough, point-by-point dramatic argument against Free Will, Redemption, and Divine Justice, among other aspects of Catholic thought." To such onslaughts other Catholic critics replied, notably Rainulf A. Stelzmann in an excellent essay in *Xavier University Studies.* (I am told that Stelzmann's interpretation of the novel received the enthusiastic approval of Miss O'Connor herself.) Stelzmann sees the struggle within Tarwater as being one between an unwillingness to accept the mission of prophecy to the ungodly, and loyalty to the spiritual conviction that the old man had sought to instill within him. The voice which throughout the novel argues with the youth, telling him that the old man's ideas were false and that he need not heed them, Stelzmann asserts was that of the Devil. The schoolteacher Rayber is seen as the weak-willed, spiritually impotent spokesman for modernity, seeking, in the name of rationality, to nullify the boy's spiritual consciousness. When the boy realizes that in drowning Bishop he has fulfilled the mission of baptism, and learns that he has not cremated the old great-uncle after all, his religious integrity reasserts itself, he defies the counsel of the Devil, and takes up the prophetic burden as his great-uncle had hoped.

Now if this is really the full meaning of *The Violent Bear It Away,* then it would seem to me that there is much to be said for the kind of criticism levelled against the novel by Bowen and others. I am no theologian, of course, and being neither Catholic nor Protestant may be said to be peculiarly ill-equipped to settle the question of the heresy, if any, in Miss O'Connor's novel; indeed, I note that Stelzmann himself has described a reading which I gave to Miss O'Connor's story "The Displaced Person" as being nihilistic and deterministic, which if true is certainly not what I had in mind. But if the struggle within young Tarwater is between whether or not to take up the prophetic mission bequeathed him by the old man, and if in attempting to negate the mission he only succeeds in trapping himself into acquiescence, then it seems to me quite arguable that it is not his own free will that makes him do so. His struggle would appear to be to avoid his destined task, much as the characters in Greek tragedy do, and the moral would seem to be that it cannot be done. Miss O'Connor speaks of "man so free that with his last breath he can say No." Yet it seems to me that the one thing that young Tarwater cannot do, if we accept the Stelzmann hypothesis, is to say No.

But is the struggle in young Tarwater precisely that proposed by Stelzmann? I think not. Rather, it seems to me that such a reading of *The Violent Bear It Away* overlooks several very important episodes, in particular the business of the revival that Tarwater attends and Rayber observes through the window. We recall that the little girl evangelist preached a sermon about God's love:

"Do you know what Jesus is?" she cried. "Jesus is the word of God and Jesus is love. The Word of God is love and do you know what love is, you people? If you don't know what love is you won't know Jesus when He comes. You won't be ready. I want to tell you people the story of the world, how it never known when love come, so when love comes again, you'll be ready."

When Tarwater comes out of the revival meeting afterward, he is for the first time in the novel genuinely open to help, desirous of his uncle Rayber's companionship and guidance. But Rayber is at that moment completely unable and unwilling to respond to the youth's overture, so shaken up and resentful is he after the episode with the little girl at the window. Why is Rayber so distraught? Not simply from embarrassment; rather, it is because Rayber had done the one thing he feared most of all doing. Listening to the little girl, he had forgotten his sophisticated rationalism and had given way to an emotional response: "Come away with me! he silently implored, and I'll teach you the truth, I'll save you, beautiful child!"

Rayber has long since learned to fear and distrust emotion. His own early exposure to the old man had so devastated him that in self-defense he has erected a wall of scientific detachment and objective rationality about himself. His reliance upon behavioral psychology is a device on his part to avoid emotional involvement in human relationships. Emotionalism, passion, violence; these are what Rayber most abhors, because he recognizes that within himself lies the latent capacity for all three. The seed of the old man's fanaticism "fell in us both alike," he tells Tarwater. "The difference is that I know it's in me and I keep it under control. I weed it out but you're too blind to know it's in you. You don't even know what makes you do the things you do." For the schoolteacher, emotion is something to be avoided, because it negates reason. There is an important passage in which Rayber thinks about his idiot son Bishop:

For the most part Rayber lived with him without being painfully aware of his presence but the moments would still come when, rushing from some inexplicable part of himself, he would experience a love for the child so outrageous that he would be left shocked and depressed for days, and trembling for his sanity. It was only a touch of the curse that lay in his blood.

.　　　.　　　.　　　.　　　.　　　.　　　.　　　.

He was not afraid of love in general. He knew the value of it and how it could be used. He had seen it transform in cases where nothing else had worked, such as with his poor sister. None of this had the least bearing on his situation. The love that would overcome him was of a different order entirely. It was not the kind that could be used for the child's improvement or his own. It was love without reason, love for something futureless, love that appeared to exist only to be itself, imperious and all demanding, the kind that would cause him to make a fool of himself in an instant. And it only began with Bishop. It began with Bishop and then like an avalanche covered everything his reason hated. He always felt with it a rush of longing to have the old man's eyes—insane, fish-colored, violent in their impossible vision of a world transfigured—turned on him once again. The longing was like an undertow in his blood dragging him backwards to what he knew to be madness.

It is the schoolteacher's fear of the emotion of love that prevents him from being able to help Tarwater. He will not give in to the irrational, the emotional; he is afraid of it. Yet it was precisely the little girl's message of a God of love that had almost broken the spell of the great-uncle's fanaticism over Tarwater; had Rayber been able to realize this, had he sought then to replace the mission of fanatical hate that the old man had instilled in Tarwater—"The Lord is preparing a prophet with fire in his hand and eye and the prophet is moving toward the city with his warning"—with the joy of God's love and mercy, he could have saved the youth from his fate. But to Rayber overmastering love was as dangerous as hatred, and he chose instead to try to combat the boy's fixation by sterile logic and specious reason, only to bring about the death of his own son and the final violation of Tarwater. The rape of the youth by the sex pervert was only the last mockery of Tarwater's failure to find in human society the love and affection he needed if he was to be saved. The remedy for the fanatical terror and wrath that had gripped the youth, then, was not the denial of emotion in favor of cold behavioristic rationalism, but the equally emotional fanaticism of love. Without love the needs of the soul are capable of being met only by wrath and violence. The violent do indeed bear it away.

The struggle within Tarwater's mind therefore is not simply that between heeding or denying the burden of prophecy bequeathed him by the old man; it is between the creative, life-giving emotion of love and the destructive, death-bringing emotion of hatred and violence. He wants to love, but he has been taught only to hate. There is another scene which bears this out: that in which the youth Tarwater, as he meditates taking Bishop out in the boat to drown him, stands on the staircase of the resort before the little boy, and Bishop asks him to tie his shoes. Before this simple act of trust and dependence, "the country boy stopped still. He hung over him like someone bewitched, his long arms bent uncertainly." As the woman resort-keeper watches, Tarwater reaches over then and ties the shoes. "When the boy finished tying them, he straightened himself and said in a querulous voice, 'Now git on and quit bothering me with them laces,' and the child flipped over on his hands and feet and scrambled up the stairs, making a great din." The woman, "confused by this kindness," calls to him then, looks into Tarwater's eyes, "and for an instant she thought she saw something fleeing across the surface of them, a lost light that came from nowhere and vanished into nothing." What is it she thinks she sees, if it is not that even at that late moment, Tarwater was almost swayed from his purpose by the simple need of the child, and the helpless affection implicit in the child's dependence upon him? But just as with Rayber at the revival, the woman will not speak gently and kindly to the youth. A few minutes previously she had admonished him:

"Mind how you talk to one of them there, you boy!" the woman hissed.

He looked at her as if it were the first time she had spoken to him. "Them there what?" he murmured.

"That there kind," she said, looking at him fiercely as if he had profaned the holy.

He looked back at the afflicted child and the woman was startled by the expression on his face. He seemed to see the little boy and nothing else, no air around him, no room, no nothing, as if his gaze had slipped and fallen into the center of the child's eyes and was still falling down and down and down.

Now, when Tarwater looks back at her after having tied the child's laces, the woman only says, "Whatever devil's work you mean to do, don't do it here." And the youth's last, forlorn chance of being rescued by the reality of love is gone. Such is the meaning of the scene, I think, and such is the true conflict within young Tarwater. The youth's spiritual integrity, invulnerable to the schoolmaster's complacent scientific rationalism, could have been directed toward love instead of wrath, had such love been offered him. But in a world ignorant and disdainful of God's love—"Suffer little children to come unto me"—the only response possible is wrath: "His singed eyes, black in their deep sockets, seemed already to envision the fate that awaited him but he moved steadily on, his face set toward the dark city, where the children of God lay sleeping."

In a world in which "faith supported by love" cannot survive the attack of secular materialism, only faith achieved through hatred is possible. Because there is no one in young Tarwater's world to instruct him in God's love, he can be won back to faith only through the passionate hatred involved in the effort to drown the boy Bishop. Extremes, Rayber tells Tarwater, "are for violent people." But in the world they inhabit, it is only the primitive fundamentalism exemplified by the old greatuncle which is violent. We recall T. S. Eliot's lines, "Remember us—if at all—not as lost / Violent souls, but only / As the hollow men / The stuffed men." For Eliot the collapse of faith in the western world has made us all hollow men, but Flannery O'Connor shows faith alive and glowing in the fanatical compulsions of the Bible Belt prophet. Yet the price that Tarwater must pay for the attainment of such faith is the denial and utter extinction of the possibility of love.

If this interpretation of the meaning of this novel is valid, then not only do the scenes at the revival and on the resort staircase make sense, but the attack on Tarwater by the sex pervert becomes something more than an act of gratuitous violence. Furthermore, it seems obvious that in such an interpretation there can be no question of Tarwater's not possessing the free will that a Catholic critic such as Robert O. Bowen declares is absent from the novel. Tarwater is not *fated* to take up the old man's burden of prophecy; he does so because the world, and not fate, compels him to do it. We can also say that he is redeemed— but at a hideous price in suffering. Nor is Divine Justice mocked, as Bowen claims; for what happens to Tarwater happens because of the refusal of those who ostensibly care for the youth to give him the love he requires if he is to be turned from his terrible purpose: "For I the Lord thy God am a jealous God, visiting the iniquities of the fathers upon the children unto the third and fourth generation of them that hate me."

But I desist from theology, and prefer to rest my case on the text of *The Violent Bear It Away*, which contains several scenes which, if the interpretation which I have offered is not admissible, seem oddly tangential to what the novel is then supposed to be about.

The Violent Bear It Away is, among other things, a critique of primitive Southern fundamentalism in action; not that Miss O'Connor set out with such a purpose in mind, for I doubt that she did. In such matters the author's conscious intention, as Austin Warren remarks of Hawthorne and the meaning of *The Scarlet Letter*, does not possess "any more authority than that of another critic: it may even, conceivably, have less." My guess is that Miss O'Connor intended the voice speaking to Tarwater to be that of the Devil himself, and I doubt that she was attempting, consciously at any rate, to set up any such schism as I have proposed between a God of Wrath and a God of Love. I rather imagine she would have considered that my emphasis on the scene at the revival and that on the staircase of the resort was misplaced, and that my insistence upon their importance was the result of my own unwillingness to believe in the reality of the Devil—that is to say, of my modern rationalistic secularism. So be it; nevertheless I persist in seeing this schism, and in believ-

ing that if there is confusion, it comes about in part at
least because of a confusion of attitude within the novel
itself. When Miss O'Connor is dealing with modern secularism, she is scathing in her satire. The scene in which
Rayber attempts to administer intelligence and aptitude
tests to Tarwater is almost too crude to be believable, and
the same is true of the scene in which the schoolmaster
tries to show Tarwater the wonder of modern science by
promising him a ride in an airplane, "the greatest engi-
neering achievement of man," only to have the youth retort that "a buzzard can fly." Miss O'Connor even supplies
a passage on the unattractiveness of modern packages of
breakfast cereal in contrast to healthy, nourishing country
food. Whenever Rayber is portrayed as the modern
rationalist attempting to reason Tarwater away from his
mission, the satire is ruthless and devastating. But the
difficulty is that this is only part of the characterization of
Rayber, and there is also the Rayber who recognizes within himself the potentiality of emotional irrationality and
tries *to protect himself from it by being scientific and
rational.* For this aspect of Rayber, satire is obviously in-
appropriate, for the satirical mode precludes any feeling
of compassion, since it diminishes the stature of the satirical object. The outcome of this is that we tend to undervalue the importance of the conflict within Rayber, who
is too often made the object of contempt rather than pity.
It is precisely this failure, I think, which has caused some
critics to ignore the importance, for example, of the scene
at the revival meeting, and thus to misunderstand where
Rayber's real failure lies, which is not in his rationalism
as such, but in his inability to counter the hold of the old
man's fanaticism upon young Tarwater with the love that
the boy craves and needs if he is to be dissuaded from
carrying out his mission. The only alternative to a God
of Wrath is a God of Love, but so savagely does Miss
O'Connor satirize Rayber the rationalist that we have difficulty in seeing his rationalism as the barrier which,

erected in defense against the Wrath, keeps out the God of Love as well.

Because Rayber's stature is diminished, Miss O'Connor's depiction of the struggle going on within Tarwater is weakened, and the suspense becomes mostly a matter of whether or not he is going to baptize Bishop. Tarwater also becomes a less complex character, and also a less sympathetic one. The result, I think, is a diminution of the potentialities for genuine tragedy; Tarwater tends to remain a freak. "No one, I think," Walter Sullivan has written, "ever identifies with Flannery O'Connor's people." This is going too far, but it is difficult to sympathize with Tarwater, and for that matter with Rayber as well, when the pity and fear that make for the tragic resolution demand just such identification. In a somewhat different way the same difficulty arises with Hazel Motes in *Wise Blood*. Like Tarwater, Haze is trying to throw off the religious bondage, but cannot do so. The only alternative offered him is the materialism and godlessness of the city of Taulkinham, which he cannot accept however much he would like to do so. But the completely satirical, one-sided picture of the modern city that Miss O'Connor gives is such that we never seriously consider that Haze will succumb. The result is that because the element of choice is removed from Haze's characterization, he remains throughout a grotesque character.

Why is this? I am not so sure but that the reason lies in part at least with Miss O'Connor's attitude, as a Roman Catholic, to Southern Protestant fundamentalism. We have seen that when it comes to a choice between primitive Protestantism and urban secular materialism, Miss O'Connor will come down on the side of Protestantism every time. As noted both in her own statements and in that by Father Gustave Weigel, fundamentalist Protestantism and Roman Catholicism share a literal approach to religious dogma. A distinguished Southern historian, Francis B. Simkins, has remarked on this as well; "the strength of the Southern Baptist church," he declared in a discussion of the fundamentalism controversy of the 1920's, "stemmed from the same cause as that of the Roman Catholic church: its utter refusal to compromise with liberal tendencies of other churches." Yet it is possible, I think, to overstress that affinity. It is true that there is agreement on the divinity of Christ, the Virgin Birth, the Redemptive Power, the physical resurrection. But there are also several important differences between Roman Catholicism and rural Southern fundamentalism. The Catholic Church emphatically does not believe in the direct and unaided revelation of prophecy that is so typical of fundamentalism; Catholicism is a liturgical faith, and the untutored and frenzied emotionalism, unchecked by dogma and unaided by reason, that characterizes primitive fundamentalism is foreign to the Catholic religious experience. Catholicism does not dispense with reason; far from it. For the Catholic, reason is a valuable tool to be used within the larger experience of faith. It is the reason of the secular mind, unaided by dogma and faith, that the Catholic Church opposes. Indeed, Miss O'Connor has been criticized by one Catholic writer for neglecting sometimes "to place enough emphasis on reason as a corrective of too much heart."

Whether this objection is valid or not, it is well to keep in mind that however much Miss O'Connor may admire certain aspects of Southern fundamentalism, she is not herself a Southern fundamentalist, and as a Roman Catholic she is both ill at ease with the messianic fervor of the direct prophetic revelation and profoundly suspicious of its consequences.

Therefore, while her fundamentalists may retain the religious spirit in an otherwise secularized society, they are nonetheless and inevitably portrayed as grotesques. Once again, we must not overlook the fact that both Hazel Motes and Francis Marion Tarwarter, in the frenzy of their warped religious experience, are driven to commit murder. Nor is Tarwater's fanatical old great-uncle an attractive or sympathetic character, for all that Miss O'Connor may approve of his religious dedication. The violent bear it away in both novels, for they are primitive Southern fundamentalist characters in the fiction of a Southern Roman Catholic author.

The truth is that, in the words of the Episcopal bishop quoted earlier, primitive Southern Protestant fundamentalism is an often violent faith, in which Satan is seemingly more real than God. All too frequently it is the kind of orgiastic, hyper-emotional religion that anyone who has ever lived in the South has heard preached on the numerous little low-wattage radio stations, interspersed with the Hillbilly Hit Parade and the anti-communistic, anti-liberal, Texas-sponsored political harangues, the last-named often delivered by ministers themselves. It is fanatical, intolerant, anti-intellectual; the God of the Old Testament and of the Book of Revelations is there, but the God of the Sermon on the Mount is seldom invoked. And for what the Virgin Mary can mean to the Catholic, there is no room at all. Its prophets agitate and exhort, shout and shriek as they seek to stir up the lagging faithful. However similar some of its tenets may be to that of Roman Catholicism, in its approach, its attitude, its appeal it is profoundly alien and antithetical to the Catholic mind and heart. Or so it seems to me.

What I would suggest is that much of the dramatic tension that makes Flannery O'Connor's fiction so gripping and memorable lies in the insight into religious experience afforded her by her double heritage as both Catholic and Southerner. The two forms of orthodoxy—the primitive fundamentalism of her region, the Roman Catholicism of her faith—work sometimes with and sometimes against each other in a literary counterpoint that has enabled her to create some of the most distinguished and exciting fiction of her time.

The Experience of Difference: Southerners and Jews

That *arbiter elegantiae* of the English-speaking world's literary disputes, the *Times Literary Supplement* of London, was editorializing, some few years ago, about the manner in which the "chief centre" of American writing had been shifting about the various regions of the United States. Most recently "it was the turn of the South," the *T.L.S.* declared, "and the 'beat' young men in San Francisco have much more to do yet before they can overthrow its dominance."

How very out-of-date such a remark seems even today; less than a decade later San Francisco Beat has gone out of fashion so rapidly that one hardly even thinks of it any more. Kerouac, Ferlinghetti, Corso—let's see, who *were* some of the others?—are almost as forgotten as are Michael Arlen, Burton Rascoe, and Hugh Walpole, who have been literarily deceased a great deal longer. And it turns out that the principal threat to the Southern hegemony is not the Beat folk at all; rather, it is the Jews. Saul Bellow, Karl Shapiro, Bernard Malamud, Howard Nemerov, Norman Mailer, Philip Roth, Herbert Gold, Alfred Kazin, Norman Podhoretz, even "Howl" Ginsberg the Zen Talmudist—a pretty formidable group all right. Where did they appear from, what are they about? The American Jewish writers haven't yet supplanted what has been so often called the Southern Renascence, but it does seem to-day that if any group is to do so, the Jewish writers are most likely to succeed. One does have the feeling about most of them that much of their best work may very well still lie ahead of them, and that a disproportionate share of the best writing now being produced in America is the work of Jewish writers.

I propose to generalize about all this. I shall do so on the strength of four books, two by Southerners and two by Jews, published within the last several years. The South-erners are William Humphrey and the late Flannery O'Connor. The Jews are Saul Bellow and the late Edward Lewis Wallant. And so that the nature of the transaction is made clear, I ought to say that I shall be approaching the matter from the vantage point, such as it is, of one who is both a Southerner and a Jew, which is to say, as one with a foot in each camp.

William Humphrey published his first novel, *Home from the Hill,* back in 1958. I have been thinking of it ever since as an example of what can happen when a younger Southern writer attempts to carry the Faulknerian primitivistic style—field and stream, the mighty hunter, etc.—into modern urban experience; halfway through, the characterization collapses as disastrously as that of Flem Snopes does in Faulkner's *The Mansion.* Humphrey's sec-ond and most recent novel, *The Ordways,* is in many re-spects much better that that first try; it isn't nearly as derivative, and it isn't pseudo-tragic. The writer's craft has improved considerably; no doubt of that. But, a seri-ous attempt to give fictional order and meaning to experi-ence? *The Ordways* starts off in true Southern style: a long scene involving the Ordway family's annual grave-tending day in East Texas, with everybody come home to take part. Various ancestral yarns, mostly humorous, are recalled by the narrator, who is the fourth-generation Ordway in the town of Clarksville. Next we get into the story of how the Ordways got there, involving a tale not at all humorous. Tom Ordway, horribly blinded and mangled at Shiloh, tries to let himself be thought dead, but his wife comes to fetch him, and they begin a long wagon trek, with the family tombstones and ashes brought along, all the way from Tennessee to Texas. Much of this is very moving: an archetypal fictional journey, at times worthy of William Faulkner himself (and sometimes suggesting *Absalom, Absalom!* and *As I Lay Dying*). The best part of the book comes next: how Sam Ordway, born the day that the family forded the river and staggered into Texas, marries, loses his wife, marries again, and has a child stolen by neighbors. This section is first-rate writing, notable for the author's sympathetic insight into the situation of the second wife, and into how Sam Ordway handles it; when at length Sam starts out after his missing son, he has our keen attention.

But at this point, or not long afterward, the novel simply seems to disintegrate. The search, at first very moving, soon becomes funny; and then the humor gets really slapstick, with Sam Ordway joining a circus and then spending a term in jail along with a phony preacher, and any importance or dignity to the search for the lost child is dissolved in vaudeville comedy. Ultimately Sam goes back home, everyone grows old, and soon we are back in modern times again, with the long missing son Ned showing up at the end for several days of joyous reunion, followed by a wild mass automobile trip to his angora goat ranch in western Texas, whereupon the story ends.

What does it all mean? It comes to mean almost nothing. As in the first novel, there is the curious grafting of the traditional Southern storytelling milieu, with its primitives who are strong and feeling human beings, onto a modern mode, this time of slapstick humor and sentimentality (Truman Capote could have composed the final sequences). Any relationship between the two parts would have to reside in the meaning it has, or implies, for the narrator. But the narrator, after the opening section, becomes merely an "I" doing the telling and can embody or present no meaning. It will not do to say that the theme of the novel is that the narrator can *discover* no meaning between the historical past and the present, as with Faulkner's Quentin Compson or Allen Tate's observer at the cemetery wall; even that realization would be a way of giving meaning to what has been told. Humphrey doesn't achieve that; there is really no connection at all, other than the facts of the family history. It winds up as no more and no less than a nostalgic stroll along memory lane and so forth, amusing, quaint, but adding up to no more than the fact that it has happened. What might have been the pathos and the drama of a family come down to a new day and forced to assume a new identity is absent, and one is led to think that it is absent because for the author there simply isn't any discernible meaning to the family's survival; the novel divides into two stories, the olden day events and the modern, with an unbridgeable artistic gulf between them. The two can't be made into one, because the historical events haven't any meaning for the narrator, who is a modern Southerner, nor does it occur to him that they should have. Gavin Stevens, in Faulkner's *Requiem for a Nun*, declares to Temple Drake that "the past is never dead. It's not even past." Not so in *The Ordways*. The past is quite dead.

My admiration and affection, both personal and literary, for Flannery O'Connor were such that it was disappointing to find that her volume of posthumously collected short stories, *Everything That Rises Must Converge*, wasn't anywhere close to being as good as *A Good Man Is Hard to Find* or portions of her two novels. Miss O'Connor's place in our literature, I think, is secure; it rests primarily on the achievement of eight or nine first-rate stories, most of them in the earlier volume, and it is difficult to think of those stories ever becoming outdated or failing to move the reader. Considering the total quantity of her life's work, that is a pretty high percentage of achievement; she utilized her talent to the fullest extent, and her performance requires neither apology nor empty adulation. It is genuine, it is singular, it will last.

In most of the posthumously collected stories, however, though the gift for language is still there—polished, muscular, the style of a talented artist—the artistic vision is notably weaker. With several notable exceptions, the stories are painfully didactic. They are theological lessons. Any human being who had to endure what Flannery O'Connor did for the last few years of her too-brief life, the years when most of these stories were written, would certainly have tended to view the human condition with more than the customary amount of distrust. In any event, what most of these stories seem to me to lack—and what most of the stories in the earlier collection did not lack—is an affection for weak humans, a sympathy for the poor proud ones, to work against the searing moral vision and thus produce the tension, the two-way emotional pull, that makes for important religious fiction. The consciously religious work of art, it seems to me, usually achieves its intensity because of the conflict set up within the work between the artist's moral convictions and his intense sympathy for the humans caught in the toils of sin. But when there isn't that conflict, what results is likely to be allegory, and very didactically set forth at that. This, alas, is apparently what happened in *Everything That Rises Must Converge*. In all of the stories except two or three, Miss O'Connor loaded the dice, as it were; she made her sinners so wretchedly obnoxious that one can't feel much compassion for their plight. The title story, for example, depicts a mean-tempered, selfish young man, who prides himself on his smug liberalism in racial matters, as he takes his racially prejudiced mother downtown on the bus to a YWCA reducing class. His contempt for his mother's bigotry is such that he actually rejoices when she is knocked down by a Negro woman after she patronizingly attempts to give a penny to the woman's little child. But the shock to the mother is such that then and there she has a stroke, and the young man suddenly realizes his own guilt and dependence as he shouts helplessly for aid. What seems wrong with this story is that the young man is made into so despicable a lout that we fail to feel any empathy for him whatever. When at last he realizes the dreadfulness of what he has been and done, we have no sense of his being caught in any kind of a tragic plight. One can hardly feel, in reading this sad story, that "there, but for the grace of God, go I." The only authorial compassion comes at the very end, and then it is a general, theological attitude, added on only as a moral and not growing organically out of the characterization. Indeed, the whole matter of the ending isn't convincing. The stroke that the mother has seems not so much inevitable as having been put there in order to make the meaning come out right. Compare this with the title story in *A Good Man Is Hard to Find*; the smug, selfish, obnoxious old grandmother in that story nevertheless has a moment, just before she is killed by The Misfit, in which she achieves genuine compassion and love; the lonely human soul breaks through the selfishness. But in "Everything That Rises Must Converge" this never happens.

The best story in this book, I think, is one entitled "Parker's Back," about a man who has a Byzantine Christ tattooed on his back to impress his fundamentalist young wife, who only shouts "Idolatry!" and routs him out of the house with a broomstick. In this fine story Miss O'Connor does what she has always done well: she shows ignorant primitives groping in their untutored way, and without knowing exactly what it is they are doing, for love and for God. Another excellent story, "The Judgment," tells of a lonely old Southern farmer living with his daughter in a Northern city, and dying there. Perhaps it is significant that in both these stories Miss O'Connor wasn't writing about the educated or the genteel. In most of the other stories, I note, she is working hard to demonstrate how middle-class smugness, modern crassness, and pseudo-intellectuality fail to cope with evil. Such a contest is always artistically unequal, because she is so thoroughly disdainful of such things that she fails to provide the characters exemplifying them with sufficient humanity to engage our emotion. This is what is wrong with her novel, *The Violent Bear It Away*; and her reworking of that situation, in the story entitled "The Lame Shall Enter First" in her posthumously published book, is even less successful, because the new version, built around the failure of an apostle of modernism to win over a juvenile delinquent, gives so little to the modernist that he becomes a stereotyped characterization rather than a believable human being. In the novel, which is a much richer story, this is only partly true.

The difficulty that these stories present, I think, is precisely the opposite of that in William Humphrey's *The Ordways*. The latter work fails because the author is unable to discover any real meaning for the human story he tells; the less successful stories by Flannery O'Connor suffer because the meaning is imposed at the expense of characterization, and the characters won't stay alive under the weight of the didactic purpose. In a sense, however, the fault in both instances is similar, namely, an artistic gulf between author and subject. In Humphrey's instance he could not make the past have any meaning, whether positive or negative, for the present; in Miss O'Connor's lesser stories she could not get inside her protagonists and make them human.

So much, for the present, for the Southerners. Now the Jews—likewise, one ought to remember, an ancestor-conscious race, strong on familial ties, and not thoroughly assimilated into the mainstream of modern American life. Case No. 1, Edward Lewis Wallant, died in 1962 at the age of thirty-six; *The Children at the Gate* was his second novel to receive posthumous publication, and the fourth Wallant novel in all. Thus far little has been written about him, a notable exception being Jonathan Baumbach's excellent chapter in his recent *The Landscape of Nightmare*, which I think is the best book-length study yet written on the contemporary novel.

Though the central character of *The Children at the Gate* is an Italian named Angelo deMarco, the novel is about a Jewish hospital attendant, Sammy Kahan, and his impact on the lives of Angelo and on others at the Sacred Heart Hospital. Sammy is a Jewish fictional type—I suspect that his origins may be found in Yiddish literature—of which we have had several examples in recent American fiction. He is a Wise Fool, the knowing innocent who won't put up with the hypocrisy and stereotyping of modern life, who asserts his individualistic humanity in the face of any and all systems, cosmologies, ideologies, and so forth. There is an element of Quixoticism in this kind of person; he spends much time storming steel mills. He differs, however, from the Knight of the Woeful Countenance in that, rather than seeking to impose any system of his own on experience, his role is always that of the defier of any such systemization. I do not recall any other kind of American fiction except that of the modern Jewish writers which has just this person in it. It is not simply that he defies systems—the protagonist of *The Ginger Man*, for example, does that, and so do Huckleberry Finn and Holden Caulfield. It is rather that he does it with a mocking sense of irony that declines to let such defiance become a system, either, and that maintains a full and humorous awareness of the threadbare nature of any such defiance. That the figure comes out of a deeply ingrained cultural instinct I greatly suspect—for one thing, it seems closely related to Jewish humor.

Of course not all Jewish American fiction features this kind of character. Yet it is interesting, and perhaps all too easy, to speculate a bit on what such a figure signifies. He grows, it seems to me, out of a process of cultural assimilation, or at any rate, out of a certain kind of cultural change. That is to say, he accepts the practical conditions and values of the dominant culture, which is the American, largely Protestant-formed society, but at the same time he feels a bit uneasy in it, cannot quite make entire sense of it, and so refuses to be engulfed in and fully defined by it. Lev, in Bernard Malamud's *A New Life*, for example, wishes to be teacher, scholar, lover, citizen, as those roles exist in the community he has chosen; but at the same time he is aware of the absurdity of some aspects of those postures and of the hypocrisy and over-simplification which they entail, and while he goes right on ahead with his plans, he is not without an ironic insight into the dubiousness of his own actions. Saul Bellow's Herzog, of whom more later, is much more disturbed by the whole thing; the contradictions between his ideals and his circumstance render him almost totally incapable of functioning. Yet he too never really becomes cynical about the values that are his; rather, he becomes confused by the apparent discrepancy between them and the kind of life he must live. And Sammy Kahan, of *The Children at the Gate*, who is an altogether less formidable and imposing person than either of the other two, nonetheless shares that essential idealism and also that irony.

A character such as Kahan is divided among two cultures. He is a Jew, from the ghetto of New York City, and he works in a Catholic hospital, where although he is to some extent set apart as a Jew he is accepted—Angelo deMarco doesn't think of him importantly as being a Jew, for example, so much as a queer fellow who happens to be Jewish. And Sammy's impact on Angelo, which is the point of the novel, is profound, for in his absurdity, his idealism, his battle-scarred humanity, Sammy breaks down the dour impasse that Angelo has reached after the cynical repudiation of his own religious faith. He forces Angelo to realize that being a "scientist," which to him means living without loyalties, isn't enough, and that not only is there an essential mystery to human life that cannot be explained through systems, but that neither may the mystery be ignored or glossed over. On that mystery rests the human condition, and it does so in and through this world, not outside, beyond, and exterior to it.

I can imagine a certain kind of critic happily working away to prove that Sammy Kahan is a Christ figure, which would probably make Angelo into Saul become Paul, and so on. That would merely be another scheme, however, and Sammy Kahan would laugh widely as he pointed out its absurdity. But then, Sammy probably wouldn't understand it anyway, for he is no intellectual. Even so, his basic humor and wisdom would doubtless be all he would need to instruct him that something was ridiculous in the idea. Yet Sammy would not deny one's right to speculate about such matters. He would recognize that he too went in for that sort of thing, in his own way, all the time. In fact, this is what kills him: it was a way of Loving, and thus of Living. Such was Sammy Kahan, and of such is Edward Lewis Wallant's fine posthumous novel constructed.

Saul Bellow is one of the three or four best novelists writing today, and he may eventually be grouped with Dreiser, Faulkner, Hemingway, Fitzgerald, Welty, Wolfe —among our foremost writers. He has that American-Russian-Jewish intellectuality, which makes him a particular kind of novelist, but along with that he has the vital mastery of living characters so that his intellectuals are men and not just embodied ideas; and this is what makes Saul Bellow so fine an artist. There are other writers, I think, who might have written *The Dangling Man, The Victim,* perhaps even *Seize the Day.* But Bellow is too imaginative a writer to settle for that part of the human spectrum, however well done. He wrote *Augie March,* which isn't a successful book but which breaks out of the grey cerebral ghetto and brings Bellow into contact with whole people. Also there is *Henderson the Rain King,* a weird kind of work but lighted throughout with humor and poetry. In his most recent novel, *Herzog,* he goes back into the urban canyons, but with the experience of other people, and the result is a great character, Moses Herzog, who can both think and breathe deeply, and for whom human experience is neither primarily a demonstrated concept nor a biological protest, but instead both and therefore much more.

Herzog's problem is to get the two into proper harmony and to learn that neither precludes the other's existence. A solitary man who craves company, he must discover the workable balance between society and self, between the need to exist among other people and the compulsion to seek to define one's identity by them. Now it seems to me that this problem, however much it is universal and constant, is for our time a characteristically Jewish-American one in its implications. Consider how Bellow has approached it again and again. *The Victim* is based squarely upon it. So is *Augie March.* In *Herzog,* Moses Herzog has left one kind of community, to which he had never fully belonged because it was in too advanced a process of dissolution, but which has left its strong markings through the impact of the parents and family on the child. Father Herzog, ne'er-do-well, failure in the Land of Opportunity, had his code of success nevertheless and had sought to pass it along to three sons. The other two brothers have proved dutiful and diligent; they have Got Ahead in business, have succeeded in being Providers. Moses can't and won't follow suit; he is impossible, a dreamer, a scholar, a born improvident. But—and here lies his trouble—he wants to be dreamer and scholar in terms of the secular American world into which the Herzog family has emerged. If Herzog had chosen the rabbinate (I don't recall that it ever crossed his mind), the value of his intellectuality and otherworldliness might have been recognizable to his father. But for Herzog any such career within the old culture would have been out of the question, for it did not deal with the real world as Herzog saw it presenting itself. So Moses Herzog pursues and achieves some distinction in a career of scholarship, in which he concerns himself with ideas of good and evil in Romanticism, and he also pursues true love, which he cannot discover. His first wife is a Jewess; she is orderly and good, and is also boring, so he leaves her. His second wife is a Christian, is disorderly and complex, and he loves her; but Herzog for her is not himself but a symbol of her own guilt and aggrandisement, and she leaves him.

So the Herzog of time present is wifeless, and is vocationless, the desire to master and give order to the intellectual history of Romanticism having faded. How very believable that is, since if Romanticism is essentially an attitude toward man as a creature of endless spiritual possibilities, then how could Moses Herzog explain its meaning? For though he feels that there ought to be possibilities—for love, for happiness, for creativity, for understanding and meaning—how on earth can he ever attain these? He has had a good, dutiful wife, and she was not enough; he has had a complex and fascinating wife, and she has betrayed him. Now he has only two children, from both of whom he is separated: the desire to be a father, to love his children, is not attainable. He has reached, in short, a point in his career at which the momentum that came from optimistic innocence and uncritical desire for success has slackened, and now it occurs to him, What is this all about? Because he is Moses Herzog, who is no egotist, he sees its comic aspects, and he is not a hero to himself. He is constantly writing imaginary letters to great and important men past and present, forcefully pointing out the inconsistencies in their attitudes and ideas: Dear Mr. Nehru, Dear Mr. King, Dear Commissioner Wilson, Dear Mr. Udall, Dear Herr Nietzsche, Dear Doktor Professor Heidegger; so much to be solved, so much simple advice to be given—if only the world, that is, were amenable to taking advice, and things were not so complex and interwoven that any effort to straighten out one set of problems only led deeper and deeper into the whole tangled mess, and toward a weary glimpse of the insolubility of anything. The letters are never finished, never posted.

It is not that Moses Herzog has been a failure in this world; within reason he is a distinguished man who need never lack for employment and recognition. Nor does he lack for love; he has a girl, Ramona, who is mature and wise, and who wants him, and for whom sexuality is the primary life art—and Herzog likes that. But Herzog cannot create. So he boards an airplane, flies to Chicago, and contemplates killing his ex-wife and his former disciple who is her lover. But he is too wise for that; he is not the killing kind, and they are not deserving of being murdered. He takes his little daughter out for a ride, becomes involved in an automobile accident, is held in arrest because of the loaded gun he is carrying, and finally calls his brother and gets out of police custody. He goes back to the old farmhouse in upstate New York which he and his second wife had occupied, and for some days he stays there by himself, sleeping, patching up the house a little, dreaming. At last he rouses himself, gets the house put into civilized working shape, assures his worried and devoted brother that he is all right, entertains his girl friend, and prepares to get ready to enter Modern Life again. But for now, he will simply rest, and be. Thus the life of Moses Herzog, scholar and Jew, as presented by Saul Bellow, novelist and Jew.

The name of Moses Herzog (borrowed no doubt from

Ulysses) is especially well chosen for what Bellow wants his man to be. There is an old Jewish saying, "From Moses to Moses to Moses, there is none like Moses," referring to the Biblical prophet and lawgiver, the medieval sage Maimonides, and the eighteenth-century scholar and philosopher Mendelssohn. Moses is surely the archetypal Jewish name (but was Moses a Jew?), and it also carries its connotations of seer and sage. But Herzog is a German name, with nothing much of savant or philosopher in its connotations. The union of the two names suggests the problem which faces Moses Herzog, which is how to be inspired prophet and practical lawgiver—meditative man, man of the hour—in a new kind of society that is not traditional and Jewish and closed, but secular and American and quite open-ended. Herzog is *in* this new society; he has crossed over and can have it no other way. But he is ill at ease in Zion, for there persists in him a spirituality, an unwillingness to concede the primacy of things, that will not let him be satisfied with the good life he has achieved. Perhaps this is the residue of several millennia of wandering engaged in by his ancestors, the idealism of Judaistic theology, the dislodgement that comes of being in two cultures and not wholly part of either. What Herzog finally does is accept the fact that he will not ever be able fully to belong to his world, and that though he is dependent on it, there is that in himself which will go on being a displaced person until he dies. Bellow's genius comes in his being able to make this special uneasiness, product as it is of an identifiable cultural condition, a symbol of man's unending discomfort with his human state.

Mr. Richard Kostelanetz, writing in the *Hudson Review* (Autumn, 1965), attacks what he considers the present overvaluation of Jewish writing; it is a species of chauvinism, he says, and he likens it (and gets most wrathful in so doing) to what he considers has been the equally chauvinistic overvaluation of Southern writers in the recent past. Such notions as "Southern writing" and "Jewish writing" are misleading, he says, because they imply a single American culture into which these so-called Movements fit, when in fact there is no one American culture, and therefore minority groups are not at all unusual but are, instead, the customary thing. The warning against chauvinism is well-taken, I think, and yet upon close examination Mr. Kostelanetz's manifesto turns out to be chauvinistic itself. For his affected horror of Jewish overpraising of Jewish writers is a way of leaning over backward not to be favorably biased, which is an acute manifestation of self-consciousness ("Don't say anything to make them mad," one Jew says to another Jew who asks for a blindfold when both are about to be executed by a firing squad). And the claim that there isn't one American culture, but a multiplicity of cultures, which Mr. Kostelanetz invokes in order to attack the idea of there being a "Southern Literary Renascence," is really an effort to maintain the very opposite; he wants to play down any thought of a Southern group dominating something known as American Literature, because he dislikes the existence of such a group, and so insists that there isn't anything special about being a member of a group. Or so I read his essay, which is well-written and very provocative.

It seems to me on the contrary that it is quite clear that there now is and for many generations has been an American culture, and that the history of American Literature in large part involves the successive accommodation of smaller groups, whether regional, religious, economic or racial, within that culture. The culture, as with all general cultures, is mainly materialistic and secular in its dominant manifestations, and the arts, which are always idealistic and religious in their source and their objectives, represent the assertion of nonmaterialistic values by a small elite during the assimilation of the group of which that elite is a part by the still larger general culture. The New England writers were not racially or even economically separated from the dominant culture of their day; they were cut off from it by religious and regional attitudes, and not only the literature of the Transcendentalists but also of more important allied writers such as Melville, Hawthorne, and Whitman represented an assertion of nonmaterialistic values during a time when an older America was being assimilated by the secular nineteenth century. The same is true of the twentieth-century Southerners, and it is true of the Jews of our own time; their writings are not only deservedly praised, but there are some quite sound reasons why such excellence existed and exists.

The Southern writers of the 1920's and 1930's and the Jewish writers have successively discovered themselves in the same place: modern, urban, secular America. Both groups have found it a strange country. The Southerner moved out of a somnolent, settled, rural kind of experience into the cosmopolitan, eclectic modern world and carried with him the sense of community, of continued historical identity in time, that went along with his earlier role. What he had to equate with that, to make part of his identity as well, was his bewildering new exposure to modern urban experience, to the ideas and intellectual attitudes of an open and secular society. That is Eugene Gant's trouble in the Wolfe novels, and Quentin Compson's and Jack Burden's, and also Cass Kinsolving's in William Styron's *Set This House on Fire.* How to accommodate traditional social and religious instincts to the reality of urban, secular experience?

It is not that the Southerner's previous experience, by which of course I mean that of his family and his tradition, was preferable to, was necessarily more religious or spiritual in nature than what he was entering. This I think has been overstated by some writers about the South (I plead guilty myself to some extent). I don't believe that the mass of Southerners in the pre-modern South were either more or less religious, or spiritually directed, than the inhabitants of modern America North or South. The point is, however, that the customs, habits, attitudes, and framework of reference were *different*, and when these began importantly changing, as they did after 1900, whatever tendencies toward the assertion of religious and spiritual values existing within the society were disrupted, and the search for redefinition, for moral ordering, that went on produced the impetus for reassertion of such values that we know as modern Southern literature. It is out of this kind of furnace experience, so to speak, that the impassioned human image emerged, with the grossness and impurities burned away; it was this that helped make possible Faulkner, Wolfe, Ransom, Warren, and others.

It is easy to see how, say, the best work of Flannery O'Connor fits into such an experience. What has been so striking about her fiction is that in the doings of backwoods fundamentalists and middle-class Southerners she has continued to discover the same burning moral image of human life that had previously characterized the work of the older writers, and which has seemed diminished, or at any rate less articulate, in the other Southern writers of her own generation. Is it an accident that Miss O'Connor was not only Southern, but also Catholic? I think not. For her Catholicism provided her with an additional and lingering impediment to the general Southern conversion to modern, secular experience. The transaction thus took longer, lasting well into another generation. She bears about the same relationship to the generation of Faulkner, Ransom, and the others, in this respect, that Emily Dickinson does to the generation of Emerson, Hawthorne, Melville, and Whitman.

Similarly, Jewish ghetto life, both in the physical ghetto of Europe and the lingering economic and social ghetto of New York and other large American cities, was traditional, familial, closed; and when the walls came down and the Jew entered into modern, secular American life, he carried with him his old identity. The highly developed inward spirituality and intellectuality of the ghetto and the synagogue needed redefinition and reassertion amid what was and still is the growing availability of unrestricted participation in a community of power and influence. This is Herzog's problem, and also Sammy Kahan's: how to equate one's spiritual identity with the role now open and available in a secular society?

Now since no set of values and beliefs can ever fully account for the reality of human experience, and yet human experience can assuredly make no sense to anyone without the continuous attempt to apply such values, the Jewish American, if he is a writer, confronts not only the constant and never ending task of the writer, which is that of giving order to experience in language and image, but confronts it in terms of a specific and concrete scheme of reference. In this respect he is like the writers of the South, who, albeit in somewhat different historical terms, have faced a similar situation: the change from one kind of cultural and social experience into another. And I think that the possibility for concreteness, the historical immediacy of the available scheme of reference, goes far toward accounting for both the flowering of Southern writing during the years between the two world wars and the outburst of fine Jewish writing since the Second World War. The experience demands the judging and weighing of one's values, and at the same time it provides a vivid and specific set of images to give form to the transaction.

There has not yet been a major Jewish American novelist, unless perhaps it is Bellow, something which is difficult to determine just now. My own guess is that if such a writer comes along, it may not be for another fifteen or twenty years, which is to say, after another generation of Jewish experience as Americans. The South has already produced Faulkner, Warren, Welty, Wolfe, Ran-

som, Tate, Porter, Lytle, McCullers, Caldwell, more recently O'Connor, Styron. To what degree any or many of
these are so-called Major Writers, it is difficult to say; Mr.
Richard Kostelanetz thinks that only Faulkner is, and
seems to begrudge even that admission; others, including
myself, have thought differently. Is the so-called Southern
Literary Renascence coming to an end, now that the South
seems pretty much assimilated into modern America, and
there is even a major league baseball team playing out of
Atlanta? Here is Flannery O'Connor, who in a series of
short stories brilliantly explored the moral and religious
dimensions of Southern experience, but in her last book
became involved with a duel with modernity that kept
many of her people from being entirely human. Here is
William Humphrey, who cannot find a way to unite his
historical insights with the life of his own time. And here
is Robert Penn Warren, one of the major literary talents
of his time, whose last several novels have been failures
because he can no longer bring what he now thinks and
feels to bear on the nature of the older Southern experience into which he was born. And so on. The best novels
written by Southerners in the last few years, it seems to
me, have been those whose writing seems least to come out
of the older modes: Styron, George Garrett, and one or
two others including a quite remarkable young man
named Donald Harington, whose first novel of several
years ago, *The Cherry Pit*, seemed like a breath of fresh
air in a sultry garden.

Does all this mean that, as Allen Tate suggested three
decades ago, distinguished Southern literary achievement
was largely the product of "the curious burst of intelligence that we get at a crossing of the ways, not unlike, on
an infinitesimal scale, the outburst of poetic genius at the
end of the sixteenth century when commercial England
had already begun to crush feudal England"? If so, the
Southerners of today seem to have reached the farther
shore, while the Jewish writers seem to be in mid-channel

yet and swimming away. Who, one wonders, will come next? The Negroes?

But this is sociology, almost, and for a literary critic a highly dubious business, and so I desist. Yet it does seem apparent that however mysterious the coming into being of literary "movements" and "schools" may seem, insofar as cultural and social factors are involved, the experience of racial and cultural "difference" would appear to be closely involved with the directions that American writing seems to take. This seems no less true of Southern and Jewish writers in the middle of the twentieth century than of certain New England young men of lingering Puritanical heritage in a rapidly-changing, rapidly-industrializing American region in the 1830's and 1840's, or of a young Virginian named Edgar Poe in an optimistic, progress-worshipping civilization during the same historical era. Well might D. H. Lawrence declare that "there is a 'different' feeling in the old American classics. It is the shifting over from the old psyche to something new, a displacement. And displacements hurt." The transaction —this Experience of Difference—is by no means complete.

The Difficulties of Being
a Southern Writer Today:
Or,
Getting Out from Under
William Faulkner

At one point during the 1930's the poet T. S. Eliot found it necessary to disapprove of the poetry of John Milton. He wrote an essay in which he declared that "many people will agree that a man may be a great artist, and yet have a bad influence." Milton, he contended, had positively ruined the poetry of the eighteenth century: "he certainly did more harm than Dryden and Pope, and perhaps a good deal of the obloquy which has fallen on these two poets, especially the latter, because of their influence, ought to be transferred to Milton."

This may be rather unfair of Eliot, but I think that if we can understand what he was trying to get at, we may be better able to understand something of what the Southern writer of the current—which is to say, the post-World War II—generation is up against. For when an author is big enough, great enough, when his style of discourse is so very imposing, the mere existence of his works creates problems for those who follow after him. Indeed, Eliot is proving just such a difficulty for the poets of the current generation; he is so formidable a poet (and so very much *like* Milton by the way, in language and attitude) that it is all that his successors can do to keep from imitating him. For a great writer teaches us how to recognize our experience, and thenceforth it is all we can do to keep from continuing to observe and to describe our own experience in exactly the way that he did.

Allowing for differences of time and place, it seems to me that very much this kind of problem exists for the present generation of Southern writers, with regard to the late William Faulkner. So distinguished is Faulkner's achievement that we habitually look at the Southern experience of his time with his language and with his values. So far as literature goes, the South of the period between 1925 and 1950 is most importantly William Faulkner's South. Compsons, Sutpens, Sartorises, Snopes, de Spains, Beauchamps, McCaslins—the image is accurate, inevitable, unforgettable. It is safe to say, I think, that few Southern writers coming after Faulkner can fail to respond to him.

This creates a problem. For if the South has been changing, then the South of our own time is no longer the South of *The Sound and the Fury,* of *Light in August,* of *Absalom, Absalom!* In certain vital respects William Faulkner's experience is not that of the present generation of Southern writers. And therefore it will not suffice for the writers of this generation to try to describe their experience by relying exclusively on the language and the insights of Faulkner and his contemporaries. The moderns have to see it in their way, and to do that they face the task of getting out from under Faulkner, so to speak. For if they do not, they will not be able to give the proper image and order to their experience.

Let me give an example. Here is the first paragraph of a novel by a Southerner of the post-World War II generation, *Home from the Hill,* by William Humphrey:

Early one morning last September the men squatting on the northeast corner of the town square looked up from their whittling to see, already halfway down the west side and passing under the shadow of the Confederate monument, a dusty long black hearse with a Dallas County license plate.

What is suspicious there? Simply that it is all too Faulknerian. For there we have the same small town, the sense of the constricted little community, the dryness, the heat, the men whittling, the Confederate monument throwing the shadow of the past upon the present, the body coming back home, and so on. It is Faulkner's milieu. But it is not really William Humphrey's world, and his novel fails to come off because, especially in the second half of his narrative, he sought to use William Faulkner's language, William Faulkner's social and human values, William Faulkner's insights, in order to describe an experience that was not really Faulknerian at all. And it fails to convince us.

"Getting out from under": if I were to select one phrase that exemplifies an important problem of the Southern writer of our own day, it would be that. I do not wish to imply that there are not other ways of looking at the South than those that Faulkner chose; I do not want to minimize the magnificent work of such writers as Thomas Wolfe, Robert Penn Warren, Eudora Welty, Katherine Anne Porter. Yet it is no more than accurate to say—surely most of those writers would agree—that Faulkner's great tragedies constitute the mainstream of modern Southern writing, and that his is the example most likely to dominate the imagination of younger writers. For that reason, part of their task has been and will be that of getting away from it, of gaining perspective, of learning to see their experience with their own eyes.

I have made this sound like a problem of literary style, or in any event a problem having primarily to do with what a nineteenth-century Virginia newspaper editor once referred to as "the *mere* beauties of the *belles lettres*." In a very real sense, however, the problem is closely connected with the state of affairs in the political, social, and historical South. For if a writer's art comes out of the life he knows, however much it may transcend the particular time and place, then there would have to be a marked difference between the literature of the High Renascence in Southern writing, and that of more recent years. If we grant that the impact of the urban, cosmopolitan, industrial experience of this century upon the settled, contained, rural society of the older South, delayed as it was by the Civil War and its aftermath, had something important to do with the way in which Faulkner and his contemporaries saw human experience, we would then have to say that the younger writers who grew up in the South during the 1930's and 1940's have undergone a very different kind of experience.

For one thing, it was not nearly so exclusively a rural or small-town experience; for even if the future writer was growing up during the 1930's and 1940's in a small town or on a farm, the same factors of isolation, the kinds of attitudes typical of a closed society were not involved, or at least not in the same way. After the First World War the rural South was not cut off in the way that it once was; it was much more closely tied to the cities. Any social study of the modern South can attest to this: the automobile, good roads, mass communications, chain stores, and so forth had even by the year 1930 all but ended, I think, the self-sufficiency, the cultural and social autonomy of the small Southern community.

"With the war of 1914–1918, the South re-entered the world—but gave a backward glance as it stepped over the border," Allen Tate has written. Tate saw the Southern Literary Renascence as the product of this backward glance, and declared that "the focus of this consciousness is quite temporary." So if the literature of Faulkner and his contemporaries is from the standpoint of cultural and social history the product of this time of transition, then the succeeding generation of Southern writers, faced with finding a meaning through language for a different kind of experience, would surely have to evolve a different way of understanding and describing it. Faulkner's way, no matter how imposing, would no longer suffice.

But even that is not quite accurate; it makes the problem seem much simpler than it perhaps is. For though there is change, there is also continuity, resistance to change, conditions that remain the same from one generation to the next, even though other factors may change utterly. So it is an oversimplification to say that Faulkner's South is no longer the present-day South, and therefore that the insights whereby Faulkner gave order and meaning to his experience will no longer suffice. If this were so, Faulkner's example, no matter how great, would not constitute an important problem for subsequent Southern writers; they could simply ignore him, as having nothing important to say to them. The difficulty comes rather in that he *does* speak in part of their own experience as well as his own—but *only* in part. So he cannot be ignored. And yet what his novels say (to the extent that novels say anything of this sort at all) will no longer serve. The Faulknerian ordering of Southern experience must be adapted, changed, revised, so that what is still valid can be used, while what is outmoded will not get in the way. That is what causes the trouble: for his example is so massive and striking, his mode, his ordering of experience is so tremendously stimulating and suggestive to the imagination, that great perseverance of effort and talent is required to keep from being dominated by his vision. Yet if the young writer is to describe his own experience accurately, if he is not to produce derivative work with insights acquired by second hand, that is what he must do.

So far I have been dealing in generalities, mostly unproved. To document my case I should have to examine the work of numerous talented writers—William Styron, Flannery O'Connor, Truman Capote, Shirley Ann Grau, Shelby Foote, Walter Sullivan, Elizabeth Spencer, George

Garrett, Peter Taylor, James Agee, Reynolds Price—and, of course, that would not be possible within the compass of this paper. What I concluded to do, instead, was to choose a single novel by a Southerner of the post-World War II generation, and to read it in terms of what I have been saying. I decided to try this out on Madison Jones's *A Buried Land.* If what I conjectured was true, I thought, then this novel ought to bear it out to some extent. So I want to talk at some length about this novel, to see what it has to show concerning this problem of changing literary generations.

A Buried Land is set in a town in the TVA region of Tennessee. Its action takes place in two parts: during the late 1930's, when the TVA lakes were being created, and some years later, after the Second World War.

The imaginative potentialities of this kind of situation—rural countryside being inundated, families being uprooted and forced to move to higher ground—with its ready-made clash between rural and urban ways, between Tradition and Progress, agrarian and commercial-industrial South, are, of course, evident, and also its potentialities for easy cliché. It has been treated before in fiction, notably by Mr. Borden Deal, who managed to develop the possibilities of cliché very thoroughly indeed.

Madison Jones's protagonist is a young man named Percy Youngblood, who works for the TVA and whose family is one of those being dispossessed by the lake waters. Percy has quarreled violently with his father over the matter, and lives at a rooming house in town. He has little sympathy with his father's dogged opposition to being ousted from the ancestral farm, and even fails to come home for the disinterment of the family's forebears from a cemetery soon to be inundated and their removal to a new burial ground. (This, by the way, is a marvelously handled scene.) Percy is much more concerned with seducing a young woman in town, Cora Kincaid, who has been discarded by his friend Jesse Hood. In this Percy succeeds, and when the young woman becomes pregnant, he and Jesse take her to an abortionist in Nashville. Unfortunately, the young woman hemorrhages and dies, and the panicky young men take her to the old burial plot, whose now empty graves will soon be flooded by the lake, and bury her there.

The remainder of the novel has to do with Percy Youngblood when he comes back, some years later, to the same town, to make a career for himself as a lawyer. He has been in the war and been wounded, has since taken his law degree, and is ready to begin practice in the town. He will forget the past; after all, it lies buried under the waters of the TVA lake. But it turns out that he cannot do so, for events combine to bring back the past. For one thing, there is a severe drought, and the water level of the lake that hides the grave is steadily receding. Another menace to Percy Youngblood's security exists in the person of Fowler Kincaid, the brother of the dead girl, who has been in prison, and who now returns to town and discovers that Percy's erstwhile friend Jesse Hood was involved in his sister's disappearance. A chain of events ensues whereby Jesse Hood is murdered. Percy Youngblood attempts to escape the moral responsibility for what he has done, but succeeds only in becoming further involved, until at length he loses control of himself while defending a murderer in a court case, takes his mother back to the lake where the family graves were once located and where the girl lies buried, and confesses his crime to her.

I have not of course done justice to this novel, which is intricately worked out and is in no sense the melodrama it may appear to be from my oversimplified summary. But what interests me here is what is involved when a young Southern writer such as Madison Jones attempts to handle this particular kind of plot situation.

First I should like to consider how Faulkner might have handled it—the Faulkner of the late 1920's and the 1930's, that is, the years when he produced the work on which his reputation primarily rests. I believe Faulkner would probably have chosen for his protagonist not Percy Young-blood at all, but the dead girl's brother, Fowler Kincaid. He would have done this, I think, because it is a character such as Fowler Kincaid who would best embody what Faulkner would find most interesting in the situation. Kincaid is a primitive, an unlettered hunter born too late, whose semi-wild existence is uprooted and ruined by the impact of change and modernity—the disappearance of his sister, the destruction of the family place by the new lake, the end of the kind of life he has known and loved. He is unable to cope with the new ways. Like Mink Snopes in Faulkner's *The Mansion*, he comes back from prison to a world now quite alien; embittered, bewildered, he knows only blind hatred, seeks personal revenge for the wrongs he has suffered. Here is Fowler Kincaid, drunk, dreaming of the long ago:

The warmth of the whiskey had spread from his belly up and down through his body. Some time later this warmth appeared to come from outside of him, against his back. A faint stirring, like whispers or rustling clothes, kept on for a long while in his ears. Once more he heard, filtered as through sleep, a voice saying, "Wake up, Fowler, son." And then the other voice: "Let him sleep on, hit's so cold tonight." Hounds' baying a long way off carried on the brittle air.

But Madison Jones made Fowler Kincaid only a supporting character in his novel, and for a very good reason, I think. As a writer, he doesn't *know* Fowler Kincaid; that is to say, he is unable imaginatively to give first priority to what a primitive such as Kincaid thinks and feels. He can only see this uneducated, simple, backwoods person from the outside, as it were; he cannot enter completely into what such a person would be like, in the sense of being able to make this reveal the most urgent, paramount meaning of the novel. The meaning of the situation as Madison Jones creates it cannot be contained in what Kincaid is and does. I venture to say that this is not because Mr. Jones's own experience does not involve knowing persons such as Kincaid, but because it also involves so many other things which Mr. Jones, because of his own time and place and experience, must take with considerably more seriousness than he does the plight of Fowler Kincaid. I mean the experience of being a human being in a South that is no longer rural and primitive, but increasingly urban and cosmopolitan, increasingly a part of the world. And the terms whereby one lives in this modern world he takes with the kind of seriousness that would make it unsatisfactory for him to do what Faulkner could do in *The Sound and the Fury*, for example: show that a decent young man who tries to live in this modern world is automatically doomed by the very conditions of that world. Mr. Jones knows better, because it is *his* world, and he is living in it. The Faulknerian tragic mode of decline and fall will not do for him, however he might wish it were possible.

Not a single one of Faulkner's characters who possesses any intellectual capacity is able to exist in the present-day South as a successfully created fictional character. The failure of Gavin Stevens to be what Faulkner wanted him to be, particularly as he appears in *The Mansion*, is proof of this. Faulkner could not write about that kind of person and make important fiction out of it. When Faulkner created a young Southerner of developed intelligence and sensitivity and placed him in the modern world, the result was always the same. Either he was a Quentin Compson or a Bayard Sartoris, overwhelmed by the modern world, unable to believe in it or cope with it, seeking in vain to adapt the outmoded values of a decaying past to a situation that will not permit or be defined by those values— or else he was Gavin Stevens, which is to say that he was a largely unconvincing creation in a largely unconvincing novel. For Faulkner, only a Snopes could survive in the modern South—and a Snopes is amoral, vicious, materialistic, without courage or honor. This is in no way a criticism of Faulkner; it is simply that his greatness lies elsewhere.

But Madison Jones, being of a different generation, is not willing or able to deal with his South, which is the present-day South, on Faulkner's terms. So he chose for his protagonist a young man who sees things through the eyes of modernity, and who tries to bury a discarded past under the water of a TVA lake. That the past comes back to bring him down, that he is unable to ignore the claims of the past with its values of family, loyalty, personal responsibility, is what makes *A Buried Land* a tragedy. What I want to stress is that it required a modern such as Percy Youngblood, educated, given to thought, acquainted with the ways and values of the contemporary South and the world beyond it, properly to embody the meaning Mr. Jones wished to give to his story. There is never any question in Percy Youngblood's mind that this South, symbolized by the TVA, is what he wants; he is never really torn between conflicting loyalties. He fails because he wants the present-day world without paying for it, which is to say that he wants to live in it without having to bring with him what he had been taught was upright and honorable.

I want to stress the difference between the two viewpoints—Jones's, and what I have conjectured would have been Faulkner's. The older novelist could view the modern, urban-oriented South only as a place in which heroism is no longer possible—in which there is no room for Compsons and Sartorises, the old families, the old values. He was able to create heroic characters for the twentieth-century South only out of primitives, Negroes, half-breeds, children. Jones, by contrast, can say what he wishes to say only through the eyes and with the imagination of a fairly sophisticated Southerner of today, one who is the result of change rather than its architect or its victim. Neither the primitive milieu of field and forest, nor yet the theme of the collapse of the old aristocracy before the materialism of the modern South, could suffice to permit Mr. Jones to give order and meaning to his experience. For his experience has not been those things at all. He is of another generation of Southerners. And his task, in which I think he succeeded in this novel, was to find the language and the milieu to give an image to *his* South.

If I have concentrated unduly on this one novel by a single Southern writer, it is because it seemed to me that the best way to show what the changing South can mean to the Southern novelist of our time would be not to deal in generalizations and capsule summaries, but to try to discover such meaning in a single novel. Of course, Madison Jones's case is not automatically true of every other Southern writer of his generation. It is not true, for example, of Reynolds Price, or Flannery O'Connor. I chose Jones because it seemed to me that of the younger Southern novelists, it was he who has seemed closest to the Faulknerian milieu in his previous published work. If I could then demonstrate the problems of the changing South in his most recent novel, the contrasts might be especially revealing. I might as readily have chosen William Styron, for example; yet it has always seemed to me that despite certain surface similarities with Faulkner in Styron's first novel, he is actually much farther away from Faulkner than Madison Jones is. In any event, if the reader will accept for purposes of argument the validity of my findings, I should like to close with a few more generalizations.

What the Southern writer confronts is a South which has greatly changed, so that he must come to grips with an experience that, while it bears certain important similarities to that of his predecessors, differs from it in crucial respects. He has before him, so that he cannot side-step or ignore it, an imposing literary tradition, which has dealt masterfully with his region's life as it was changing, and which, when he begins to write his novels, tells him that this change has meant certain important truths about human experience. Part of his job is therefore to test the validity of this meaning. He cannot accept it uncritically, because if he does he will be unable to describe what he sees and knows with sufficent accuracy. He must determine for himself what is still usable, and what is no longer so.

I suggest that this is not an entirely enviable situation that he finds himself in. For he has some very persuasive elders, who were able magnificently to describe what they saw, and since much of what they saw is still very much true in his own time, there is every temptation for him to accept their account as still entirely true. Yet the South has changed, and even what so great a writer as William Faulkner has said was true of Southern experience is no longer fully true in his day. It is his job to decide what *is* true. This means that he must write novels which seek to discover, through language and image, what the world that he knows is all about. He must find out the meaning of his experience for himself—which is what good writers always have to do. It will be interesting to see how well he succeeds.

Index